SEVEN SUMMERS

Seven Summers

A Naturalist Homesteads in the Modern West

Julia Corbett

The University of Utah Press

Salt Lake City

The Defiance House Man colophon is a registered trademark
of the University of Utah Press. It is based on a four-foot-tall
Ancient Puebloan pictograph (late PIII) near Glen Canyon, Utah.

17 16 15 14 13   1 2 3 4 5

LIBRARY OF CONGRESS CATALOGING-IN-PUBLICATION DATA
Corbett, Julia B.
  Seven summers : a naturalist homesteads in the modern West / Julia Corbett.
    pages cm
  ISBN 978-1-60781-249-4 (paper : alkaline paper)
  ISBN 978-1-60781-250-0 (ebook)
  1. Corbett, Julia B. 2. Corbett, Julia B.—Homes and haunts—Wyoming—Wind
River Range. 3. Frontier and pioneer life—Wyoming—Wind River Range. 4. Log
cabins—Wyoming—Wind River Range. 5. Summer—Wyoming—Wind River
Range. 6. Women naturalists—Wyoming—Wind River Range—Biography. 7.
Naturalists—Wyoming—Wind River Range—Biography. 8. Wind River Range
(Wyo.)—Biography. 9. Natural history—Wyoming—Wind River Range. 10. Wind
River Range (Wyo.)—Description and travel. I. Title.
  F767.W5C67 2013
  508.092—dc23
  [B]

                                                          2012045263

An earlier version of "A Finger of Owls" appeared in *Camas: The Nature of the West*
17, no. 2 (2009): 6–8.
"Are *You* an Environmentalist?" is based on "Dirty Little Words" in *OnEarth
Magazine* 28, no. 2 (2006): 48.

Printed and bound by Sheridan Books, Inc., Ann Arbor, Michigan.

*For Dad and Sara, who love me
and support me in such different and essential ways*

Contents

Acknowledgments

I honor and sincerely thank:

- my parents, who gave me a childhood in the woods and the freedom to explore it, and my brothers, Scott and Jim, who shared it with me.
- writing-group members and friends Debora Threedy and Sylvia Torti, who helped immensely to shape and envision a book, and Maria Melendez, insightful and encouraging editor-advocate.
- Winifred Gallagher, who provided a challenging exercise at the Jackson Hole Writers Conference that helped me see the larger and unique story of "a professor and a chain saw."
- all my superb friends, who visited the cabin in various stages and donated all manner of furnishings, and who understand and have shared what this place means to me. And Sara, who is an extraordinary role model for a human being.
- the entire cast of builders, who taught me so much and did such fine work on this magnificent, humble structure.
- my Wyoming neighbors who supported and befriended me during construction and continue to provide social, intellectual, and woodsy fun.
- my students and colleagues at the University of Utah.
- the woods, meadow, and all the creatures therein that have permitted my dwelling among them and given me such solace and grounding. It still feels more like home than any place on earth.

All the personal names in Wyoming (and some of the locations) have been changed. These people did not ask to be put in a book, and I respect their privacy, as well as the privacy of this place.

SEVEN SUMMERS

ONE

Chain Saw Dreams

The smell of sawdust and gas met me at the door when my dad and I strode into the dimly lit room. I stood for a moment, my eyes adjusting from the blazing summer sun outside. Arctic Cat and Polaris posters lined the wood walls, displaying helmeted bodies astride gleaming dark machines flying through clouds of sparkling snow. A man emerged, wiping his hands on a grimy rag.

"We want to look at your chain saws," I said.

"So what kinda saw you looking for?" he asked my dad, a tall, thin man with a shock of wavy, white hair.

"Oh, it's not for me," Dad said, grinning widely. "It's for *her*," and poked my upper arm with his index finger. This confusion rather pleased him, someone underestimating his forty-seven-year-old daughter.

The shop owner's assumption didn't surprise me. Twenty-first century or not, reactions like his sprouted like dandelions: assign a woman a role and deposit her in the background. In conservative Utah (where I teach) some students automatically address me as Mrs. instead of Ms. or Professor. Store clerks ask whether I'm purchasing a tool or a two-by-four for my husband, though I plainly wear no ring. And here in western Wyoming, similar presumptions proliferate—about spouse, children, and what a woman might be doing, wanting, or buying.

"Yep, it's for me," I confirmed. "And I want something with a medium-sized bar, not too heavy."

"Oh. Okay then," the man said, avoiding my eyes. He led us through the snowmobile room—his winter business—into a room filled with chain saws and dirt bikes, his summer business. We stopped before a wall with several shelves of shiny machines. A few with absurdly long bars were parked on the floor. How strange to see them so pristine without blackened grease and sawdust.

"So, you used a saw before?" he asked, plucking one from the shelf and turning toward me.

"Yes, but it's been quite a few years. It was a Stihl, about that size," and I nodded at the silver one he held. He offered a couple of recommendations and pointed out all the current safety features: chain brake, throttle lock, chain catcher, and the stop switch, which was always bright red. I ambled down the row and hefted one saw and then another, holding the handle in my curved grip, appraising the weight.

I decided on a Husqvarna, a "Husky," which came in bright orange—not something you'd be losing in the duff. It idled at about 2,000 rpm and revved up to 9,000 rpm, and I could imagine it propelling that silver chain around and around on the eighteen-inch bar. Fully gassed, it would weigh about eleven pounds, and I regretted not working more with my hand weights last winter.

While the man retrieved a new saw from the back, Dad selected small bottles of chain oil and engine oil, and I fingered the sleek chain on a big floor model. The essence of a chain saw was the chain, an ingenious collection of links: notched cutting links on top, pointed links on the bottom that drove the sprocket wheel and propelled the chain, and side links that held the whole chain together. An amazing invention, this gas-powered tree-felling machine, patented in 1929 by Andrew Stihl (which I learned when researching chain saw brands). It was hard to believe that homesteaders once cleared land and built log cabins without them.

When I sauntered toward my truck toting the shiny orange machine, I drawled, "Golly, I got me a chain saw. Thanks, Dad."

"Happy early birthday, daughter," he said.

~~~~~~

A chain saw was a logical choice for my first power tool after buying ten acres of forested land in western Wyoming the autumn before. The saw may have been a practical purchase, but my father wasn't convinced that the land purchase was. When I first discovered the parcel of high-elevation woods and meadow and was poised to make an offer on it, I called Dad, bubbling over with excitement.

"What are you going to do with ten acres of land?" he asked.

"Well, live on it," I said. "I'll live up there each summer when spring semester ends."

"Live in what?"

"I don't know. A tent at first. Maybe a little trailer. Someday a cabin."

"And where are you going to get the money for all this?"

"Dad, I don't know. You already asked me that."

"And how are you going to build this cabin?"

I paused. I had already interrogated myself with all these questions and hadn't come up with many answers.

"Dad, this is my dream and it always has been—to live and write in a cabin in the woods. You said I talked about it when I was a little girl, remember? So, no, I don't know how it's all going to work. And I know it sounds crazy, but this is what I want."

"Oh, daughter," he said, his voice trailing off.

～～～～～

Dad refused to sell the family home in the Iowa woods after Mom died seven years ago and still rattled around in the four-bedroom rambler, so I knew he understood my desire at some level. I grew up in those deciduous woods, and the naturalist in me was birthed there. I knew every deer trail in the nearby creek valley and where the dogtooth violets bloomed each spring. In the several-mile radius I explored on foot and bike, I learned the bugs and the birds, the plants and the critters— if not by name, by sight, location, and habits. After college, I worked as a bona fide naturalist in Olympic National Park, and a decade later, as a naturalist for the Raptor Center in Minnesota.

Now, I was a naturalist-turned-professor stuck in major metropolitan Salt Lake City, a woman whose life revolved around the natural world—by profession, avocation, passion, religion. Every Sunday morning, my dog, Tobie, and I hiked the nearby Wasatch Mountains for "church." The woods provided a compass to navigate the larger landscape of my life and world, to steer me through deep canyons and windswept plateaus and rediscover where I fit. Each Sunday in the woods, I regained my footing. By comparison, the city sent my footsteps scattershot through miles of concrete corridors. I longed to live in the woods, not just visit them.

In that sense, my land purchase felt like striking out for new, uncharted territory far from streetlights and sidewalks. Unlike my homesteading predecessors whose land was the linchpin of their

existence, of their ability to survive, I had the luxury of not wrest-
ing my subsistence from my acres. I was a twenty-first-century homesteader, more interested in immersing myself in the rich life of meadow
and forest, sentinel to seasons unfolding as they had for millennia—
a naturalist homesteading a West that was much emended yet con-
solingly familiar and unchanged. Someday I would build something
modest and learn to live in tandem with the creatures who already
occupied this precious piece of ground. On its face, it was such a pure
and simple dream.

Nevertheless, cutting some timber for firewood would be help-
ful. I tried christening the saw on several dead lodgepole pines and a
Douglas fir about halfway up the faint two-track driveway. I opened
the choke, braced the saw on the ground with one foot, and yanked
the starter cord. Put-put-cough. I pulled again. It yowled to life and I
grinned. I set the blade on a downed log and revved it some gas, but
Dad, who had come to visit for a week and check out the place, shook
his head and mimed something and pointed. I tried again, and he
yelled something unintelligible over the wail of the saw and my ear-
plugs. After thirty minutes of this halting and unproductive scenario,
I passed him the chain saw without a word and started hauling cut
sections to a woodpile we were stacking between two standing trees.
He handed me the saw a few more times, but each time the panto-
mimed pedagogy began anew. Move this hand down, no, that one up;
at times the advice seemed contradictory and confusing. I tried, but
only seemed to get it wrong.

Several hours later, we trudged up the driveway to Dory, my ancient
little motor home, for some lunch. All morning, Dad had pointed out
everything I was doing wrong, and what little confidence I had for
handling a chain saw had drained away.

I knew from training Tobie, my headstrong golden retriever, that
what delivered success was positive reinforcement for the desired
behavior. If she heard scolding or displeasure in my voice when I said

her name, she wouldn't bother to turn her head. I knew Dad was concerned about my safety and about the infamous kickback (the abrupt ricochet of whirling saw from log to logger), but I couldn't learn with the constant criticism. He was his own harshest critic, I knew that, but I wearied of him being mine.

As I watched my father chainsaw that afternoon, I thought about the other men I'd sawed with, particularly my ex in Idaho. Each autumn we drove to the nearby forests to cut and cart fir and aspen for a winter's worth of heat. We started work in the chill of the morning; the sun soon warmed the damp earth, releasing smells of frost and decay and all that sweet sawdust. He sawed while I hauled and loaded. Nate taught me how to operate the saw, but I was too quick to put the machine—and its dangers, its thrills, and its power—in his hands. In the woods, the kitchen, and the bedroom, I was a twenty-something woman who believed it necessary to relinquish my wishes and please this man to hold on to him.

I didn't understand then the dangers of operating a relationship so passively. He could be as critical as my father, though the welt was slower to rise, like chuckling that his mother would die if she saw my kitchen floor. He didn't lift a finger to mop it, and I never asked. The more I acquiesced and the harder I tried, the more my person faded into the background.

<hr />

Dad snored so loudly in the motor home that on the second night of his visit, Tobie and I retreated to a tent in the meadow. I woke refreshed by the plaintive warbles of hermit thrushes and fresh breezes. After breakfast, he knelt outside Dory, refilling the chain saw's gas and oil.

"Dad, I need you to tell me today what I'm doing *right* with the saw—not just wrong," I said sternly.

He started to argue why his teaching method was prudent.

"Dad, I mean it!"

"Yes, daughter," he muttered.

In my first forty years of life, Mom was the peace broker between my father and me. "Now John," she'd gently intervene when she witnessed my wounds from a barrage of criticism. In many respects, my relationship with Dad didn't begin until she died. In her final months, Mom made me promise to take care of him when she was gone. It quickly became clear that what I needed most was to learn to take care of Me.

By midmorning, after struggling to incorporate Dad's myriad advice about angles and positions, the saw settled better in my hands. Dad nodded occasionally, for which I was grateful. The blade slipped through each trunk like a hot knife through butter, chips flying, the saw whining and straining. Between cuts, the saw hummed its contented putt-putter-putt until I squeezed the trigger and it tore into the next log. My arms ached. Though I wore steel-toed boots, jeans, and leather gloves, it would take only a misstep, a poorly placed log, or just bad luck for that whirling chain to make mincemeat of some body part. Yet the saw was in my hands now, responding to my grip, my direction. Its flash and destruction still scared me, but it thrilled me once again.

~~~~~

When I told people about the land and building a cabin, more than one person interjected, "Oh, you want to live in the woods like Thoreau, living deliberately and all that." Since the bookmark in my copy of *Walden* is a hall pass from high school, he's actually not the first person who springs to mind. Since honors lit class, I've heard more about Thoreau than I've read him, particularly oft-quoted phrases like men leading lives of quiet desperation.

There is much about Thoreau I admire: living simply and shunning excess, finding beauty and power and freedom in nature, and immersing oneself in sensory nature experiences. He was a man of principle; he abhorred slavery and preached and practiced civil disobedience, and he hated impostors and distrusted men of wealth. I even have a refrigerator magnet with a favorite Thoreau quote: "Go confidently in the direction of your dreams! Live the life you've imagined."

So why isn't Thoreau more of a hero for me? Walden was his short-term experiment, where he lived simply and alone for eighteen months, yet walked the railroad tracks into town for lunch at his mother's. I'm seeking a long-term relationship with my land, and I do not intend to just try and then relinquish it. And frankly, what interests me more is how, say, Thoreau's *sister* might have contemplated leaving present society and its cultural constraints to make a life in the woods by herself. A man building a cabin—whether mid-1800s Concord or twenty-first-century Wyoming—isn't the same story or filled with the same consequences. Thus, I have other role models.

Twelve percent of all the individuals who filed claims under the 1862 Homestead Act were single women, and they were just as likely to "prove up" their 160-acre (and later 320-acre) claims and get the title as were men. The gender-neutral language that "any person who is head of a family" (and over twenty-one years old) was controversial, but it was deemed important to attract women to the uncivilized West who would help organize churches, schools, and town socials and provide alternatives to drinking, gambling, and prostitution. The Homestead Act had a stipulation, however, that if a woman married between the time of filing her claim and proving up on it, the property reverted to her husband. Even so, almost three-quarters of women homesteaders were still single by the time they earned the deed to their property.

This fascinated me, for I carried the stereotype of pioneer women as the self-sacrificing, compromising helpmates who set aside their own qualms and fears and went West with their husbands. In general, women were largely absent from texts of western history. One history textbook devoted only two sentences to the role of women in the settlement of the West, another text just half a page. I was invisible at the chain saw shop; they were invisible en masse.

It was obvious to me what attracted single women to head West and homestead. In the 1860s, women wore corsets and long skirts, rode sidesaddle (if at all), and had few choices beyond "wife" and "mother." Fathers (and sometimes brothers) dictated whom a woman should marry. Homesteading offered single women freedom and economic security on land of their very own, a chance to choose something of their own making and to create their own experiences. That was indeed a new and heady notion.

May Holaday wrote that she felt this in the air as soon as she crossed the Rockies: "My former ideas of the importance of class distinction and the observance of social conventions seemed to fall from me like a heavy cloak, which had long been a burden—and I was free! Free to live my own life in my own way…"

Alice Day Pratt, who homesteaded in Oregon in 1910, wrote that when she boarded the train to head West, she had no regret of what she was leaving behind—the competition and life at high pressure—and she anticipated instead "calm…freedom…limitless spaces…hope and opportunity."

The cloak of social conventions is less heavy now, but a single woman building a cabin in the woods is still a highly unusual occurrence. Sure, Dad would visit each summer for a week, but I was embarking on this venture alone without husband or partner. The land title was in my name, I weathered life in that meadow by myself, and my future there sat on my shoulders.

~~~~~

Toting my own chain saw and knowing a bit about using it hardly qualified me for building a cabin. For starters, I knew nothing about construction. In my Salt Lake City basement, I had a hammer, some pliers and a wrench, a pruning saw, and an electric screwdriver. I was pretty handy with the Martha Stewart–type arts and could paint a room, nail things on walls, cook and can, sew curtains, and tend a yard and garden. But knowledge of building? Nope. I loved log cabins and had bedded in a fair number of them, but I never gave a second thought to how those logs went together. Though I grew up with a well and a septic system, I knew nothing about their operation other than the fact that sewage could back up in the bathtub if the septic tank overfilled, as it once did when I was a child.

My typical approach to any new project or goal was to plan, research, and plan some more, to approach the subject practically and methodically. It's how I moved through six states and became a tenured professor. But this? I wanted the end result—a cabin—but hadn't a clue how to get there. After buying the ten acres, my savings were scraping bottom, and I had no visible means of buying logs, windows, well, or woodstove. At this stage, I couldn't imagine all I had to learn and the thousands of decisions I would render before this dream of a cabin was palpable.

Perhaps it was a crazy, insane dream, really—the idle daydreaming of a single woman approaching middle age and feeling mislaid in a big city. After all, professors know scads about esoteric topics, but by and large they are more accustomed to creating things with their brains than with their bodies. Even if my area of teaching and research was fairly down to earth and a bit more useful (communication and environmental studies), it wasn't going to be much help in erecting a cabin.

But for all the apparent foolhardiness of it, I trusted this dream wholeheartedly. It wasn't religious faith; it wasn't confidence in my abilities. Yet I didn't question it incessantly or weigh the pros and cons as I did with some difficult decisions. The trust of this dream came from some deep and visceral intuitive place that simply couldn't be interrogated. I could see it, feel it, taste it. Each spring I would do as I had this spring: post spring semester grades, pack up my truck, and head north with my dog and cat (and now my chain saw). Each summer, I would transform from a pen-wielding professor into a chain saw–toting naturalist-homesteader, seeking to make a life and home in the new West.

Dad knew that once his daughter got something in her head, it was tough to shake it loose. Extremely determined, he called me, and with great focus. As our week in July progressed, his admiration— if not attachment—to this place deepened. I spied him sitting in the meadow, an arm draped across Tobie, man and dog quietly contemplating the expanse of forest and mountains that opened beyond the meadow. A lifelong angler (of the old-fashioned spin-cast variety), he discovered a good fishing hole near the bar-store where I sometimes showered. One evening after dinner, I spread the national forest map on the little table in Dory and pointed out nearby features.

"Wow, you're only ten miles from the Green River!" he said, knowing the river's reputation for trout fishing.

I never dreamed I'd become a professor like my father. At seventy-seven, he was still doing inorganic chemistry seven days a week, a passion made all the more essential since Mom died. My career path was circuitous. After college, I left journalism for Olympic National Park, then other federal and state environmental jobs, freelance writing, a brief stint as a political staffer, and then fell into college teaching in a roundabout way. Only then did I consider graduate school and academia.

A quote from Eleanor Roosevelt traverses the top stones on a Salt Lake library where I often walk with Tobie: "The future belongs to those who believe in the beauty of their dreams." Mine was indeed a beautiful dream, though for much of the remainder of that first summer on what I dubbed Mouse Meadow, it was hard to believe I could make it happen. Was this dream strong enough? Did I yearn for it more than other dreams, of husband and family? I wondered about this while sitting on a log outside Dory, watching the sun leave long pink streaks as it slipped behind the distant peaks. Sandhill cranes warbled from the wetland below, and I knew only that this felt more like home than any place on earth.

TWO

The Picture in My Mind's Eye

Though I took no pictures the very first time my feet touched those acres and I gazed across the meadow to distant peaks, I have one all the same. I imagine many people have such a picture of such a place to which they can magically transport themselves, body and soul, in a heartbeat. There it is—the way a breeze touches your cheek, the pulse of color, the murmuring of leaves—placed deep within and recorded, perfectly, eternally.

The picture I possess of this place must somehow reveal itself when I mention it to others, for they always ask the story of how I found the land, of how it came to be in my life. The truth is, the journey unspooled messily like thread from a bobbin that rolled around table legs and under the sofa. You could say it began the fall before I got the chain saw; you could say it began in my childhood.

~~~~~~

"I think it's this way," shouted my realtor, Cindy, forging up the far side of a small draw.

We worked our way through the whortleberry and wild rose, around lodgepole pine and Douglas fir, looking for the corner property marker on this ten-acre parcel about an hour from Pinedale. Since I was of no use route finding, I was soaking in the musky scents of frosts and thaws on this high mountain hillside. The aspen were glowing in the slanted September sun. The earth was fragrant, damp, in some manner familiar.

It was our second day looking at land. On the winding gravel road to this place, I saw three cow elk bound across the dirt road. I spied ducks on every small pond, even a muskrat. When we crested a small ridge, a red fox popped up from the ditch, paused with one paw in midair to glance in our direction, and disappeared down the other side.

"Found it!" Cindy called, pulling grasses away from the brass marker. We turned north, climbed a small, wooded knoll, and walked into a clearing. Sloping away from us was a large meadow, swaying with tall tan grasses and dotted with dried yarrow heads, rabbitbrush, and a few sagebrush. Beyond, the tops of the Wyoming Range wore dark clouds, and north through the trees rose the rocky face of the Gros Ventre range. Conifers and aspen surrounded and sheltered the soft meadow, which opened to views of advancing weather and hawks on the wing. Elevation 7,685. It was perfect.

"Wow," I said softly. My eyes brimmed over. "You know, this is the picture I've had in my mind's eye since I was a child, the exact picture…"

Cindy smiled. The following summer, a little 1975 motor home was parked on that very spot.

~~~~~~

There's a black-and-white photo of me—I look about seven or eight—standing alone at one end of a wide meadow. I'm holding in both hands a bunch of wild white daisies, the grasses are up to my shins, and I'm wearing a sweet, brown calico dress my mom made. What strikes me is my look—gazing over the top of my bouquet across the meadow, looking so, what, serene? Content? Perhaps just entirely at home. "That's my nature girl," Mom used to say.

That photo (and my childhood memories) gives me reason to believe that I did indeed carry a sensorial picture in my mind's eye for much of my life of a place in the woods such as this. As old memories are wont to do, it probably morphed over time, commingling the green woodlands of my rural Iowa childhood with numerous adult residences. The wet, dense coniferous forests of the Pacific Northwest. The high-desert sagebrush plains of Idaho, punctuated by upwelling mountains. And the basin and ranges of northwestern Utah and the long north-south ribbon of the Wasatch Mountains. My picture contained information not just about how such a place would look, but how it would make me feel.

When I stepped onto that meadow, it was more than a simple picture in my mind; it was a triggering smell, a sense of a deep comfort for a place that was entirely unknown to me just a few minutes ago. It was like meeting a person for the first time, yet feeling like you've known her for ages and have skipped over the initial years to a place of familiarity. I felt instantly and utterly at home and at peace on that land, so much so that there was no resisting it, no second-guessing. This was it.

By late October, I drove up from Salt Lake with my friend Camille and Tobie, signed the title papers for 10.3 acres, and drove out to the parcel to christen it. Snow lay on the shaded parts of the road and in the deep timber. Tobie's nose went into overdrive with the wild scents, and even though she was a female, she marked a great many spots, perhaps sensing that she now had ownership as well.

Camille and I first met in the woods, so she was the perfect companion for this embarkation. When I first moved to Salt Lake, I joined the Wasatch Mountain Club to meet people and learn the hiking trails, and here was this short and cheery woman with an impish grin and hearty laugh who didn't care how slow or fast she hiked. She just enjoyed the journey and the people she met along the way. A social worker for the state with compassion to spare and a love of good food and wine, Camille quickly became a friend. She was eager to explore my new land and shared my excitement.

Under the dry base of a large Doug fir at the highest point on the meadow, Camille and I drank champagne in plastic flutes and said "Clink!" when we toasted. We ate strawberries, Tobie too, who was thrilled with the treat and devoured them stem and all. Then we walked the boundaries corner to corner to corner, posing for pictures at each post.

〰〰〰

"Woods" may not be what many people associate with central Iowa, but I grew up surrounded by them. Our 1960 rambler four miles south of town opened onto a dirt lane, surrounded on all other sides by woods. There were basswoods (which were great for climbing), hickories (which, with patience, had nuts good for eating), maples (good for shade), and the limbs of all that were good for making forts. The tangled, largely deciduous forests were thick with chlorophyll and humidity, deer, raccoon, toads, and bugs. There were mosquitoes, of course, also fat, brown June bugs buzzing and clinging to the screen door and, to the delight of us children, fireflies. Owls hooted beyond my bedroom window. The nights were the blackest of black when the moon was absent.

I chronicle these bits of childhood because it was so unlike childhood today. There were no cell phones for constant oversight, no adult supervisors, no fear of abduction or harm. My play territory extended a couple of miles beyond our half-acre lot, and friends and I wandered at will—as long as we told Mom roughly where we were going and made it home by dinnertime. Without this comfortable immersion, I don't know if my land and cabin adventure would have come to pass.

Across the road was a park where my two brothers and I and assorted playmates played capture the flag at dusk and held important meetings in the trees. We had innumerable trails through the woods—to forts, to friends' houses, to the creek. The easiest way to navigate the little creek valley was via the train track, whose trestles gave us great thrills. In the creek we engineered diversions and created impoundments for crawdads.

Bikes were the other mode of exploration. We peddled up to Mrs. Plaggman's farm to climb in the hayloft and eat green apples. We biked to Mr. Christopherson's farm to pet the horses, see what treasures emerged from his rock polisher, and visit the mural of stallions he had painted on the interior barn wall. Though my best friend, Susie, and I played with dolls and made elaborate dollhouses and clothes, we were probably considered tomboys. That had much to do with the available and engaging playthings like sticks and creeks and critters. Friends in town could walk to the movies, the mall, or the swimming pool; we walked into the woods.

~~~~~

When I was granted tenure at the University of Utah, a professor friend said, "Guess you're stuck here now, huh?" The thought was sobering: what if I am indeed stuck behind the Zion Curtain with its hellishly hot summers? What can I do to survive here?

Wallace Stegner wrote fondly about his time among Mormons in the "city of the saints"; I am less magnanimous. Even though just half of Salt Lakers are Mormon, Mormonism nevertheless forms the "default" for Utah culture at large, prescribing such things as the acceptable "family," the myriad rules about liquor, and the "proper" role of women. The church shapes the stance of news media they own and the legislature, where three of four lawmakers are Mormon. Church doctrine promotes a consistent rightness and obedience to chosen norms that belie the heterogeneity of a large city. Though I formed a nice community of like-minded souls in Salt Lake, the saintly backdrop remained and chafed.

My survival wasn't just about Salt Lake per se, which is a vibrant city full of the arts and great food, with mountains so close by. It was about me as a country mouse living as a city mouse, feeling suffocated in a city that was never quiet, never dark, that smelled of metal and oil and was packed with structures that blocked the sun and wind. It closed in on me; it created a busy, dizzy hum in my head. So yes, survival meant getting out—at least in summers when a professor's nine-month contract was a delicious advantage. With tenure, the push to publish had finally eased; now, I could really write anywhere, like in a cabin in the woods.

My initial plan was to look for land (with or without a cabin) near the Uinta Mountains east of Salt Lake City. Before the searching began, my truck was T-boned at an intersection by a woman who claimed she sneezed (but had run several red lights before this one). The only loaner car my insurance covered was a small two-door, not really a backwoods exploration vehicle. I'll look later this summer, I said. Six weeks later when my truck was finally repaired, I was pulling the lawnmower to the front yard when I tripped up a step and severely sprained my ankle. It was several more weeks before I could walk normally. Maybe next summer I'll look for land, I said.

That fall was my first sabbatical, which I used to begin an academic book. To commence, I rented a friend's cabin on Fremont Lake at the foot of the Wind River Mountains in Wyoming for two weeks in

September. When I lived in Idaho, the Winds were one of my favorite backpacking destinations. Even during graduate school in Minnesota, I'd fly back to rendezvous with a friend in the Wind Rivers. It is a magical place. One night nestled in the tent, I lay awake for hours listening to the wind flow down the valley, enchanted with how the sound mimicked flowing water. Far up the drainage, the breezes tumbled off the highest peaks with gusto, flowing down, down. When the wind reached the tent, it seemed to eddy, swirling and circling, before journeying on. After a brief and quiet calm, the flow commenced again.

Near the end of my stay at the cabin, a stay full of strange and fantastical dreams and several intense storms, a friend from Salt Lake drove up for the weekend. Over a glass of wine on the deck, I told Donna my foiled land-hunting saga.

"Why don't you look around here?" she asked.

"I can't afford it around here," I replied.

"Are you sure? You just really love it here. It might be worth a shot."

Donna was a nurse, which must have had something to do with her ability to read situations and people. After our paths repeatedly crossed while walking our young dogs, we learned that we lived just blocks apart and became fast friends.

After Donna returned to Salt Lake, I found myself slowly cruising the main street in Pinedale; I spotted three real-estate offices. I stopped at the one with three women visible through the picture windows.

I walked in the office wanting a cabin but soon learned that most parcels with dwellings were legions above my budget; one small A-frame entirely encircled by dark woods was more than triple the cost of my house in Salt Lake. But one agent, Cindy, who was about my age with short-cropped brown hair and a sweet, genuine smile, suggested that we go look at a few. She drove me first to several parcels of more affordable land sans cabin; each was a flat sagebrush square on

a wide-open plain, skimpy on trees and with neighbors in full view—
though some had great views of the Wind Rivers. The last one on her
list our first day of touring had a dozen cows foraging on it. In Wyoming, cattle essentially have the right-of-way, and it's the landowner's
responsibility to fence them out, not the cattleman's to contain them. I
explained to Cindy that after four years working for the federal Bureau
of Land Management, referred to by some as the Bureau of Livestock
and Mining, I couldn't handle cows and their pies just out the front
door. Perhaps this was a crazy idea. She sensed my discouragement.

"Let's go out again tomorrow morning," she said. "I'm getting a
much better idea of what you want and don't want. There are a few
more sites I want you to see—they're a bit farther from the Winds, but
I really think they might be what you're looking for."

<hr />

Quite a few of my Salt Lake friends are professed "desert rats," wax-
ing eloquently about the serenity of the red-rock and sandstone country of southern Utah. When I lived in Port Angeles, west of Seattle,
I met a lot of "ocean people." Though I like to visit and hike the desert, I do not feel at home there, nor do I have an affinity for the open
ocean beyond the beach. I loved my time living in the Pacific Northwest but sometimes felt downright claustrophobic driving or hiking
through a solid tunnel of trees, wanting to get up or out, wanting a
clearing or opening, wanting some perspective. In Iowa, because it
was flat, flat, flat and lacked any elevation outside of the few creek
valleys, I felt slightly agoraphobic and wanted to climb up on something to get some perspective. One's sense of place in a landscape is
part familiarity, but perhaps also part biology; biologist E. O. Wil-
son claimed that wanting to dwell up high with a view may have had
evolutionary survival value. Whatever the reason, my favored habitat
is mountain woods with a view and variety—not solid trees but the

blend provided by extremes of temperature, moisture, and exposure: open south slopes clothed in sage and browse, timbered north slopes, and the rest in ever-shifting allegiances. In all kinds of western habitats, I've witnessed a fierce "native" pride. Decades ago when I was testifying at a hearing in the capitol in Boise, a legislator interrupted to ask me where I was from. I paused, confused, because I had said I was from Idaho Falls. "No, how long have you lived in Idaho?" he needled. "About four years," I replied. He snorted and threw glances to his colleagues seated left and right. To him, I was not native enough.

But like Wallace Stegner and John Wesley Powell, my line is drawn not at a state boundary but at the one hundredth meridian, a demarcation of the West that includes most all the places I've lived since college: two towns in Washington, three in Idaho, one in Utah, and now Wyoming. Though I spent the first third of my life in the Midwest, I feel through and through—biologically and philosophically—like a westerner. Some people aren't born in the place they are really "from" or where their soul belongs.

A neighbor and hiking friend of mine who spends eight months a year working in Florida and four months in Wyoming, said a Florida friend of hers always asks, "So, how's Montana?" Janet has given up correcting her and replies, "It's good." Part of that may be regionalism—as when people learn I'm heading to Iowa for Christmas and say, "Have a good time back East."

Wyoming registers little for most people. It's the least-populous state in the nation, and for anyone who has traveled the state solely on I-80, they surmise why: it's mile after blessed mile of sagebrush. Flat, windy, boring. Look at a relief map instead of a road map, and the other Wyoming becomes apparent: mountain ranges rising from those sagebrush plains, the Bighorns, Medicine Bow, Bear Lodge, and in the West, the Winds, Absaroka, Gros Ventre, Snake, Teton. The state has nearly as many pronghorn antelope as people, three times as many cows, and a fair number of sheep. I was driving my dad to the airport once when my truck was surrounded by a herd of sheep being driven down the highway; there was nothing to do but shut off the engine and wait as the woolly bodies brushed by, rocking us gently and leaving a buff line along both sides. In the Cowboy State you can also see cattle driven by chaps-spurs-and-Stetson-wearing horsemen and -women, sometimes next to the highway. An earlier moniker was the Equality State, because this independent-minded place was the first to grant women the right to vote in 1869, a full fifty years before the entire nation.

In my Wyoming county, there are just 1.2 people per square mile and not a single stoplight. My land is fifty minutes from a grocery store and, in the opposite direction, thirty minutes from my post office box. It's closely nestled by Forest Service land a half-mile north and scattered parcels of BLM land to the southwest. Most roads aren't plowed in the winter (though a hardy handful snowmobile in and out). No hunting is allowed and fencing (though uncommon) must be wildlife friendly. Many mornings I hike to my own little geologic formation, the Ridge, which acts as a mini Continental Divide, draining what falls on its east slopes into the Green River and the Colorado, while its west slope drains to the Snake and Columbia Rivers and the Pacific Ocean.

The contrast of this "empty" place with fully occupied Salt Lake is intoxicating to me. If I lived here year-round, however, that emptiness might include a measure of inconvenience, with the nearest dentist, hospital, and department store more than an hour away.

〜〜〜〜

During the first winter in Salt Lake after I bought the land, I oscillated between giddiness and sheer panic. I am a landowner of woods and meadow! A patch of earth and dreams! No more waiting for a man in my life before I pursue a dream such as this. After my ex left years ago, the longer I was partnerless, the more accustomed I became to making decisions without having to negotiate—what house to rent or where to move for graduate school. Some of it was difficult and lonely, but it was also heady and fed my independent streak.

After a period of land-baron exuberance, I had to ask myself, "What on earth have I done?" I knew how to hike and backpack and basically play in the woods, but not how to live there, let alone build there. I hadn't a clue where to begin. What made me think I could do this? It was overwhelming, all of it.

It must have been that picture in my mind's eye that propelled me forward, despite overwhelming naïveté. The situation could have easily paralyzed me and made me more painfully conscious of my shortcomings: ignorance, lack of money, no firm plan, and a host of other obstacles of which I was not yet aware.

One Saturday in late February I found myself in the classified ads, scrolling my thumb down the RV section. Just for fun. Just curious. Most were very big and very expensive. Except one: a 1975 eighteen-foot Ford Eldorado motor home.

When I went to see it, it was clear that the vehicle soon to be known to me as "Dory" had seen a lot of country. The motor part of her was in fine shape; it was the home part that was ragged around every edge. There was water damage in the tiny galley kitchen and tinier bathroom, stains on the gold shag carpet, and patched places here, and there, and there. The seller boasted about the low miles and great engine and said that "she sleeps five." Well, five if most of the people were very small. The little couch folded into a barely double bed that was a few inches longer than I was. The tiny table could be lowered to span the two padded seats for a single bed. And in the "loft" over the truck cab, one could perhaps hoist two small children. Dory felt a bit like a hand-me-down dollhouse where I would be playing house, but she nevertheless was the answer—at least tem-porarily—to my lack of a dwelling on the land. I had envisioned tent camping up there periodically but knew that would get tiresome and be hard on my back.

I bought Dory for a song, parked her in front of my house, and, with the promise of spring in the air, went to work on her interior. After all, like in bridge, you lead with your strong suit. In the process of an exceedingly thorough cleaning, I found a few more surprises: rotten floorboards under the cupboards below the kitchen sink, scads of mouse droppings (aided by the holes in the floorboards), water damage and mold on the ceiling, broken window latches and frayed screens. I also discovered some sweet souvenirs. A flowery cotton sheet cut with pinking shears that fit inside the front windshield for pri-vacy. Two toys. And my favorite, swinging from the rearview mirror, an Indian headdress of sorts, fashioned from beads strung along a row of large, folded safety pins, with small faded pom-poms swinging from each side.

I was so ready to nest in that mountain meadow that I had the kitchen stocked and the curtains stenciled long before I thought about tires or testing the water system. I visited dollar stores and thrift shops for kitchen items—a tiny salt-and-pepper grinder, a little tea-pot, and spices in cute diminutive jars. I invited Salt Lake friends over to celebrate with candles, wine, and appetizers inside Dory, parked at the curb, my new summer home. When I finally attended to the sewer line and electrical system, I had many more surprises, but that's another story.

What Dory made possible was a life in the woods. Since my child-hood ensconced in those tame Iowa woods, woods had been a place to play, not live, a place to visit and then leave. An afternoon hike, even a weeklong backpack—both are such temporary relationships, like a long-distance love affair whose reunions are enchanting but whose absences are tortuous. I wanted to start and end the day in woods, to witness their spring bloom and fall frosts, welcome the warblers and bid adieu the frogs, to internalize the basal rhythms of light and wind.

~~~~~~~

In the seven summers since the land purchase, since Dory, and since cabin construction, friends have reminded me of the low points, of the accident, of the setbacks. I have vivid memories of all that, but nonetheless what I remember most are the growing and unfolding of a physical structure and of myself.

Each May when I arrive at my land, summer stretches before me but arrives in fits and starts: snow squalls, cloudbursts, sun, windstorms, more snow. On the heels of a frenetic school year, my body is tight, my mind tighter. The day planner that orchestrated my life in Salt Lake is blank and empty, and each day yawns wide and open. I read, tend the woodstove, and watch the meadow for visitors, while my body and mind spill into the hours, seep into the evenings, loosening.

One bright May evening, a visitor, an elk, lingered. Chocolate-brown fur hung from his chin like an oversize goatee that continued down the length of his thick neck. It was the best-looking part of him. His body was covered with mangy, matted fur, loosening in uneven clumps to reveal dark new growth below.

The best chance of seeing elk was the fall when the males were bugling and crashing through the woods in search of females. Once, one snorted and huffed at the edge of the timber, his breath steaming, his neck bulging under a magnificent rack, a sleek, dark hunk of an ungulate. He was so unlike this spring one that grazed on the bright new grasses, occasionally raising his head to survey, the mane swinging gently below his neck. Next to his ears were fuzzy nubs, the promise of antlers. His ribs were filling out after the long, frigid, and snowy winter, and each mouthful replenished heart and marrow and muscle inside, and fur and antler outside.

My recall of this picture is as complete and deep as that very first picture of this place. Both images held the promise of things yet to come.

THREE

Faith in the Witcher

"I wasn't sure you was here," he said, "until I seen your outfit."

It took me a moment to realize that he didn't mean my fleece sweats but was talking about my little motor home. His ball cap said Wheeler Drilling, the cloth faded to a vague color and rimmed with a thick band of accumulated grime and sweat. It was hard to tell how old he was; there were deep wrinkles on his ruddy face and his posture was a bit bent, but that could just be Wyoming, not years. Maybe he was fifty-five, perhaps seventy-five. A shirt and quilted jacket poked from the neck of his coat. He wore black jeans and black leather boots with squared toes, not pointy. In his hand he carried two thin steel rods with handles bent ninety degrees and a fairly thick willow switch.

"Nice to meet you, Sam," I said.

It was the first official day of summer, the summer solstice, but Tobie and I had gotten caught that morning in the weather, leaving Dory in a thick fog and returning coated in wet snow. After I'd crawled beneath the sleeping bag to warm up with the dog curled next to me, we awoke to his rapping on the trailer door. Sam said a week ago he might come up "sometime Sundee," but he hadn't returned my phone calls so I wasn't counting on a visitor.

I had heard about Sam through various sources: my realtor, the road-grader operator, a neighbor. He was the only driller who'd never drilled a dry hole in this area, unlike the two companies from Pinedale, who I'd also heard didn't show sometimes. The Internet said Sam was on the board of the Wyoming Well Drillers Association, and I learned in our first phone call that he wanted to come out first and witch for water.

Dowsing has been around for centuries and many people swear it works. And now, I wanted to believe it, too. But all my scientific training—how to design valid tests, gather data, and accurately evaluate evidence—made me skeptical. I was schooled to have faith in statistical probability, to look beyond random occurrence, and not to put stock in post hoc reasoning. From all that I'd read about witching to locate deep water, it was a matter of opinion and, to a certain degree, faith, whether it really worked. But I really wanted to put my faith in this seasoned man and his divining rods.

When I followed Sam into the snow-dappled meadow, he asked me where the house would be. "Uh, right here," I said, holding my arms in front of me in a V. Tobie thought my open arms were a sign of some significance, and she took off at an eager run in my designated direction.

It was the first time I had pronounced the location out loud.

If there was no water deep beneath this meadow, I might not build a cabin, I told myself. It wasn't just Hollywood and novels that depicted the doom awaiting homesteaders if their parcel had no water.

Throughout the West, I'd seen a lot of abandoned homesteader cabins and shelters on dry, dry land. A lack of water was no doubt one reason that only 40 percent of all homesteaders ever got their titles a century ago. I had the advantage of a professional well driller; if he couldn't find water, perhaps there should be no cabin.

~~~~~

Cecelia Weiss told a reporter for *Sunset* magazine that "the water problem is still with us." She and her sister homesteaded adjacent parcels in the Escalante Valley of southern Utah in 1912 and quickly concluded that the lack of desire for this land was caused by the lack of water.

> There is no running water of any kind for miles and miles and miles. To survive one must drill a well and set up a pump, which is an expensive undertaking. Sister and I have no well, but the neighbor who lives three-quarters of a mile away has.... Until I had to walk a mile and a half and carry every drop I had no conception of the value of water, and I never knew how much of the precious fluid is wasted criminally when you only have to turn the faucet to wash your hands. Water conservation became a religion with me.

Since I hauled water, I understood her religion, though I put my water in closed poly containers and drove them back to my 'stead in the truck. (Cecelia's homesteading story was also compelling because she said, "I had to go to the city every winter to earn enough money to keep myself and the homestead going in summer.")

John Wesley Powell concluded the same thing in his 1878 report to the secretary of the interior about potential settlement in the West: "The mere land is of no value, what is really valuable is the water privilege." He recognized that because moisture from the sky was unreliable, farmers in lowland areas needed to corral moisture that fell somewhere else, namely, as snow in the mountains. This required coordination, which he argued was most dependably achieved if municipal and regional boundaries were drawn according to watersheds.

Yet the first step in creating a system for homesteading was a survey that carved up North America into what some have called an immaculate grid of perfect squares, completely ignoring watersheds and stretching like a neat human-constructed quilt from the Rio Grande to the Arctic. The federal government was then poised to become a real-estate developer on an immense scale, parceling and disposing of great amounts of dry land that never should have been considered for settlement.

〰〰〰

Sam looked northwest, looked southwest, walked twenty yards, planted his feet wide, and held the steel rods from his sides pointing forward, one in each hand. He kept talking; he asked me whether there was another house over thataway with a jerk of his head. Then, one rod crossed on top of the other. He walked a few yards downslope, faced south, and held the rods out again. He turned his cheek and shot a brown stream from the corner of his mouth.

"Yep, there's water here," he said matter-of-factly. "Better'n I thought."

Water witching depends on the witcher's ability to sense buried objects with high electrical conductance, which travels through rods and implements and into the witcher's body. Yes, there's evidence that some people can detect changes in an electromagnetic field and changes in electric current. And maybe human senses are far keener than we've been able to measure. It also makes sense that we don't understand everything about human perceptions. I wasn't sure if my reasoning amounted to faith in the witcher tromping through my meadow, but it was at least positive thinking.

Although I was raised in the Episcopal Church, I never absorbed its beliefs, its faith in a forgiving God and Jesus dying for my sins. The Bible had many good stories and nice parables for how to treat one another, but I wasn't convinced about the life-everlasting part or the rewards in heaven. If anything, my faith lay with the daily turning of this planet toward the sun, birds returning in spring, and accepting a great deal of unknown and unknowable. It seemed plausible—highly likely even—that there were forces and powers much greater than I could imagine, but they didn't have a name or a face with a long beard.

Perhaps I could view Sam as a modern-day geologic shaman, providing a bridge between humans and the higher powers of nature and universe—or rather here, between humans and the lower powers of underlying strata. In every culture, there have been individuals who knew how to heal, those more connected to nature and spirit who provided wisdom and guidance, and those who knew how to find water.

I asked Sam where he learned to witch for water.

"Well, I learnt it from my dad, and he's been practicing it since 'bout 1947."

He then trotted through a tale about how his dad had learnt witching, but I caught only pieces of it as I followed him around the wet meadow. His dad fell off something in the dead of winter and broke something.

"Word 'ventually got out, and a plane with snow runners landed at our place, just glided right in. We were 'bout fifty miles from Laramie. And after my dad got his cast put on, it was a whole week before the big storm died down and the plane could fly back to Laramie, and that's when Dad met the old-time water witcher."

It sounded like the pilot was also the doctor and the witcher, but I couldn't be certain.

Sam leaned the steel rods against a tree and turned his attention to the willow stick. With an ancient, gleaming pocketknife he whittled a couple of inches off the narrow end to make a sharp point.

I asked him about the geology of water around here and why he was pessimistic on the phone, warning me there wasn't much water in the area.

"Well," he started slowly, "it's all a bit tricky, ya see. On the highest part of the ridgeline, water could be just fifty feet down. But if ya don't tap into one of the sand folds coming off there, you might be outta luck." The more he talked about geology, the better I felt.

He grasped the pointed willow end and wrapped his hands firmly around it, then grounded both fists near his navel. The switch end began to bob and Sam's lips moved silently, counting. I quit asking questions and watched his hands.

I tried to imagine that his hands were just an instrument of the willow and of whatever forces or water spirits were involved. Some skeptics say the dowsing tools are essentially a conduit for the diviner's subconscious knowledge or perception, tapping into what the diviner expects to find. Perhaps it was both: feeling the pull of the earth deep below and reading the sand folds and fractures for possible pockets under his feet.

The willow switch stilled.

"Hundred-'n-fifty feet," he announced. "But this is the measure that's sometimes a bit off."

Water just 150 feet below our feet. I grinned. The willow began to move again. When it stilled, he said, "Eleven feet. Looks like you've got a second stream 'bout eleven feet away. That's good news that there're two down there. Yep, we should be okay."

I was pleased with his pronouncement, of course, and for the moment was willing to put stock in it. Faith calls for confident optimism, even when the evidence for doing so seems a bit shy.

We sat at the little table in Dory while Sam did some figuring. His hands fascinated me—heavily wrinkled but slightly shiny and stiff looking, like they were covered with a layer of shellac. On his left hand was a stub where a thumb once was.

"Just being careless," he explained. He was drilling a well in December, which is deep winter up here.

"I had a trailer so I was okay, didn't think too much about the snow. Well, this piece of rigging came loose, and I just didn't see it…It was snowing real hard by then, and my hands, they were real cold. And that rigging flung around and sliced my thumb clean off."

"My god," I said. "What did you do?"

"Well, the snow by then was up past the winders of my car, but at least it was still loose, not too settled and thick. And I made it."

To attempt a self-rescue in those conditions, he must have thought that he could die. His right hand gripped his pencil awkwardly and the writing trembled some. He must have sensed my audience, and he explained that he had injured his right shoulder a few years back, and ever since, his handwriting had gotten worse and worse.

"I don't know why it shakes now. Boy, ya shoulda seen my signature on some checks a few weeks ago," he said, shaking his head.

He handed me the penciled estimate: $7,920. I stared at the paper as if this were a number I had expected. (I had budgeted barely half that much.) Based on drilling two hundred feet, with fifty extra feet for increased storage and better flow. Included: forty feet of eight-inch steel casing nearest the surface, PVC casing below that, and filing the state groundwater permit. His charge per foot was several dollars more than the other two estimates I'd gotten, and I still didn't know how to compute what the witching was worth, but Sam hadn't drilled dry holes around here. He was booked until the very end of the summer.

After Sam's visit, I went to the library and thumbed through *Geology of Wyoming*. Although my land is rimmed by mountain ranges, the area in between is considered part of the extensive Green River Basin, whose bedrock consists of fairly flat-lying, alternating layers of sandstone and shale and some other rock types. Because my land was raised up from the valley floor, some of these sedimentary layers were folded and broken by faults, creating complex patterns of ridges and valleys. When I hiked around here, the abrupt rises and descents were pretty obvious, and now I envisioned them folding around pockets of water, pushing streams between layers far beneath the surface. One night I dreamed that deep underneath my meadow lay mile upon mile of just sand and sandstone, and water drained away, farther and farther toward the center of Earth, through Tertiary, into Mesozoic, past Paleozoic, deep and out of reach. I woke up thirsty.

~~~~~

In the month I'd lived on my land in Dory, I'd taken a lot of notes about wildflowers discovered in the meadow, birds identified, and the vagaries of weather and wind. And because the walls of the motor home were the thinnest of thin, I also noted the night sounds: coyotes yipping in distant draws, hermit thrush putting me to sleep, and little red squirrels waking me up with a chatter that sounded like a windup alarm clock winding down. At various times of day, I'd park myself in different places in the meadow, with coffee, with a book, with binoculars, the dog beside me, watching the sun move and shadows play. I watched where the breezes came from and where they blew too much (at the tip-top of the meadow), too little (at the meadow bottom), and where they were just the right amount to discourage mosquitoes. I found where morning light first peeked into the meadow and where it departed over the mountains.

So by the time Sam asked me, I could see where a cabin might sit: southwest of the knoll, tucked down by the aspens, where the sweet, light clattering of their leaves was such music. Big windows would face the wide-open west and catch the last light of day. And if Sam now had a location for the well, I needed a location for the "used" water: the septic tank and drain field.

When I explained the "perc test" to Dad over the phone, he said, "No problem. Sounds straightforward. We can do it. You don't need to hire anyone for that."

The only building-related things the State of Wyoming and my county troubled themselves with concerned water: a ground- or surface-water permit and a perc test—a test to figure out how quickly water percolated into the soil, which was used to design your septic system. The only government official who personally inspected anything related to the entire building process was the one who signed off on your septic design and actually looked at the tank and drain field before you shoveled the dirt back over. Unlike witching to discern properties hidden from view, we would dig into the earth to test and measure visible properties, a scientific process more aligned with my experience.

Though in most all respects my father lived by the maxim "If you keep track of the pennies, the dollars take care of themselves," he was eventually supportive of my 'stead in the woods. At first he sputtered and muttered over the impracticality of the land purchase and questioned how on earth I would handle all this by myself, but when convinced of my resolve, he e-mailed one day, "You only live once, but you happily go into debt several times." I read the words several times before I printed out the e-mail and tucked it into my journal. When I was growing up, a plaque hung over the desk where Mom budgeted and paid bills that declared: "The worst place in the world to live is beyond your means." Dad's e-mail seemed to give me permission to set aside that family maxim; he did indeed understand my dream, and if he could see the necessity of debt to get there, I could get used to the well bill (and many other bills yet to come).

A perc test was the perfect chore for a man who finds great satisfaction in figuring out the path of a problem. Dad's methodical questioning and deliberate progression could drive me crazy, though I knew that I had learned or subconsciously mimicked some of this very ability. For example, my first project upon parking Dory in the meadow was to build a small deck outside her door to lessen the mud tracked inside and to have a dry, flat space to put a small table. Friends asked me, "How did you know how to build a deck?" "I don't know. I just figured it out," I said.

When Dad flew out in early July, after breaking in my new chain saw, we read through the detailed instruction sheet and examined the sketch for a perc test. Dig three holes, three to four feet deep, in the proposed leach site. Line the bottom of each hole with sand or gravel. Thoroughly presoak each hole. Lower a stiff measuring tape into a hole, pour in twelve to eighteen inches of water, and start timing. Calculate the minutes it takes the water to drop one inch. Repeat five times at each of the three holes. The slower they drain, the bigger the drain field needed.

We bought a shovel and a spade and filled my two five-gallon water containers at a gas station in town. Digging the holes was no small task, chopping through assorted roots and tough meadow sod. The presoaking step used all ten gallons and we returned to town to refill. How ironic that we needed so much water for these tests, but didn't yet have a well to provide it. Guess that's true for most investments: you need some seeds to grow more seeds, some love to find more love. And it takes faith that the investment will pay off somewhere down the road.

My chemistry-professor father soon encountered a potpourri of confounding variables that were not addressed in the instruction sheet and potentially affected the results of our experiment. How level should the bottom of the pit be, for that would affect where the measurement was taken? How should the water be poured in—all at once or in increments? If we had to stop to go fetch more water, would we need to presoak again? And how exactly did a person actually see the inch marks at the bottom of a deep, muddy hole?

Once these variables had been standardized to his satisfaction, we began. I sat next to the hole with a notepad and watch. He lay prone, manning the ruler. Two of the holes percolated fairly quickly, but the third was like a plugged drain, sluggishly seeping away in fifty or sixty minutes, which disturbed him.

"I think two holes are fairly sandy, and the other one is full of clay or something," I concluded.

He shook his head. "There's got to be a problem with our method or execution. There's got to be some logical explanation."

I walked to Dory to make sandwiches.

For the entire afternoon, and part of the next morning, I watched this gray, slight seventy-seven-year-old man lying prone on the dirt, lowering a ruler into a hole. While waiting for the holes to drain, he gazed into the meadow, Tobie at his side, engaged in thought but more peaceful and unoccupied than I usually see him. Between trips to town for more water, and sometimes missing the exact time when each hole went dry, the test process was long, but the results no doubt far more accurate than most submitted to the state engineer's office. His tenacity for the task he pronounced as "easy" over the phone was admirable. A scientist at work.

~~~~~~

I got a call in early August that Sam would start drilling the following week, a month earlier than scheduled. I tracked down the guy who graded our roads and pleaded for a rush job: bulldoze a fairly level pad for the well rig and knock down two trees from the bottom turn in the dirt path that served as a driveway that Sam said the drill rig couldn't get around. The grader guy came through with great speed and enthusiasm.

The drill rig chugged up the driveway late Monday, driven by Sam's son. It was a fantastical machine; when positioned, its two front wheels were high off the ground, and the tall column of steel at the rear stood ready to bite the earth. Around here, drilling a well was a bit like a barn raising; neighbors I didn't know I had dropped by—not to help, but to watch, and to share their own well stories and prognosticate about my chances of finding water.

On Tuesday morning, the machine began to chew with deafening gusto. Tobie was alarmed at the sound and ran back to Dory and sat on the little deck, watching. The first three feet were brown topsoil, spit out in a slurry that drained down the slope. Next came gray dirt, then brown again. Every so often, Sam's son stuck a large wire basket under the slurry stream to inspect the type of rock and record it in a logbook. At thirty-nine feet, brown sandstone, and again at fifty-two feet. Sadly, I had to leave for Salt Lake shortly after noon to attend a daylong faculty meeting the next day, and it felt like leaving a good action movie just when things were heating up.

On Wednesday I borrowed cell phones during the faculty meeting to check on the well's progress. One hundred feet, nothing yet. After lunch I called again. One hundred seventy feet, still no water; Sam had said the depth measurement was the one that was a bit off. "Trust them," I told myself. "You hired the best guys around." In our midafternoon break I called again, but no one answered the phone.

～～～～～

From an airplane traversing the West, you can easily see that settlements sprouted where water was. The plane floats past miles and miles of dry rangeland, and then boom, there's a green oasis of river, a ribbon of life for the people planted there. Settlements were made—or broken—by water. Indian tribes that moved seasonally were less dependent on one reliable source of water than were homesteaders who stayed put with crops and herds. Thus, much of the West was simply off-limits to permanent dwellings—until well-drilling technology. Even so, my future settlement depended on striking water in amounts beyond the few gallons stored in Dory's tank.

I got a call late that afternoon—they struck water! At 205 feet. It felt like striking gold. My head and heart were in Wyoming, and I remembered little of the remaining faculty discussion. But Sam said the flow wasn't great—less than two gallons a minute—and they wanted to keep drilling to try to improve that. At 220 feet, gray sandstone and shale, and again at 240. At 263, gray sandstone. They stopping drilling at 300 feet; the water flow hadn't improved much, but now there was more storage in this amazing hole in the ground. They lowered the pump into place, deep into the earth.

When I returned several weeks later in late August, the two-foot-tall well pipe was capped, the permits filed, and I could only imagine the water, how it would taste, how cold it might be. I had no cabin, no pipes, no faucets to send it to. For months I had lived with the uncertainty and unpredictability of finding water; now I would live with a legion of brand-new uncertainties—not the least of which was pouring a foundation and finding builders. But at the very least, I assured myself, I had now traveled this path once and was minutely more comfortable with it. I had relied on a little bit science, a little bit magic, and as much faith as I could muster.

If they hadn't hit water, would I have progressed and built a cabin? Or would I have lived in that sorry motor home for a couple of summers and then, like many others (past and present) who have taken small settlement steps, lost interest, visited less and less, and found other places to summer? Every time I lugged five-gallon water containers to my property and hauled Dory and her septic waste out, I asked myself, how much did I really want this? What was I willing to endure, and of course, what was I able to spend? But I still dreamed of water flowing from a faucet and down a drain.

The fact that I'll never know what role witching played in my striking water is the very essence of its power. That fact has no doubt helped witchers the world over continue their craft. It may be just pure odds, no more, no less. Or it may have been infinitesimal pulses of energy and particles moving into Sam. Or a subconscious reading of the land and decades of experience of doing so. Or his faith in this art-and-science practice handed down by his father.

Such is the nature of faith in general: I'll never know whether the faith I mustered in witching (or well drilling, I guess) worked or what role it played. Was it the result of my believing and trusting something or someone, or did that matter not at all? Even if my faith in witching was only akin to the "power of positive thinking," isn't that as much control as one ever has over anything?

Today, it still feels like magic when I open the faucet and am delivered this pure, clean, very cold water. I imagine the pump clicking on three hundred feet down, pushing the liquid up, up, up from deep in the earth, through pipe, through pressure tank, through faucet, into glass. No chlorine, no bacteria, little discernible taste. Simply amazing.

Sometimes, I imagine what it would be like if I turned the faucet handle...and nothing came out. How would a person ever know if the pocket or fold of water she tapped deep, deep in the ground was just that—a pocket not connected to other streams or formations, or whether other wells tapped the same stream and drew it dry? I have faith that my well will continue to flow, but I still keep two five-gallon containers of water on hand.

FOUR

If You Want to Make God Laugh

I was awakened at two Wednesday morning by two simultaneous sounds: heavy rain clattering on Dory's roof and Tobie climbing over pet food tins to get into the front seat, trying to escape her soggy dog bed. Then I heard the drips, splashing with syncopated rhythms into a variety of bowls and tins strategically placed on carpet, table, and counter. My sleeping bag was wet, presumably from a brand-new leak. Another night of sleepless water torture.

It was June of my second summer and log cabin construction was slated to begin, but June was on its way to becoming the wettest in a quarter century. Pouring the concrete basement floor was delayed four times (though, thankfully, the skies held for three days so the "mud" cured). Delivery of the cabin logs was postponed twice, as was the interior framing lumber. The freight delivery was scheduled two days ago but hadn't arrived.

When the logs were finally delivered, my builder ferried the log bundles up the hill from the road, but the lack of other material forced him to move on to another job in the interim. So every day I worked the phone, conveying urgency, encouraging prompt rescheduling. Every day, I walked to the meadow and lifted tarp corners to drain the accumulated rain (or snow) from the stacks of building material that had been delivered, and I replaced large anchoring rocks that the wind kept flinging aside. I had soggy two-by-fours and wet tongue-and-groove pine, and moisture soaked into the top row of stacked logs.

In the morning when the storm subsided, I emptied the assorted drip buckets and catchers onto the meadow. I removed the cover from the dog bed and hung it up to dry on the rope clothesline I strung between two Doug firs, along with the wet towels used to catch rainwater in places where bowls didn't fit. I swept the mud from the deck outside the trailer. And as I did several times a day, I walked over to the basement wall and peered down at the floor; there was one very large puddle. When I walked back to Dory to fetch the broom, the phone rang.

"You doing okay over there?" Betty asked. "You know, this really isn't normal. Bob said we've had over three inches in our rain gauge in just three weeks. That's just unheard of up here."

Betty and Bob were my nearest neighbors, about a half mile up the road, and one of the first to build up here several decades ago. They were my dad's age and had two grown daughters back East who were a bit younger than I. Each summer Betty and Bob flew out for the summer from their winter home in Florida.

"Normal or not," I said, "it's totally messing up all the deliveries and the construction schedule."

"I know, dear, I know. Well, I just called to make sure you were okay after that big storm last night."

"I'm okay—wet, but okay. But I would like to take up your offer to borrow the space heater. I just can't get Dory warm, let alone dry."

"Of course, dear. Why don't you come over for a drink later?"

~~~~~

When I left my land last October after my first summer, I had a foundation—literally. It wasn't very sexy, certainly not like a cabin, but it was a meaningful stage: you don't just pour a foundation and then stop. No, a foundation says, this is the beginning of something long term; there's a plan behind this. There it stands, rising from the soil, this concrete sign of something larger yet to come. A foundation may sometimes seem like a mirage—the closer you get, the farther away it seems—but it is built to last.

This second summer was to be all about building upon that foundation. I had spent the winter researching, first with books. My favorite, *Log Homes Made Easy: Contracting and Building Your Own Log Home,* introduced me to a dizzying array of foreign vocabulary. "Shrinkage" and "settlement" were straightforward, but who knew that log corners came in four styles (dovetail, butt-and-pass, saddle-notched, and corner post) and that there are a dozen ways for logs to "interface" each other? I combed every log-home website, which both excited me with possibilities and depressed me with prices. I even visited a log-home show, feeling horribly out of place with the McMansions and their Persian rugs and gleaming brass. But I pestered the reps with questions, and eventually came away knowing the difference between "dry-in" and "turn-key" and that I could save money and energy by forgoing lofts and cathedral ceilings.

By late winter, I signed a contract with a log-home company in Colorado and started shelling out money. They used dead standing logs cut nearby and sold the most complete "kit" I could find, with logs, interior lumber, tongue-and-groove pine ceiling, doors, energy-efficient windows, a roof package, and even stain and caulk. They accommodated my design changes to their standard plans, and I really liked the folks I talked to. The main floor would be 720 square feet on top of a cement walk-out basement. (I had learned that a cement basement was far cheaper than a second story of logs and a more efficient space than sleeping lofts, which in my experience were always too hot or too cold, too noisy with company, and poorly insulated with little attic space.) I extended the deck partway around two more sides to extend my summer living space and provide options for sun and shade. I chose medium-diameter "D logs" (rounded on the outside but flat on the inside), butt-and-pass corners, and scissor trusses in the main room for height that were lower than cathedral ceilings and thus could accommodate insulation. I happily put delivery dates on my calendar, beginning in late May.

~~~~~~

When the art museum at the University of Minnesota was dedicated when I was in graduate school there years ago, I made sure to attend the ceremony—not because I admired the gaudy new steel building, but because the program included a "Dance of the Bobcats." There they were, six of those compact little machines driven by six hard-hatted men, spinning in tight circles, zooming in and out in lovely patterns and formations. When they formed a circle and lifted their scoop shovels in unison, and then bowed and backed gracefully away, it reminded me of a flower formation in synchronized swimming.

Maybe that's where I got the idea that construction could be choreographed. The very short summers in the mountains called for a fair amount of coordination and timing: cement, logs, lumber, roof, windows, and doors, not to mention plumbing and electrical work. But

I was unsure of all the individual steps in this dance and could visualize only the end.

So when the dance began this soggy June, I grew more and more anxious. With each cloudburst, it felt like my well-planned choreography was collapsing, as dancers missed entrances time and time again. During sleepless nights in Dory, each new drip in the musical score reminded me of an added expense I failed to budget for: off-loading logs, roof insulation, a woodstove, doorknobs, porch railings. When fitful sleep arrived, I had a repeating nightmare about logs and lumber rotting in the meadow and having to start over. I knew this was a subconscious fear of failure, but it was hard to imagine how a phoenix could ever rise from such soggy ruin.

My anxiety about building also muted the moments of joy I felt at the stirrings and sightings of early summer. Last week in a break in the rain, Tobie and I hiked over to the forestland, and from a tall ridge where we stopped to rest, I spied a female elk in the wetland below. Only her back and head were visible above the dense willows. As I watched her browse through my binoculars, a perfect miniature version appeared. The calf's back end was bony, its limbs spindly, and it had to be only days—or hours—old. But even this incredible treat faded far too quickly when I returned to the wet and empty building site.

~~~~~

When I arrived at Bob and Betty's that afternoon, the space heater and an extra sleeping bag sat by the door. Betty ushered me to a waiting chair and asked me what I wanted to drink. "Bob, she wants white wine," she shouted over to the kitchen. Her outfit was always variations of the same combination, a polo shirt draped over her thick middle and khaki slacks. Her white hair, parted on the side and held near her ear with a silver barrette, was flipped under in a curl just below her chin line.

Bob brought me a glass of white wine and joked, "Maybe I should warm that up for you." He was a tall, thin man, sporting a few days' worth of whiskers; he loved infrequent shaving at the cabin.

"So how are ya doing?" he asked as he sat in the rocker.

"Oh, overwhelmed, anxious, with a headache that won't let up. I mean, this rain, and all the lumber just sits there, and…" I stopped, on the verge of tears.

They reminded me how much I'd already accomplished, that I was making good decisions and hiring good people.

"I know, but…"

The conversation soon shifted, to recent animal sightings, to shenanigans by the Forest Service, to neighborly gossip. As usual, they interrupted each other and squabbled, but I felt rather numb to it all, wondering instead why the freight truck hadn't arrived this week.

〰〰〰

On Thursday morning, another storm ushered in strong, steady winds, and it snowed and rained for twenty-eight hours without stopping. In a not-so-positive way, it reminded me of living in the Pacific Northwest, when a storm got a grip and simply wouldn't budge, dumping more moisture than it seemed possible for a cloud to hold. The sky was solid and gray and nondimensional and impenetrable and utterly without definition. Dory found new places to leak (this time around the skylight), despite the tubes and tubes of caulk and a slathering of rubber roof coat I'd applied. Tobie wearied of the drips, too. No sooner had she gotten comfortable in one spot on the floor or her dog bed when she'd notice that her fur was getting wet and slink off to a new location.

By early afternoon, there was a new drip in Dory each hour and I was running out of ways and containers to catch them. Dory's sorry roof had a sag in the middle, which pooled water into a lake on top of the trailer. Every hour or so, I'd climb the ladder to broom off some of the accumulation. I even tried to circumvent the roof sag by placing the metal cat carrier on the roof's low spot and draping plastic sheeting over it (with the edges anchored by rocks) to encourage runoff instead of ponding. With innumerable trips up and down the ladder and moving the ladder from side to side, I was soaked. That solution lasted about two hours before drip, drip, drip.

I gave up and wrapped myself in both sleeping bags and donned a second pair of thick socks. I tried to read, but I kept thinking about all the times I'd been really, really wet. Of course, there were many, many wet times when I worked in the Olympic Peninsula, which now seemed like one big, soggy memory of a wet tent, wet sleeping bag, wet food bag, and perennially cold feet, rather than distinct wet trips. Then there was a backpack with an Idaho friend in the Eagle Cap Wilderness in northeastern Oregon; the storm hit just as we cleared the pass, and we knew we needed to get down in elevation quickly and bundle up. By the time we did, we were both slightly hypothermic and erected the tent in lightning speed. We sat inside in our sleeping bags, jaws chattering, making cup after cup of tea in the tent vestibule, trying to warm up. Thankfully, the storm was intense but brief, and by morning, we spread our wet laundry over the rocks and shrubs where it steamed in the bright sun. There was also the time in the Pahsayten Wilderness of Washington with an old roommate, where it sprinkled hiking in, and I saw my first spotted owl. But the rain kept up for two straight days, and everything she owned was saturated; she convinced me to hike out early, and we found a B&B with a hot tub.

I went to sleep that night curled tightly on Dory's couch, unable to fold it down into a bed because of the assortment of drip buckets on the floor. Kaya, an easygoing cat who'd adapted quite well to motor-home life, abandoned her cat bed and lay on my stomach, her ears twitching nervously at every hint of thunder. Tobie slept on the passenger seat in the cab, displaced once again from her still-wet dog bed. Please, please, please let this be the end of this storm. My lip quivered and I fought back tears. To quit feeling so sorry for myself, I fell asleep thinking about the sandhill crane I saw on its nest, not able to move from its appointed post, keeping eggs warm and protected.

~~~~~~

The phone rang at 5:05 Friday morning; it was the driver of the freight semi, and I needed to drive out to the main highway to meet him. I put my truck in 4 WD-low to get out of the mud and drove with the heater on full blast. I was dry and warm for the first time in days. From the back of his semi, he handed me boxes of bolts, dowels, and augers, which I loaded into my truck. Still no caulk or construction glue, which was supposed to be in this shipment.

When I returned to Dory, I inspected the evening's leakage. The top of my sleeping bag was fairly wet. Water had run down the vent pipes in the bathroom and ponded at the back of the sink. Containers had caught most everything during the night, though there was yet a new leak in the cubby above the cab near the cat's bed and the phone. There was water under my laptop, a terrifying sight, though none of the papers on top of it were wet. I made coffee and curled up with the pets. I knew that no other deliveries, no other progress, would be made for days and days.

I am one of the more organized people I know, and a certain amount of it I think I was somehow born with. When I was perhaps ten, I organized a family hike and cookout up the dry bed of Onion Creek. I brought plaster of paris to cast animal tracks. I brought my pocketknife for carving sticks for roasting hot dogs and marshmallows. And when I sliced my wrist carving those sticks, I pulled out my first-aid kit, which had sufficient supplies to stem the blood until we got to the emergency room. My parents shook their heads and smiled at "Little Miss Organized."

The organizational challenges are probably why I love to entertain, too. The details, the planning, the timing—it drives many people to cater or never send out invitations, but I love it. The choreography of myriad details (and thus the illusion of control) is in your own two hands. And I've done it so many times—since helping my mom at her elegant summer dinner parties on the patio, serving and clearing in my little maid's apron—that the rush of adrenaline feels good, brings a flush to my cheeks, gets me excited at the first ring of the doorbell.

But at construction, I felt like such an unskilled choreographer who had never done this kind of dancing. So far, I'd managed, step by step, to make a lot of decisions: the cabin location, the cabin design and supplier, an excavation contractor, the concrete contractor, the type of basement wall (who knew there were so many choices?), a plumber to lay drainpipe underneath the basement floor, and, crucially, a builder. But now it felt like it was all busting apart, as my logs sat in the sodden meadow and my builder moved on to other jobs. It was hard to be content with what materials had arrived; all I could think about was what was not yet here. The longer I waited for those arrivals, the longer the pauses yawned before me, and the more I feared that this dazzling bright bubble would burst and I would awaken from a dream: there was no cabin; there was no way to build it. It continued to rain, and rain some more.

~~~~~~~

The phone rang late morning on Friday. It was Linda at the log-home company, who told me that the roof trusses were five weeks out.

"What?" I sputtered. "You've got to be kidding! Why the delay? You told me, what, two weeks ago that everything was on track for those, that they'd be here by the end of next week."

"Well, there are only so many hours in the day," she said.

Her excuses all sounded lame. While she talked, I visualized rain collecting on the subfloor, rotting and leaking into the basement. I reminded her that my contract said I must accept delivery of The Kit by June 15. (I thought about making a standard I'll-contact-my-lawyer threat, but I didn't have one to contact.)

"I realize that," she said, "and we're doing the best we can, but there are only so many hours in the day."

With this news, I had to get out of that saturated motor home. I started down the driveway-path when I ran into "Lake Corbett," which had grown significantly during the twenty-eight-hour storm. A series of puddles at a low spot in the half-completed driveway had now grown to one continuous lake about six feet wide, twelve feet long, and half a foot deep at the center. My truck got stuck there briefly that morning when I drove out to meet the freight.

I started my engineering work with a stick, pulling it through the mud and pebbles to open a channel, but it wasn't very effective. I walked back to Dory for the spade to scrape through the ridges between puddle portions so they'd drain into each other and onto the meadow. While it slowly drained, I went for a little walk with Tobie, but when we returned, several inches of muddy water remained. Time to get serious. I dug a deep channel a couple of feet long from puddle to meadow. It was admittedly gratifying when the puddle bottoms were again visible, and I scolded myself for not getting into the true spirit of mud-puddle engineering. Just look at Tobie—to her, this was a really fun game in the water. I wiped my muddy hands on the grass. Next week will be better, I told myself, and I started to cry.

In my youth, mud puddles were magnets, transforming my brothers and me into hydrological engineers after Iowa downpours. With sticks and sharp rocks, we dug into the thick black soup, cutting channels between pools. For hours, oblivious to the mud, cold water, and icy fingers, we worked our waterways, created tiny pour-offs, and drained driveway swamps. The sounds of sucking mud, the swirling eddies of chocolate and mocha, and the joy and satisfaction when the water broke through, flowed, and emptied made us feel like saviors of some larger than life hydrological crisis. We were the self-appointed guardians of the miniature watershed of our rural woods—well, at least the driveway.

Those youthful mud-engineering experiences were fun; this was not. I felt no adventure, no accomplishment, no camaraderie with my brothers in mud. Lake Corbett was drudgery, a chore. My goal for the week was to quit fretting about the weather, and I was falling far short.

I propped the spade against Dory and went inside for some lunch. It started to rain. I popped two ibuprofen and lay down on the sofa bed, waiting for the drips. As sleep overtook me, I was worrying about the lumber that wasn't up on pallets, most notably the OSB waferboard held together by glue.

~~~~~

The phone rang about three that afternoon; it was Scott, my older brother, awake after day-sleeping following a night shift at the hospital. Scott and I had not been close, with issues yawning into the past. By adulthood, we had probed, washed, and stitched the wounds from childhood as best we could, but they never healed entirely, like proud flesh that remains raised and conspicuous and sensitive to the touch. But since I bought the land and began the construction process, he'd gotten more interested and called more often. This was a subject where he shone, having worked in construction for years before nursing, and he dispensed reams of brotherly advice. He put me on the mailing list for the Tool Crib catalog and bought me a subscription to *Fine Homebuilding*. The magazine articles were way over my head; all I truly understood were the ads.

I was happy he called, not mildly annoyed as I was sometimes with his voluminous advice. I needed his wisdom, but what I really needed was support. I launched into my headaches: deliveries, weather, trying to be my own general contractor. Choking back tears, I explained the "additional charges" my builders billed for off-loading the logs and putting in deck footings. No, Scott said, that was reasonable. It was becoming clear that I had assumed a lot, assumed they'd put the entire cabin up no matter what. I also told him about the log-home company and their screw-ups in deliveries, how things had been dribbling in, how they now said trusses would be five to six weeks out and how I got angry.

For a brother who for much of my life had said or done the wrong things—or said the right things but didn't follow through with them— he said exactly all the right things, and there was enough in his voice that I knew they were true, that they came from a real place.

"Good for you. That's bullshit about the trusses. They screwed up."

I told him about the mud-puddle engineering to drain Lake Corbett and how it wasn't fun like when we were kids, and he laughed.

"Sis, you need to go find that little kid again," he said.

"She's turned into an adult and she's worried about money. Scott, there are all these extras I didn't budget for—and I don't even have anything built yet!"

"Hey, go back to that dream of yours. It's only money. Big deal," he said. "And think of the money you're saving by being your own general contractor and having to deal with all these headaches—I bet you're saving like 30 percent."

"Yeah, but I still don't have the money."

"Hey, you've never done this before, remember? It's okay not to know everything. Limber up your arm and reach around and pat yourself on the back."

"Yeah, but 'it's only money' and 'you're not supposed to know everything' is not what we Corbetts were taught," I said.

Scott said, "Quit the 'yeah buts.' You're doing it—you're following your dream. Most people would only talk about it, not get up and do it. I'm really proud of you, Sis. And you know, they've found that a really good way to help cure basement concrete is if you go dance on it with your dog, just get down and funky. It really compacts it amazingly well. You might try it."

"That's sweet. Maybe I will." I paused and pulled a new tissue from the soggy box. "You know, I was reading a story last night and it quoted this Yiddish proverb: 'If you want to make God laugh, tell Him your plans.'"

Scott laughed uncontrollably. "That's perfect! I want you to make a sign of that and put it in your cabin."

I began to kvetch and said I didn't have a cabin to put it in and nothing to make the sign with.

"You got some cardboard? You got some duct tape? Go make that sign, and whenever you walk past it, laugh and go back to the simple stuff, go back to that little kid," he said.

I smiled, wiped my eyes, thanked him, hung up, and cried some more, releasing a flood of fears that I was in over my head, that I would fail at this. Weeks of sitting in that soggy motor home, surrounded by even soggier lumber, had threatened to drown me. Happily, life preservers take many forms: furry and four-legged, kind neighbors down the road, and a brother who for so many years drifted far, far away but had now sailed into my port.

I went to find some cardboard—some dry cardboard.

FIVE

Blackwater Run

I could ignore the stench no longer. All the windows in Dory were open and the curtains fluttered in the breeze, but it stunk. Sewage fumes. I was trying to read at the table, using one hand to hold the book and the other hand cupped to cover my mouth and nose to block the fumes. I had even taken to peeing in the trees to save space in the tank for the big jobs. But full or not, it stunk. I had been postponing the inevitable, wanting to coordinate the toilsome dump trip with another errand, such as a shower, groceries, or beer.

Yesterday I emptied Dory's gray-water tank, the tank that collects what goes down the kitchen and bathroom sinks, hoping that would diminish the stench. Under the rear end of Dory I attached a short hose to its drain and emptied the contents into a bucket, while holding my breath. I carried the pail a good distance from Dory and dumped the slurry on an unsuspecting shrub. It may have been just sink water, but between dishwashing and toothbrushing and the particles of assorted biomass they produced, it reeked foully. Draining this line never emptied as much as I thought it should; I suspected a clog somewhere trapped much of the water and fermented it. Draining it and adding an extra packet of sewage digester to the toilet did nothing to lessen the smell coming from the other holding tank, the blackwater.

I put down my book. "Tobie, we gotta do it," I said, and she looked at me with expectant eyes. "It's time for a blackwater run." Her tail thumped on Dory's gold shag carpet, knowing that whatever this meant, it involved going somewhere.

The journey to empty Dory's blackwater tank was one of necessity and self-sufficiency, of course, but the journey always tested my mettle. My parents taught me to be a self-reliant and capable woman, but in my heart of hearts, I sometimes wished there were a man in my life to deal with chores that were not my strong suit, not my cup of tea, or just plain gross—like auto repair, the stock market, electrical things, and sewage. Or, lacking a man with such talents and proclivities, I wished I had lots of money and could pay someone to undertake undesirable tasks, like sewage.

When I first began backpacking in my early twenties, it was a matter of pride how self-sufficient the entire enterprise was. You carried on your back everything needed to survive: food, shelter, clothing, and equipment for cooking and filtering water. You also were responsible for your waste—packing out all garbage from meal making, and disposing of your own bodily wastes. I carried a fluorescent orange plastic trowel for digging "cat" holes and a partial roll of TP in a ziplock bag.

With the prodigious exercise of backpacking and the water consumption required for it, regularity was, shall we say, never a problem. And with mosquitoes and precipitation to contend with, speed was desirable—no magazines to read or navels to contemplate.

By comparison, sitting on the toilet in Dory was highly civilized. Dory's toilet was like an outhouse with a plastic trap door. Open the door, and the waste descended into the blackness below. There was a button to release a stream of water to help the waste on its descent, but I closed the valve because it leaked on the floor; I now chased the waste as needed with a cup of water from the sink. To save space in the tank, pee paper went in the wastebasket. By and large, I was free to forget about my remains and where they traveled. But unlike the animal scat that peppered the hiking trails and backpackers' waste buried hither and yon in the great woods, the remains in Dory, well, remained, accumulating and fermenting in the plastic holding tanks.

I postponed blackwater runs because they were a major production for a mobile home that I used as a stationary one. It was thirty miles to the dump station, four on gravel, and it required battening down the hatches and removing everything that would slide or fly. For my first two summers, Dory remained parked on the flattest spot on top of the bumpy meadow and didn't move until the blackwater tank demanded it. I even hauled water to fill Dory's water tank, rather than drive Dory to water.

To prepare for the journey, I unplugged my laptop and the phone and placed them in the storage area beneath the bench seat at the table. I took the tea kettle and salt and pepper from the stove and parked them in the sink and emptied all the pet bowls. In the bathroom, I shoved all the items on the countertop into the little sink. I carried the dishes from the high cupboard to the deck outside (true mobile-home life would require plastic). Then I hauled out everything stored underneath Dory—broom, shovel, ax, water jugs, chain saw, and gas—and moved them all to the deck.

It was the beginning of our second summer, but this would be Kaya's first blackwater run. Last summer, she was in Salt Lake when I did one run, and for a couple of runs, the weather was cold and rainy and I left her in the SUV. But it was hot today and that wouldn't work. I couldn't leave her outside to roam, either. I briefly thought about putting her in the cat carrier under a tree, but I pictured a bear rolling it around like a backpacker's food tube, trying to get the goodies out. No, I decided it would be less stressful for her to accompany the dog and me for the blackwater run. She rode well in the car, and she had taken quite well to Dory, exploring all the cupboards, napping contentedly in her cat bed, looking out the windows.

"Let's get this over with," I announced to the pets. Kaya, asleep in her kitty basket above the cab, opened one eye and then closed it again. I turned the key and Dory's engine (no doubt the most reliable part of her) roared to life.

~~~~~~

I learned the ins and outs, shall we say, of Dory and her holding tanks the spring I bought her in Salt Lake City. Like much of her creaky body, her plumbing was stiff from sitting in the elements and needed some work. One spring Saturday, I donned my disposable latex gloves and went out to Dory, parked at the curb, to get acquainted with her plumbing. About six inches back from each holding tank's end cap was a lever that lifted a sluice gate. Leaving the end cap in place, I slowly lifted the sluice gate for the gray-water tank; nothing slid through to the end cap. Good; it had been emptied. The sluice lever for the blackwater tank, however, wouldn't budge. I tapped it with a screwdriver; I squatted in different angles and pulled. Nothing—no movement. There wasn't a place to spray WD-40, either, so I sat in the street, legs in a V, and jiggled and wiggled and strained to lift the sluice gate.

When it eventually gave way, the protective end cap went flying into my lap, followed by a slurry of orange-brown slop. I slammed the sluice gate shut and sucked in my breath from shock and surprise, which meant that I inhaled the aroma of the mixture most foul that now covered me from the waist down. I gagged slightly; it certainly didn't smell or look like what one sees below the outhouse seat. It was rather slimy and viscous with unrecognizable softened chunks. And it certainly wasn't black. With a gloved hand, I removed the end cap from my lap—ah-ha, broken threads—and proceeded to scoot backward into the street. For some reason, I looked up and down the street—either to seek aid or check for witnesses. I stood up, and the glutinous mixture oozed down my legs and onto my shoes. I started walking bowlegged to the front porch, dripping a slimy trail, where I removed my shoes and socks and attempted to hide behind the large screen door before I dropped my shorts and headed to the shower.

After buying a new end cap and some flexible black tubing, I drove Dory to a Flying J truck stop in western Salt Lake. It took me several maneuvers to drive the rig into position so the black tubing (which I fitted over the drainpipe) reached the hole in the ground. The nicely lubricated blackwater sluice gate slid open and glug, glug, glug went the remaining slop into the hole. I surmised that the garden hose hanging nearby was to flush the system from above, so I maneuvered Dory once more and snaked the hose in through the tiny bathroom window and pinned it into place under the toilet seat.

A gargantuan, gleaming white motor home towing an SUV idled behind me, and the driver, watching my numerous trips in and out of Dory, leaned out and inquired, "You 'bout done there, honey?"

"Gettin' there," I replied.

~~~~~

When my mother was a child during the Depression, her family moved from town to town, looking for work. Her favorite residence was an orchard and farm in eastern Washington, which her father managed. Like most farms of the era, this one had an outhouse, a simple wood shack set back a fair piece from the house, and a crescent moon cut out on the door. One day someone—no one ever fessed up—left the outhouse door open and a chicken fell down the hole. Her dad eventually got the chicken out, but she wasn't sure how. Mom also remembered sitting in the outhouse, perusing the Sears catalog pages and dreaming about the dresses and the dolls, before ripping out a page to use as TP.

I could imagine catalog pages as toilet paper because of my experience with toilet paper in London. I spent a semester studying there in 1976 and returned to the States with a collection of the odd sheets. Most resembled stiff parchment or thin writing paper, some with bumpy ribbing or ridges, and all were really noisy when you crumpled them. None were white; most were nondescript tans, but several samples were a lovely deep rose. Many had writing on them. The scratchy sheets from the loo in the House of Parliament said "Government Property." One intoned, "NOW WASH YOUR HANDS, PLEASE."

With or without toilet paper, for most of human history, how you dealt with your waste was largely dictated by your social class. Servants emptied chamber pots of their master's "nightsoil." People without servants dumped their waste into open ditches (often flowing right through the center of town) and cesspools. Ladies held perfumed hankies to their noses (I should have tried that in Dory) as they walked to their carriages. Plumbing originated in several ancient civilizations—most notably the Roman, with its system of water aqueducts and lead pipe to transport waste—but virtually no plumbing progress was made by subsequent civilizations until the nineteenth century.

In this country, outhouses remained well into the twentieth century. During the Depression, Franklin D. Roosevelt's Works Progress Administration built more than two million "Sanitary Privies" across the country. As late as 1950, about fifty million American families still had outhouses; by 1990, approximately four million outhouses were still in use.

If you had the means, you hired someone to haul away your waste. In China after World War II, a waste collector hung full "honey buckets" on each end of a pole, which he carried on his shoulders through the streets to some collection point. In Australia, as recently as the 1970s, some large cities like Brisbane lacked modern plumbing. Their version of an outhouse was a metal can beneath the toilet seat, and each week, contractors (hired by the local town council) collected the "dunny" cans and emptied, washed, and replaced them. In India, the government said in 2003 that 676,000 people were employed in the manual collection of human waste.

Anyone—a poor Indian, my mother, and to a certain extent me—who sees, smells, and negotiates her waste aboveground is delighted when those bodily excretions move belowground, out of sight and smell, out of mind. But I wonder, too, if something is lost, even a simple understanding of a very real and corporeal recycling; what is no longer needed by our bodies is nevertheless full of nutrients to enrich soil and grow food that we will once again put in our bodies. Of course, over the centuries, we've learned that human waste is full of pathogens and bacteria and must first be treated, but like the manure of other species, it can fertilize the earth.

〜〜〜〜

In Wyoming, I soon perfected the blackwater procedure: attach, open, dump, rinse. Whoosh gurgle glug, and the black flexi-tube wiggled and wriggled as everything slooshed into the pit. There was something satisfying about the operation. Done properly, you never saw or smelled anything whilst dumping. What went in came out—outta me and now outta Dory. Such a healthy cleansing.

Despite my perfected technique, it didn't mean that blackwater runs always occurred without a hitch. One time when I turned from the gravel road onto the highway, the little fridge door popped open and the contents went flying—soup on the carpet, cantaloupe against the cupboards, milk everywhere. Tobie gladly helped clean up the mess. On another run, a highway patrol car spun around and turned on its lights in pursuit, which surprised me because it was virtually impossible to speed in Dory. The bolt attaching the spare tire had broken, and I was dragging the tire down the highway. Dory's ride was so loud and bumpy that a mere rubber drag didn't catch my attention. The officer burned his hand on the sizzling rubber when he propped the tire back up; we reattached the ruined spare with bailing wire. And once, I didn't attach the flexi-tube securely and it flew off when the sluice gate opened. I felt sheepish in a campground full of Dory's wealthy relatives—what an amateur—but I was grateful there was a hose for washing the splattered overflow into the black hole.

~~~~~

With Kaya still in her basket in the loft, Dory bumped down the driveway. Tobie sat happily at the table, sniffing out the window; unlike me, she loved blackwater runs. This was probably the best of all possible worlds for a dog: not only riding in the car, but riding in your house at the same time. The building thunderheads made me glad the journey was under way; there was one very steep pitch that even on dry gravel and with a bit of a run, Dory struggled up at five miles an hour with the gas pedal to the floor.

Suddenly Kaya appeared looking frazzled and a bit puffed up. She tried to get in her litter box on the floor in front of the passenger seat—must be nerves, I thought. The top to the litter box had lodged against the dashboard, so I reached over with one hand and placed the lid on the passenger seat. Kaya zipped across the litter...and disappeared toward the engine. I looked again. Yep, she was gone, totally gone.

I pulled over—it was not a good stopping place, but if she had somehow gotten into the engine, I didn't want fried or diced cat. "Kaya! Kitty kitty!" I called several times. No response, no plaintive mew, no freaked yowl. I cooed several more times. Nothing. The engine was already hot.

I walked back to the kitchen and got a can of tuna. Kaya usually materialized out of the ether at the sound of the can opener—never mind that only one can in forty cans opened was actually tuna fish and she would get the juice. I called, tapped the can with the spoon, walked outside to the engine, called some more. No movement, no sound.

My "what if" panic kicked into high gear. What if she flew into the engine, got burned on something hot, and skedaddled out through the floorboards? My god, she could be anywhere! What if she were running through the deep woods in kitty terror? What if she were snatched by a roadside coyote? She could be embarking on an Incredible Journey back to Salt Lake to rival Disney. I popped open the hood; no sign of cat. I trotted back down the road, calling. A car slowed but didn't stop. The woods were thick and this looked hopeless.

I ran back to Dory and decided to look at the engine from inside the cab. Like a minivan, Dory had a brown plastic hump between the two front bucket seats fastened at the sides with latches and to the floor with screws. I worked out the rusty screws, pulled off the hump, swept aside dust and leaf litter—no cat. I shoved the hump back and walked down the road, now in a full panic, guilt and fear constricting my throat. Oh, wait, I forgot the tuna can.

Kaya was sitting on the floor between the bucket seats, looking put out and pissed off, but not singed or sliced. I hugged her, then shut her in the stinky bathroom for the remainder of the blackwater run. When Dory was parked and leveled once again upon the meadow, I discovered the open heater vent, big enough for a cat.

~~~~~~~

By mid-July of this second summer, all was not right with Dory's tanks. One day, blue-treated-sewage water backed up through the shower drain, which supposedly drained to the gray-water tank, not the black. Obviously, there was a nasty breach somewhere. (I only tried showering twice in Dory. The shower drain, which doubled as the bathroom floor, plugged before I got my hair wet, and the pitiful spray was rather like being peed upon.) I drained two large bucketfuls from the blackwater drain just by opening the end cap (not even lifting the sluice). I had had it with Dory and her so-called plumbing.

I called my friend Dennis and explained my sewage woes.

"I can't take it," I said. "After I make a blackwater run, it's okay for several days, but then it stinks again. Can I borrow that little porta-potty you store in your cabin basement?"

"Of course," he said. "You know where it is, and the key's in the same place."

Dennis liked to claim partial credit for my cabin adventure because it was his cabin north of Pinedale where I stayed during my sabbatical almost two years ago when I found and bought my land. Dennis was one of the first people I met in Salt Lake, a fun and compassionate man who did IT work for a corporation. He and I shared a love of cooking and entertaining, and now landownership in Wyoming.

I parked the squat little potty under a fir near Dory and used it whenever workmen (who had begun work on the cabin that second summer) were not around. Elimination al fresco.

By late August, I gleefully sold Dory (who in addition to her plumbing deficits was a magnet for meadow mice) and moved into the bare basement of the cabin shell. I parked the porta-potty in the corner near my mattress, tied a blue tarp in front, hung a roll of TP from a piece of reinforcing steel sticking out of the concrete, and christened it "the blue room." Tobie liked this arrangement, for it was easy to barge in under the tarp for a visit with anyone sitting there.

This little potty didn't smell—thanks to a packet of digester that melted everything into a green soup—but it nevertheless required a blackwater run, and more frequently. But in comparison, carrying the little holding tank to my SUV and driving it to the nearest campground was gravy.

~~~~~

In August of my third summer after the first blackwater run, I had a party to celebrate my first real flush in the cabin. Neighbors came bearing gifts of toilet paper and septic-tank treatment. Tobie christened it with the first drink of toilet water. We took pictures. I understood why the toilet was called "the throne." I understood the joy felt by millions of people the world over at the sound of their very first flush.

When I flush, I still think sometimes about the journey of my waste down the pipes, into the big yellow septic tank, then spilling down the hill and out into the drain field at the bottom of the meadow. It sounds strange, but I like having my waste right here. Perhaps it's a nod to the total self-containment of backpacking, and of putting food in your body and dealing with what comes out. Maybe it's a sense that the cycle is more complete here, that a physical part of me is left here, a small amount of biomass nourishment given in return for all the nourishment this place gives me.

Occasionally, I slip outside at night to pee under a canopy of stars horizon to horizon and a meadow washed in moonlight. But then mosquitoes seek the soft white flesh of my bare butt, and a bit of nightsoil splashes my feet, and I reconsider and head back inside to my comfort-height, low-flow, gleaming-white toilet.

SIX

The Wild Within

It was late morning when Tobie and I reached the overlook. The granite slabs jutted out from the cliff face, surrounded by sheer and electric drop-offs. The Wind River Mountains rimmed us on three sides, and breezes rising up from the valley more than a thousand feet below kept the mosquitoes at bay. I took off my pack and settled, and Tobie came and sat close, our flanks touching. I never tired of hiking to this viewpoint: snow crowned the jagged peaks, thick cumulus were stacked above them, and bees worked the flowers around us. Tobie looked too, her nose working the wind and her ears perked (as much as floppy ears can) and twitching ever so slightly. We were two creatures utterly enamored of the wild around us and feeling a bit of it ourselves.

"Isn't it gorgeous?" I said and gave her a squeeze. And then I realized that her answer would be "No."

To Tobie, the magnificent view was of little consequence. Her "picture" was composed largely of smells and sounds, not sights. I faintly heard the waterfall far, far below us, more than a mile away. Tobie could have heard a waterfall four miles away, aided by the dozen distinct ear muscles that moved this way and that to direct the sound to her. To me, the air smelled sweet and fresh, slightly piney. Her sense of smell was a staggering one hundred thousand times more powerful, and I couldn't even fathom what her smell-picture of this place included. Right here on this rocky ledge, she must have detected dozens of previous human visitors, and of course their dogs and the "pee-mail" they left her.

How my dog and cat experienced the wild in Wyoming was a source of constant wonderment. Tobie and Kaya seemed to keep two paws easily in domestic life and two paws beyond it, connected and attuned to this wild place with their powerful senses and bodily intelligence. In our culture, we give domestic animals like them an intermediary position between oh-so-civilized humans and undomesticated "wild" animals. But over two summers living with Tobie and Kaya in the little motor home, this continuum became far too simple and confining and raised a lot of questions. What is "wild" anyway? And for them and me, how much of our wild selves comes from some predetermined amount decreed us by biology, and how much is from experience? And to what degree is wildness—wherever it comes from—a key to our fundamental relations with all that occupies this planet?

~~~~~~

To many of my acquaintances and work colleagues, where I spend my summers is a very wild place, and thus, rather fearful. They ask if I get scared up there all alone, with the wild animals and such, where it gets so dark. Before I bought the land, I heard similar worries from my mom when I backpacked by myself on backcountry patrols in Olympic National Park.

"Mom, I've got a park radio with me."

"I know, but you said you couldn't always get reception, couldn't always hit the repeater thing. And what about bears? And what about other people, you know, bad people?"

"Mom, I feel safer in those woods than I do walking around in any big city. I really do."

She still worried; I still backpacked. I had a few scares: getting pretty lost once, making some dicey river crossings, and approaching hypothermia when all my gear was soaked by days of rain. Once when my flashlight went dead, I stumbled into a bull elk surrounded by his harem. But other than sore muscles and some scraps and scratches, I was fine—thriving even.

It's peculiar to me that some folks are more fearful of places where humans are not, rather than of places full of humans. There's actually a greater risk of being harmed by our own species than by other species, whether bears or falling trees. Just because humans and their structures, vehicles, and concrete don't dominate these woods doesn't mean uncontrolled "nature" is out to get me. If "wild" is everything external to humans and their touch, that's a whole lot of the planet to spend time fearing, rather than getting to know.

I recognize that spending my childhood playing in woods gave me a head start being comfortable in them. Tobie's puppyhood also had wild experiences that shaped her; her first was a backpack in the Winds when she was just eight months old. One afternoon my friend Hester and I raced back to camp after cresting a high ridge, chased by a storm. We zipped ourselves (and Tobie) in the tent just as the skies opened and lightning crackled and split around us, so close that the electricity raised hairs on our arms. That night a bull elk snorted and bugled so close to camp that Tobie was sure he was coming for us. She stayed awake all night, growling soft and deep in her throat at the slightest sound, long after the elk had moved on. These two encounters had lifelong effects on her: a fear of lightning and thunder, and a desire to bark at sounds in the night. Otherwise, she became a woods-wise dog and thrived there, too.

～～～～

That evening after our hike to the overlook, Tobie lay on her dog bed, twitching in dreams, but still cracking open an eye to sudden sounds outside. Nearby, two trees groaned and creaked when the wind ascending the meadow moved their limbs against each other. When a boreal owl started its rapid-fire staccato hoots, Tobie lifted her head, alert. Through it all, Kaya slept soundly in her basket in the loft above the cab.

Only the loudest sounds rise above the city's big hum: the rumble of trucks, the wail of sirens, and the ever-present chorus of barking dogs. In the woods, even the softest sounds popped out of the dark night: leaves soughing, the crack of a stick, rodents rustling. During our first summers in Dory, Tobie looked to me for cues as to what night sounds were welcome, but of course, sometimes when she queried, I had heard nothing at all.

When I first brought Tobie and Kaya here, I kept a tight rein on them, not knowing how this citified pair would adapt to this place, but also to protect the current residents; I didn't want the cat to kill songbirds, or the dog to chase away deer and other animals. I let Kaya outside briefly during midday and under my supervision. She was a savvy cat outdoors (daytime only) in Salt Lake, perhaps honed of necessity before she landed in the shelter. When I first took her from her cage at the shelter and held the nine-month-old, she looked in my eyes, ignored the cacophony of barking dogs and yowling cats, and purred. This is a kitty who could handle a new puppy, I thought. And she did, allowing the four-month-old Tobie to pin her down and wash her with only plaintive protests. (Once released, Kaya would commence a thorough rewash.) In turn, Tobie protected her kitty fiercely from the marauding city toms. Their partnership of sorts continued in Wyoming. If I momentarily lost track of Kaya outside, I'd ask Tobie, "Where's your kitty?" and she'd course the meadow, sniffing her out.

I let Tobie outside during the day but not in early morning and evening when wilder animals deserved to wander the woods. Much of the daytime she stayed right around Dory, listening, napping, and sniffing the wind. She even preferred to eat her meals outside and began to leave a few pieces in her dish. The only reason I could surmise for this behavior was that she knew the gray jays would soon fly by to claim them, and she would watch them intently or make a quick charge. It seemed that both species profited from this little game.

About one in the morning a different night sound woke us: a spirited romping of cat and mouse. There was no moonlight to see this chase, but the chorus was undeniable: a muted shuffle of mouse over carpet, followed by the flurry of a pounce, a brief, high-intensity skirmish (sometimes accompanied by a mouse squeal), then quiet. The volleys continued for hours, perhaps with multiple mice. Tobie left her dog bed and crept paw by paw up on the trailer's sofa bed with me. Most nights, I would have shooed her from the tiny bed back to the floor, but the dog was obviously tired of being traversed by the pair.

There is something hardwired in most cats to stalk and kill mice, and Kaya's switch was fully tripped in the woods of Wyoming. Cats' age-old hunting instinct is the reason humans have brought them indoors for centuries. And I did indeed appreciate her keeping Dory—with rotten floorboards under the sink and rusty openings between the cab and engine—mouse free.

There were times, I must admit, that I wished there were an "off" switch to Kaya's hunter. She discerned no difference between mice in Dory and a meadow full of mice beyond; of course, mice were mice. She loved the chase and capture, not the keeping (or eating). It was as though she were in some fishing derby where the winner was determined by the total catch, not by the size, health, or later release of the fish. As soon as she deposited a fresh victim under Dory, she was back in the meadow for more.

Still, my appreciation for her hunting skills was renewed twice after Kaya left Dory for a weekend in Salt Lake. One time, we returned to the remains of a mouse bacchanalia. Entire packages of pasta were nibbled to bits and pouches of pizza sauce sucked dry. Tufts of pink Kleenex were spread hither and thither like confetti. Half the buttons on the phone had small divots gnawed away, as did the ends of the plastic spatulas. Kaya went to work. The second time was in early September when I discovered an elaborate nest and storage cache in my sock and underwear drawer. Thousands of seeds—no doubt collected painstakingly from the meadow—were interspersed with turquoise d-CON pellets. (Just during our absence, I had put a container of d-CON in the closed kitchen cabinet.) The nest was an orb of brown and white fluff—the brown chewed from my favorite wool cap, the white from shredded panty liners.

Kaya hunted in Dory at night when the mice were most active. And to her, even a pitch-black night appeared about five times brighter and was thus no impediment to hunting. Both cats and dogs have an extra layer of cells in their eyes (called the tapetum lucidum) that reflects light back into the eyes' receptors and increases their night vision. Animals with this low-light advantage have that spooky appearance of their eyes glowing in the dark. Kaya's whiskers also provided sensory information about the slightest air movement around her, valuable for nocturnal hunting.

By the time light crept into the meadow, Kaya had retreated to her sleeping post. I imagined her kitty thoughts and dreams after a wild night of hunting that her feline body was designed for. I imagined her hunting pose: eyes wide and gleaming, her back end slightly raised and wriggling and ready, her entire body focused and fully attuned.

Although we assume that human "intelligence" comes through our thoughts and brains (independent of our bodies, really), this cat smartly moved with the whole of her body. She never separated her senses, her paws, or her storied movements from the constantly unfolding scenario of mouse moving on the motor-home floor. "Instinct" alone doesn't explain the uninterrupted improvisation, the continuous minute adjustments, moment to moment, needed to catch a mouse. Kaya had wild intelligence.

As I made a large mug of coffee, I mused how my own "intelligence" is too often sequestered between my ears, and not in full interaction and dialogue with my entire body and all that it encounters. Kaya dwelt fully in her wild self last night; I was the creature feeling too fully domesticated. I decided to take a hike after breakfast to shake the cobwebs.

〜〜〜〜

Someone once commented to me that I must be a hermit to enjoy life up there by myself in Wyoming. "Hermit" is a curious cultural label for someone who chooses to live surrounded by things other than humans. We picture a hermit as someone who lives cut off from civilization, eking out a rugged existence, avoiding human contact. Actually, I can understand wanting to escape what people call civilization; cities can make me anxious and wound up, negotiating all that traffic and constant noise, surrounded and penned in by cement, lights, machines, and the mass of humanity. But am I a hermit? No. I don't seek to isolate myself from humans, just to connect with much more than my species.

At my usual pit stop at a little park midway between Salt Lake and the cabin, I once saw a border collie with a piece of broken red nylon rope around its neck. It cautiously approached Tobie on her leash but kept its distance. The fur on its neck and belly was matted to dreadlocks, and the sockets of its eyes were bright red. A local teenage girl drove up; she had been following the dog and trying to catch it. We teamed up to lure it with some cat treats I had in the car. The dog crept forward time and again, only to bound away out of reach. It looked haunted and hungry, like it was unable to find food or comfort or fall asleep soundly. Perhaps it'd escaped abuse; perhaps it just wanted to explore and taste the wild world beyond.

The name for a cat or dog returned entirely to the wild is feral. The dictionary gives synonyms for feral—*savage, fierce,* and *brutal*— and notes that a wild population of animals can descend from individuals that escaped captivity or domestication. Escaped to the wild. Humans "rescue" feral dogs and cats, both for population control and because we assume they are not thriving and happy. That is probably true for most; centuries of domestication have accustomed them to human companionship and care and a life largely indoors. But the fact that some domesticated pets can survive as feral animals suggests that enough of their wild within is still reasonably functional. The border collie was surviving (through instincts or luck), but he didn't look ferocious or savage—just miserable. He smelled stale and sour to me. To Tobie, he no doubt smelled like a story, whose fur collected dirt and odors and blended them into something complex and intangible.

Another way to think about feral is that it's a limbo of sorts between "domesticated" and "wild," a no-creatures-land where one has forgotten how to keep one foot/paw in both worlds and is therefore unhappy and unqualified for either. When I see humans at wits end when the electricity goes out, or terrified of insects, or ill-equipped to walk from one end of a field to the other without GPS or a tour guide, they are feral in their own world. They have run away from the world's wild essence; they are pretending that the wild isn't involved in absolutely all their experiences. I exchange the same air, feel the same rain, and reside in the same animal's body whether I'm hermiting in the woods or standing at the bus stop.

~~~~~~

As I rinsed out my coffee mug and cereal bowl, Kaya growled. She had just finished her breakfast and sat on the little table, washing up. Right on the other side of the table was a cow moose staring in the window. She looked dopey and sweet with her long ears and dark shiny eyes, just peering in.

I had never been that close to a moose, through a window or otherwise, and I was excited. "Well, good morning, you," I said. The moose cocked her head slightly, but my salutation also alerted the dog, who put her front paws on the table and uttered one small "woof." The moose, curiosity satisfied, took a series of quick-steps deep into the woods behind Dory. Kaya stayed hunched on the little table, growling deep in her throat. For much of the day, she sat high in the loft, fearful that the creature might return. I thought it smart that she was alarmed at something that was utterly foreign to her, though it made me wonder if she'd react similarly to an up-close horse; was it mere size, or a smell, or just its sudden appearance that frightened her?

I like to talk to creatures. Just last week at the nearby pond, when a Canada goose clucked and honked at my approach—alerting its mate who swam nearby with three fuzzy yellow goslings bumping up beside her—I said softly, "Hello. It's okay. I mean no harm." And the goose stopped honking. Sometimes there is little or no reaction, like from the juncos in the branches and brush around Dory who continue their tik-tik-tik when I speak to them. Some animals have better hearing than eyesight (like moose), so my saying something helps them evaluate me. But I also offer words as acknowledgment of their presence, like prayer, speaking words directly to them rather than about them. It's a respectful way of recognizing our paths have crossed.

The most intense conversation I ever had was with a cougar. Two girlfriends and I were in southeastern Utah one spring. They were drying off in the tiny cabin; I was sitting alone, meditating at the edge of a cliff, when I felt the undeniable presence of another. When I turned and stood, there was a cougar, just fifteen to twenty feet away.

"Wow," I whispered. "You are so beautiful."

She stared and began to flick the dark tip of her tail, left, right, left.

"Were you watching me on that rock?" I asked. "My god, you are so gorgeous..." And I unzipped my camera case.

She took three steps to the side, turned, and sat facing me. Dramatically regal. She wrapped her tail around herself and blinked her eyes, slowly, deliberately, like the relaxed "I love you blinks" you get from your cat.

I took several pictures—flash pictures, no less—and the cougar sat there blinking.

"Thank you," I said. "Thank you so much."

In that moment, neither of us was afraid. I knew that more than I'd ever known anything. It was the most pure and powerful moment I ever shared with another creature. My words conveyed something, I don't know what exactly, but they were direct and undeniably—unintentionally—honest.

Chief Dan George said if you talk to the animals, they will talk with you, and you will know each other. Beyond indigenous wisdom, there is also scientific evidence to support an authentic connection between humans and other creatures. Charles Darwin (and innumerable scientists after him) concluded that humans didn't have an entirely different path of origin but were in fact closely kindred to all other creatures; call it a wildly diverse "family tree." So when an Indian talks about "brother salmon," there are bits of both belief and science behind that, which I find highly satisfying.

~~~~~

"Okay Tobie, finally, let's go for a walk!" She raced to the trailer door and whined excitedly.

We began walking up the gravel road, not sure of our destination. For some walks, I let Tobie's nose and my discoveries guide our route, which creates a circuitous journey. When Tobie coursed the woods, it was as though there were an invisible string attached to her nose, pulling her here for a sniff and abruptly over there for a closer whiff. A pine bough overhanging a path might deserve intense scrutiny; it amazed me that just a few needles could hold molecules of deer dander or fox essence.

Suddenly, Tobie bounded over the road edge, I presumed after a darting chipmunk. But it was a smell that led her, not a movement. A mule deer doe emerged below her and for some reason turned uphill, made another pass near Tobie, sprang onto the road, and stopped, waiting for the dog to give chase. But Tobie was distracted and started sniffing the ground intently at the base of a tree. Then I got it—there was a fawn somewhere! Why else would the mother double-back but to lead Tobie in the opposite direction? The sniff spot must have been where the fawn was bedded down. The doe then made a wide arc around me on the other side of the road, and eventually cut across and down, presumably to reunite with her baby somewhere downslope. I leashed Tobie, still sniffing around the tree. I worried about Tobie bothering wildlife, especially during baby season, and did my best to prevent encounters. If we ended up near the pond later, I'd leash her near the reeds that might house duck nests.

The gravel was speckled with last night's shower droplets and various hoof and paw prints—deer, chipmunk, a couple of large birds, and one print I guessed might be a pine marten. Around the next wide bend, I unleashed her, and she bounded up the road. "Tobie, this way!" I called, and we left the road for a rough path through a vacant piece of property that connected on the far side with public land. Tobie raced past me.

Though as a former park ranger I understood the importance of keeping people on established trails, I delighted here in making my own. The slow pace of route finding meant that I needed to read the landscape in a way not necessary on human paths, as I followed animal trails, negotiated obstacles, and paid attention to direction and topography.

A constable of ravens cawed from the hillside above, cackling and swooping from the treetops to the ground and back, perhaps protecting a carcass and alerting other individuals to the find. "Caw! Caw!" I croaked up to them. They were silent for a moment—one eyed me briefly from its branch—then they resumed and crescendoed. Ravens here cruised the woods in raucous groups, like feathered gangs patrolling a home turf, their noisy wing beats rowing the air and alerting all to their approach.

For the past twenty-five years that I've been a student and scholar of communication, I've learned that much of our communication about the environment is not expressed through language. Think of what the landscaping of a city park, or roads without sidewalks, or monstrous garbage cans communicate. Our daily practices, our actions, and our objects—big and small—communicate just as much as what comes out of our mouths, and articulate what we value and the place we claim in a world full of others.

As I listened to the ruckus of ravens above me, it struck me that all the academic research I've conducted has tried to understand humans' perceptions of the environment—such as in public opinion, media coverage, or behavior change—as a one-way street. Perhaps that's necessary, particularly when statistics are involved. But it nevertheless treated the nonhuman as disembodied objects with nothing to say. Communication, really, is all the ways that someone or something radiates a sense of who or what they are, of what they are experiencing. That could (loosely) include moss on a boulder rocketing out of dormancy with a dousing of rain, as it could chatty ravens. They both certainly communicate something to me.

Near the top of a rise, I climbed over two large Douglas firs whose fall had opened the sky and allowed morning light to reach the forest floor. Beyond them, I spied a large layered bracket fungus on the base of a towering fir and knelt in the duff before it. The dense, firm growth was moist to the touch, a muted painting of colored rings with scalloped edges bulging horizontally from the trunk. I leaned back and gazed at the treetop; it was still thick with branches. The presence of the fungus meant the heartwood was rotten, though the tree lived on. Once the fungus digests the dead wood (not harming the living wood), it is available in a form the tree can absorb. I like the symbiosis that this pair provide as each ages: the bracket fungus growing and adding beautiful rings, the tree getting nutrients. As David Attenborough wrote, "Tree and fungus, each pursuing its own best interests, have come together to the benefit of both." And the aging tree is more resilient with its hollow, rotten center; the removal of tons of timber from its core reduces the strain on its elderly root system, and a tree with a hollow center is often able to withstand a gale better than a younger, solid pillar. Perhaps that was the fate of the stout firs over which I just climbed.

A small explosion from the brush interrupted my fungus fantasizing; a pair of ruffed grouse flapped furiously past me and lighted in a tree. Tobie raced to the tree, put her front paws on the trunk, and gazed up and then over at me, wagging, proud of her flushing them.

"Wow, thanks Tobie! I wouldn't have seen those."

We followed a series of animal trails up the opposite slope, Tobie coursing this way and that, happily driven and diverted by scent after scent. I paused to watch the activity at a tall thatched mound where hundreds of red-black Formica ants frenetically milled about. The ants in the ant farm we had as kids were sluggish compared to these, which zipped up and down and over each other. I tried to track the path of various individuals, but repeatedly failed. I stood, took a swig of water, and continued the climb up the ridge.

Near the top, I saw two distinct piles of scat on the same rock, one small and gray and the other bigger and black, an obvious territorial one-upmanship. Tobie nosed in to take a whiff, then dropped the side of her head onto the poop and rubbed her ears, her neck, and her shoulders past it, then repeated on the other side. I knew the reason for this, but it still struck me as gross, especially when I knew I'd be stuck in close quarters with her afterward. A dog's roll—whether onto a decomposing carcass or the feces of another animal—is thought to be a leftover behavior from when domestic dogs had to hunt for a living and needed to disguise their own scent; the behavior is still practiced by wolves.

Hunting or working dog breeds tend to roll in smelly stuff more often. The golden retriever breed was developed in Scotland in the mid-1800s as gun dogs to retrieve shot waterfowl and upland game birds. They were bred from several kinds of dogs (tweed water spaniel, Irish setter, bloodhound, St. John's water dog of Newfoundland, and wavy-coated black retrievers) to have a soft mouth to retrieve game and with an instinctive love of water, loyalty, intelligence, gentleness, and hunting and tracking ability. When I watched the becoming-one-with-poop behavior, I wanted to question the "intelligence" part, but then I'm not a hunter.

Tobie's occasional roll in dead fish was also foul, but her worst "roll" ever was fresh bear poop. Despite several soapy washings, Tobie's neck and back were green for more than a week, and the smell lingered for two. It was a testament to her powerful sense of smell that being coated in such a stench didn't compromise her sniffer in the least.

As we descended the south slope, completing a long, rambling loop back to the 'stead, I saw several aspen trunks rubbed down to bare wood on one side. A few trunks also bore teeth marks. Antlered mammals used the young trees as rubbing and scratching posts, and some of them (particularly moose in winter) gnawed at the bark and the sweet layer of cambium beneath. Below me, I saw Tobie sniffing intently. With each short sniff, mouth closed, she saved some scent and didn't exhale it, allowing for more intense scrutiny. I joined her; the object of her sniff fest was a large, batted-down area in the tall grass. Nearby were pellets that looked like those of a large deer, still shiny and moist.

"They must have bedded here last night." Tobie looked at me, smiling, and resumed her olfactory investigation.

While Tobie's nose mostly led her to such pleasant discoveries, it also led her into the back end of trouble. Tobie's perennial curiosity at slow-moving, small mammals meant she had been skunked once and porcupined thrice.

〰〰〰

Later that afternoon, the three of us sat outside Dory in the sun. Kaya and Tobie lay quietly, eyes closed and resting, then watching and listening. I had trouble concentrating on my book, looking up when I heard bird wings or sounds in the woods, lifting my chin to feel the sun and breeze on my face.

I leaned down to stroke Tobie's broad head. I lacked her powerful senses and wild sensibilities, Kaya's too. But, I smiled, this is my wild. Days like this are how I step out of what I know as human and endeavor to learn of another. It's not a giant sense of smell or sound, but a sense keenly seen and felt, pondered and awed. When I come to know elements of the wild—the beauty of bracket fungus, the nighttime activities of deer—I feel their existence as part of my own. The connection gives me a richness—of life, of lessons, of ingenuity of process and intricacies of place—that I cannot get solely through interaction with my own species. Without it, in a safe and sterile bubble of all that is "civilized" and human, isolated from such natural profusion just beyond the membrane, I would literally ache.

〰〰〰

The more my students learn about environmental issues, particularly the science of climate change, the more upset they become. After one such discussion last spring about climate-related changes already observed in the West, the room grew quiet and then exploded with questions. "What can we do?" they asked. "It's just so big, so enormous."

"Well, identify one thing you think contributes the most, that's a big cause or reason for it, and then do something about it," I suggested.

"Cars," a young man in the front row said. "That's the biggest problem."

"I'd say fossil fuels, period," another chimed in. "Oil, but also coal, natural gas, all that stuff."

"I think the biggest thing is our lifestyles," a young woman offered. "I mean the way Americans just plain live large—cars, houses, electronics, just all the consumerism, it's ridiculous."

"Yeah, and now the Chinese want the same lifestyle," a voice from the back added.

"To me the biggest problem is politics," another student said. "All the fighting about it and nothing ever gets done."

"Okay, so what do you think it is?" an older student asked.

"Fair enough," I said. "All of those things contribute, of course, and all need to be addressed. But just one thing that would help the most? God, that's hard. Well…"

Forty-four pairs of eyes were on me, waiting for words of wisdom.

I smiled. "Be more wild." I was a bit surprised at my own answer—"wild" as the Answer to all environmental problems?—but in the moment it made perfect sense. They sat blinking, perplexed at my answer.

"You mean, what, like setting aside more wilderness?" offered one tattooed girl, perennially sleepy in class but fully awake for this conversation.

"No, not wilderness, but wildness—like the Thoreau quote, 'In wildness is the preservation of the world.' How do you suppose wildness could do that—preserve the world, even change it?"

More blinking; no one spoke.

"I don't mean wildness like running around the woods in a loincloth, disengaged from society. Being wild—to me, anyway—is acknowledging that the earth, the environment, whatever you want to call it, is fundamentally involved in every single experience you have. Every single one. Being wild is about carrying that with you, about remembering that in absolutely everything you do, no matter where you are. I mean, isn't the stuff of the earth right in this room? Air, paper, clay, plant fiber, oil, metals, water, food, and...," I grinned, "wild creatures! So don't the seeds of change have a lot to do with being able to see that, to feel that wildness?"

Ecologist and philosopher David Abram suggested we add an *i* to our planet's name to remind ourselves that "Eairth" includes the "air" that swirls above the planet's surface. We live right in the middle of this elixir that is generated by soils, oceans, and organisms, all exchanging ingredients as they inhale and exhale, all contributing to the composition of what he called a phantasmagoric brew. We don't just live on the surface of the earth; we live fully immersed and enveloped in it.

Though it makes me smile to imagine exchanging air with ravens, cougars, and pines (how utterly wild is that!), I also recognize that connecting with and learning from the wild other is far easier for me here in the woods than in the city. It's far easier when the city's big hum doesn't drown out raven caws and its lights don't obscure the stars. I wish I knew how to evoke the wild more fully in me and my students when in the midst of a million humans—other than just escaping them. The wild is that important. As author Richard Louv proclaimed, we need to get children into the woods. And we need adults there more than ever. I fear that too many humans of all ages have lost touch with the biological part of their wild and lack the wild experiences to find it again. As the world's population shifts to cities (and "sustainability" experts proclaim we must live more densely), will we remember that city life doesn't keep us "safe" from the wild but instead can dangerously estrange us from it? If we're elbow to elbow in tall buildings, will we be too high to hear the wind in trees? In noisy, concrete monocultures, will we hear birdsong?

Our appetites drove me and the pets from our sun posts. After dinner, as a slice of moon served itself up over the horizon, a coyote yipped from a nearby drainage. One long howl and a series of yips were followed by an interlude of silence as he loped through the sagebrush, stopped, and called again. Kaya heard it from the window by the table where she watched the night awaken; she didn't growl, but she left for her bed above the cab. Tobie and I went outside to listen. The lone coyote was answered to the north by a boisterous chorus of yowls and yelps that might have included young ones. Tobie listened intently, alertly, silently. There was no fear, no aggression, perhaps even a sense of familiarity. Maybe to her it was similar to barking dogs in the city, where word was passed from block to block of an approaching meter reader or distant siren, a canine network of information sharing, gossip, and camaraderie.

Earlier in the summer, Tobie and I heard a single wolf call, drawn out and mournful, softened by distance but unmistakable. From low in Tobie's throat came a long, rumbling growl, audible, but faint enough for my ears only.

I don't know why Tobie reacted so uniquely to these different distant canines, what she heard in their tongues, what they said to her. I would love to know and understand. But I do know that communication isn't solely a human possession, and ours is only one faint way to speak the wild within.

SEVEN

Becoming a General

The remodel of my 1917 Salt Lake kitchen was my first experience with builders and the construction trade, and it sadly fitted all the negative stereotypes, including the right-wing talk radio blaring from paint-splattered radios. Workmen didn't show up. Workmen didn't communicate yet blamed me for not understanding their process or choices. Workmen didn't respect my space, or me as a woman. Workmen came up with extra charges and unexplained delays.

Thus, a decade later, the part that scared me the most about building a cabin was my ability to deal with the male-dominated construction industry and culture. Every woman has had interactions with workmen of various types that are unpleasant and intimidating—whether a wolf whistle when she walks by a construction site, workmen who patronize "the little lady" as if she lacks a head on her shoulders, or an auto mechanic who takes advantage of her ignorance of engine operation. It was a foreign culture with a seemingly foreign language and operation. And for me, it involved a rather foreign sex; though I grew up with men, to a certain extent they still confounded me. Far too often, they were short on communicating and I couldn't read them, couldn't figure out what made them tick. I had no reason to believe that the men who would work on my cabin would be any different.

Plus, the notion of building a cabin on my land took a while to grow. I lacked the money, and I had trouble foreseeing how some magnificent yet modest structure would rise from the ground. So, my first summer began with a few small steps—steps that would add some value to the property (whether I ever built a cabin or not) and help me get acquainted. The first was a driveway, for I needed something more than the faint two-track path leading up to the meadow.

The driveway project didn't go well. I hired a fellow who was recommended to me, and he arrived with his dog and young boys one Saturday in mid-May to discuss the project and walk the length of the intended driveway. I pointed out where I would park Dory on top, and where the cabin might eventually go. A week later back in Salt Lake, I got his bill and paid it, happy that my first project was completed so quickly and easily.

But when I drove Dory up two weeks later, the new driveway ended abruptly only partway up the hill. I was mad, but also extremely perplexed. We had walked the entire path for the driveway, and I thought I had communicated clearly all the details and certainly the entire route. For reasoning that I can't now recall or make sense of, I thought it must have been my fault. There must have been some language I didn't understand, some key thing I didn't hear, some way I didn't make myself clear. No matter how I turned over and replayed our meeting, I was baffled how my first encounter with construction had gone so wrong. Although I wanted to, I didn't say anything, didn't call him. And I seriously doubted whether I could ever pull the cabin thing off.

Yet after my first few months of living on that meadow, of watching the sun slip behind the mountains and listening to owls locate each other on a dark night, a seed had sent down roots. When a notion gets planted in your head, suddenly brain cells and thoughts drift in and take up space whether you think you're devoting much energy to it or not. I wanted a cabin on that meadow, period. So, I committed to another step—to see if there was water up there. And after the well drillers struck water, the seed and its roots were watered, and I could finally envision four walls and a roof and me inside, right over there.

Of course, for two summers, I had four walls and a roof in Dory, but all her systems were failing. She was, nevertheless, head and shoulders above historical choices of dwellings in the West. Sod houses were well insulated, but a good rainstorm brought streams of mud into your living room. Tepees were nice and portable, but even with a vent hole there was all that smoke. Some homesteaders in Alaska lived in canvas tents through the winter, for god's sake. So in comparison, a log cabin would be an enormous step up.

I was nevertheless still baffled and anxious about building a dwelling—or, more accurately, dealing with the men who would help me build one. How did those single women homesteaders in the late 1800s manage to construct their dwellings? I went back to the library. Well, of course, they hired men. Some hired men to erect a prefab shed, or they hired men to nail up rough pine boards and then cover it with tar paper, or they hired men to dig out a sodie. Men were also hired to break sod and to plant and harvest crops.

But those women worked, too, big time. Cecilia Weiss and her sister dug and set more than six hundred fence posts on her 'stead in southern Utah; she also chopped all her own wood (no chain saw!) and grew a large garden. Other women spoke of similar cooperation from brothers, friends, relatives, and yes, hired help. Kate Heizer said her success homesteading in the Uinta Basin in Utah was not just luck, but also her own sagacity: "I had questioned and listened to every man who could give me any information, and it required judgment to determine which were giving honest advice, and which…had interested motives." If these women could manage and negotiate this hiring and building, so could I.

〜〜〜〜

In September after my first summer on the meadow, I called Fred to excavate a hole for the Foundation. That word, and taking that step, was like the grand, symbolic gesture of an epic adventure—the Orient Express pulling out of the station, the *Queen Mary* slowly steaming away from the dock—only with a 720-square-foot expanse of cement.

Fred was a cheery fellow who had the contract to grade the main road. Every time I passed him on the road, I'd see his round face up there on the grader, grinning from ear to ear like a little kid with a fun and fancy toy. There's a man who likes moving dirt, I thought.

When he drove up to the meadow in his pickup to see the foundation site, he was wearing a clean plaid shirt and some cologne. I showed him the stakes I'd tapped in, roughly marking the four corners of the cabin. He was earnest in his inspection, gesturing this way and that, asking questions and repeating what he heard me say. "So ya want this over here," he said with a long sweep of his arm. When he felt he fully comprehended what I was saying, he responded with a long-drawn-out "ahhh."

Fred asked me if I wanted him to save the topsoil in a separate pile—"so's you kin spread it on top, see, after I come back and back-fill around the basement wall, ya see. Some people don't do that, and it just gets all mixed in, and then they can't git nothin' to grow there again."

He was obviously proud both of his understanding of moving dirt and of what happened on top of it. And he dug me a great hole— on time, no surprises, for the agreed-upon price. Tobie loved the tall, wide pile of dirt saved for backfilling, running up to the top and fly- ing down the other side, streams of soil flowing around her paws like little avalanches.

By the time the snow flew in October, I had four stem walls, back- filled against a tarred foundation. It was time to think about cabin building the following summer and how I was going to manage that. The concern was the money, of course, but also identifying the vari- ous tasks, the order in which they needed to occur, and finding men to undertake them. I fully expected to take on some chores myself but knew I needed to depend on others for the bulk of it.

~~~~~

Dad said that I've worried about things since I was a little girl. "Just like your mom," he said. "You know, when you were in the third grade, you even worried about your grades."

That wasn't pleasant to hear and I felt sad for that little girl, but it was revealing. I fancied myself a very organized woman who was able to accomplish a great deal. A modicum of worrying seemed a crucial driver, an internal push, a sign that if something was important, it mer- ited at least a little brooding. Of course, that was easy to take too far, which I did far too often.

Thus, for an experienced worrier, the title of General Contractor was a good fit and seemed to match the job at hand: worry about costs, fuss over late deliveries, fret over synchronizing people and tasks, and eventually, speak up and even raise hell.

It wasn't until my Salt Lake kitchen remodel that I learned what a General Contractor even was. There, I thought I had hired one guy, but he was just the overseer, the title head, who farmed out each task and got his hands dirty only a time or two. He brought in a plumber, an electrician, guys to reframe a new window, guys to hang the cabinets. And for each guy's service, he tacked on a bit to my bill. Ah, so my shoestring cabin budget would benefit if I found and hired the various workmen myself. But frankly, most full-service builders in this sparse and rural setting probably wouldn't take on my modest cabin, preferring to hire a large crew for a full season or two to build a gargantuan, high-end log home.

At first, it seemed straightforward, this General Contractor thing. However, imagine hiring yourself for a job for which you have zero experience and about as much understanding. I knew next to nothing of excavation, cement and foundations, plumbing, electrical, and roofing—not to mention erecting a log cabin—yet I was now the General, running the whole army of them, responsible for hiring them, scheduling them, advising them, paying them. And, of course, communicating with them. I worried my ignorance would get me in hot water and I would be taken advantage of.

However, the more I learned about construction and its components, the less I worried. On the flip side, the more I learned, the more aware I became of what could go wrong, and of how much more— legions more—I didn't know.

The vocabulary alone was a foreign language with no dictionary. The half-a-driveway guy had asked me, "You want pit-run or crusher-run?" Not knowing the difference, I asked, "What would you recommend?" "Most folks go with pit-run 'cause it makes a good base and it's a far sight cheaper." Okay then. Months later I learned that pit-run is what's scooped directly from the gravel pit, an amalgamation of dirt, small boulders, and rocks. Crusher-run is the evenly sized gravel produced by a rock crusher that you see on dirt roads. And pea gravel is even smaller uniform pebbles that I eventually had spread underneath the basement-floor cement.

When I was hunting for log-home suppliers, I kept seeing the word "turn-key." I eventually learned that this was a cabin whose interior was entirely finished, not just stain and flooring, but light fixtures, kitchens and baths, and locks in the doors. Well, I certainly couldn't afford that. Besides, I reasoned, I could do much of the finish work myself.

So I would find a builder to get me to the other option, "dry-in," the rough, unfinished weather-tight shell. I took out a large line of credit on my Salt Lake house and sucked in my breath as I wrote a really large check for a down payment on a log kit.

In the spring before construction started, I'd spread the cabin blueprints on my Salt Lake dining table and pore over them, trying to match footnotes to diagrams and decipher codes and instructions. Nowadays, blueprints were not just blue but multicolored, and each color represented a different layer or angle. I peeled the pages back like layers of a sweet onion: basement, floor, deck, log walls, roof.

Years ago, when things were slow in the Olympic National Park visitor center, I'd pull out a topographical map and entertain myself, interpreting elevation lines, transforming symbols into pictures, a cliff face here and a swampy meadow there. The cabin blueprints similarly had scale and labels, side notes and instructions, though sometimes the explanations for the symbols and instructions were just as confusing. Yet unfurling each page and its layers full of mysterious codes felt like a trail of sorts that one could follow from the deepest footing to the highest peak of the roof. I tried to picture the round logs that would form the beams over the porch and how the scissor trusses would join the regular trusses. I learned where the OSB waferboard would go, though I had to call my brother Scott to find out what OSB was.

After each delivery of building materials that soggy May and June, I walked from pile to pile stacked in the meadow and basement with my pencil and the inventory list. My kit contract said I had twenty-four hours after each delivery to note missing or damaged items for free replacement. Some things were easy to locate, count, and check off the list: fir floor joists, Qty 15, 2x8, 8'; redwood decking, Qty 36, 2x6, 16'; and #10 x 1½" screws, Qty 1,000. But I couldn't identify a lot of what was on the list: Simpson angles, belly band, sill plates, follow plate, LSSU 210 hangers, gable and eave fascia, truss freeze blocking, and outriggers. Why didn't the inventory have diagrams or labels? By the time the summer ended, I knew most of the names and had a vague inkling how they were used. However, I didn't learn until late summer that I was shorted one long piece of metal roof flashing, which I had to buy and have shipped because I missed the twenty-four-hour window.

〰〰〰

Overall, I made very good choices in the men I hired, and they chiseled away at my workmen stereotypes. Given the dearth of choices in the region, I was also exceedingly lucky. Fred was a cheerful and reliable dirt man whom I hired on several occasions. The plumber Bill was a large man with a full beard touched with gray who loved trout fishing. He had a sweet smile, really listened to me, and, as my brother Scott later noted, did excellent work. He was expensive, but he arrived when he said he would—from laying out the sewer pipes under the basement floor to hooking up the sinks—and he brought all the right equipment and worked until he was done.

Not one electrical contractor in the county phone book could guarantee an electrician until fall, so I prepared my argument and called Harvey, my electrician from Salt Lake.

"Harvey, I'll pay your gas and time to get up here. And you can sleep in the basement—it's not done, of course, but there's a futon down there now. And I'll cook for you—just tell me what you like to eat. And best of all, Harvey, it's in the mountains, and I know you love the mountains! Why, it's probably twenty degrees cooler here than in Salt Lake."

He chuckled; he probably would have come for less, once telling a mutual friend that I was "a very special lady." (I assumed that meant he had a little crush on me, since he once asked me to go bowling with him.) Harvey could have retired decades ago but was far too energetic for that. He had a shock of silver hair that he slicked back lightly and twinkly Paul Newman–blue eyes. He was in a couple of bowling leagues, loved cats, and was very active in his church. When he arrived at the cabin late one evening in a downpour, Tobie wriggled and whined, relieved that a familiar friend had come, not another Wyoming stranger who must be sidled up to and evaluated for their dog friendliness.

Harvey learned his trade when most current-day electricians weren't yet born, and his techniques were decidedly old school and amusing to watch. The builder shook his head at the way Harvey configured the breaker box—both its overall small size and amp choices—but he assured me none of it was dangerous, just different. I was just so grateful that he came.

〜〜〜〜〜

Perhaps the smartest thing I did as a General was to hire the Lamberts as builders. As with all my hires, I asked all the neighbors I knew who was good and who to avoid, narrowing a list that was meager to begin with. I avoided the guy who kept soliciting my bid (and even told others he had the job) but whose own house had never been finished and who was known for bouncing checks and stopping work before it was done. And I stayed away from the builder used by a neighbor whose logs settled wrong and lacked sufficient headspace above doors and windows, pinching them so that they wouldn't open. Everyone said, if I could get them, hire the Lamberts.

Although I signed a contract with Joe and Daisy, what I had hired was a whole family. Joe and Daisy lived several miles away and built custom log furniture, but also garages, additions, remodels, and assorted projects for quite a few cabin owners in the area. Joe was a lean, mustachioed man with a ready smile, I guessed near sixty, and his wife, Daisy, with long white hair pulled back was not just bookkeeper but able woodworker and finisher. Though their youngest son, Peter, did the majority of the log work, and older son Dan and other siblings and in-laws helped out in a pinch, it was the parents who directed the show and supplied prodigious advice and expertise.

As in every family, they had their squabbles and quirks, and I was witness to some. But it felt good to have a family working on something that was to become so intimate and personal as a home. When I descend the basement stairs, I picture Joe scribbling measurements on their angles. At my kitchen table, I imagine Peter working at the top of the west wall when it was just rough logs joined around large empty holes that would hold windows. When I'm in the kitchen, I remember the entire family working the boom truck to hoist roof trusses into place over this room. The Lamberts and their work are in the rafters and the floorboards.

I knew from my remodel experience in Salt Lake that plumbers and electricians typically came and worked solidly until they finished. Not so with the culture of builders, including the Lamberts. The only analogy that made sense to me was the process of getting a perm. A perm takes a couple of hours start to finish, so your appointment is layered with the appointments of other customers. While you sit with curlers for the first chemical cook, the beautician cuts someone else's hair. When the neutralizer soaks, you wait again while someone else gets her attention. Such layering works reasonably well—until one person is late, and then the sequenced timing goes to hell and all of you are now running late. You have no choice; you have to share the beautician's time. At least since you're all in the same salon, you can see all this juggling take place and know what's going on. At the cabin site,

I could only wonder. Maybe Peter was at the lumberyard. Perhaps he was working on my stairs in his shop.

And like the Salt Lake builders, the Lamberts didn't say, "We'll work Monday and Tuesday, but not Wednesday and Thursday, and we'll let you know about Friday." As a professor who likewise didn't have a typical nine-to-five day, I don't know why this was so hard for me. Sometimes when I heard them loading up the truck, I'd come out from Dory and ask whether they'd be back tomorrow, but their answers didn't correlate well with what happened. Get used to it, I told myself; they show up when they show up. I still listened each morning for a truck coming up the driveway.

Sometimes during a day they worked, a rap on Dory's door meant I was needed to make some little decision or choice, and we'd walk down to the cabin where I'd hear their explanation, ask their advice, and make a decision. I also made a fair number of runs to the lumberyard (a two-hour round-trip). But otherwise, they worked and I waited.

To satisfy myself in the interim that progress was being made, I'd walk about the cabin when they drove down the road at day's end. Tobie thought this routine great fun, and she'd sniff every corner and piece of equipment and take in every view; sometimes she scored a half-eaten snack. Sometimes, Kaya came along as well and would sit on the decking or a stem wall in the setting sun like a sentry watching the meadow beyond. As I walked around, I tried to picture a cabin on top, like a tennis player tries to picture where the ball will land. Some days I found an exciting completion or addition, but many days reminded me of highway work, when you can hardly tell if anything's been done since the last time you drove by.

The biggest cause for worry for the first several months was not their work, but the weather. My stomach was in knots with the delays that forced the Lamberts to go work on other jobs. By the summer solstice, I needed to celebrate and take note of what had been done and not dwell on what had not. The cabin had a subfloor and three courses of logs. I invited some neighbors for a potluck, and we climbed the ramp to literally party on the house. We sat huddled in fleece jackets, but at least it wasn't raining.

By July 4, the log walls rose their full eight feet with gaping cutouts for windows and doors. The following week, the roof trusses stood like soldiers in formation, and they readied the boom truck to lift plywood over the trusses. But a storm rolled in, complete with lightning, and since the boom served nicely as a lightning rod, they left. I spent an hour sucking up water and wet sawdust from the basement and main floor with my shop vac.

<hr />

As July ticked by, each day began with birdsong and ended with lavender-gray skies, and I grew more anxious. My family of builders had shrunk, often to just Peter, who found it too hard to work on some things by himself, like the roof. As accomplished as Peter was, he didn't appear to be greatly experienced in reading blueprints and made two mistakes that were costly timewise. I marveled watching the structure rise, but the pile of materials still awaiting attention was significant: plywood for roof, metal roof, soffits, deck piers, the entire deck, porch column supports, and all this before interior stud walls, windows, and doors. Just breathe, I reminded myself; go walk through the woods.

During some delays, Peter worked on the deck. One task that brought Joe and Daisy to watch was the installation of Sonotubes for the deck footings. In the *Fine Homebuilding* magazine that Scott bought me, one advertisement intrigued me: deck footings that didn't require concrete. The Sonotubes were high-strength plastic tubes, certified by engineers to hold great weight and built to stand all manner of frost heaves. After a bit more research, I ordered a set.

"Well I'll be," Joe said, amazed but a tad suspicious.

I also worried how the slow pace might delay the work of the plumber and electrician, and my brothers, who would arrive the last week of July for a week of nailing up tongue-and-groove ceilings and drywall on interior walls (work I learned was not included in the dry-in price). I expressed my concern to Joe but didn't feel like I could push him much more (though Scott disagreed). I talked a lot with myself: be patient, have faith, trust that they've heard you and are trying their best to come through.

A day or two before the electrician came, Joe and Dan worked on the roof, finishing the log facing up the back side near the top and starting the fascia board over the soffits. Joe said he would lay the titanium roof paper soon.

"Yeah, those electricians don't like to get wet," he said with a smile. Hallelujah.

～～～～

One evening, I carried my dinner from Dory to eat on a finished portion of the deck and found myself grinning at the large, round beams above me. It was ineffable, this structure rising from the earth. My anxiety undoubtedly had subdued some of the wonder and joy that went with every screw and nail driven and every board or log placed. But what had seemed improbable at summer's beginning was now something to be tasted, mulled over tongue and mouth, and swallowed with great delight.

It was also satisfying that what was arising was not a surprise. I was struck time and again how similar an angle or a shape or a room was to what was in my head. When I walked up the meadow early one morning with Tobie, the layout of the deck and how it looked in front of the house were precisely what I expected. The size and arrangement of the guest room–office was just as I imagined it would be. My mom

also had the ability to look at a pattern and a bolt of cloth—or a rec-
ipe and its ingredients—and see or taste the finished product, a skill
Dad marveled over. It was also due in no small measure to how much
I thought and dreamed into this space each school year when I was
back in Salt Lake, gathering paint swatches and researching the effi-
ciency of toilets.

～～～

As the summer advanced, so did my understanding of the pattern
and style of interaction with the workmen, especially upon meeting.
Unlike walking into a store or meeting a workman for the first time
in the Big City where time is money and then some, you didn't jump
right in here. Up here, it wasn't just about business, but about con-
ducting business with a particular person, business with someone you
needed to take stock of and establish some accord. At first, I was a
bit impatient about the time this chitchat took, especially with steep
hourly rates and travel time, and I just wanted to get down to pounding nails and cutting pipe. But here, you might run into this person
again—at the lumberyard, on the sidewalk in town, at a barbecue. The
light conversation moved the relationship across the border of mere
business associates.

Often the chitchat concerned the weather, the woods, or the
neighbors.

"That was some rain last night, wasn't it?"

"Had a moose at the salt lick last night."

"Heard there was a fire down near Cottonwood Creek."

"Thompsons have had company from back East most all month."

"Somebody bought the property down Forest Drive."

The exchanges made for a healthy grapevine, and this interpersonal
communication often grew into a modest form of mass communication in this sparsely populated place. A workman might have heard

through several people something about me—the cow elk and calf I saw, whom I hired for the electrical, or what brand of chop saw I bought.

Another strategy that worked well with my workmen—not just for rapport, but to help me learn more about the work I was paying for—was to get curious. Asking questions isn't threatening, and most folks rather like talking about their work. The more questions I asked, the more curious I got, and the more enamored I became with how this cabin was put together—its specialized parts and pieces, and all the tools and machines used along the way.

A time or two, my questions prompted a workman to remember something. When the concrete guy was setting up the red metal frames into which the concrete would be poured for basement walls, I asked, "What are those square boxes in the blueprint, and when do they get taken care of?" He looked up at me, glanced toward the third wall taking shape, and said sheepishly, "I'm glad you reminded me about that." Two basement walls were tucked into the hillside, but two walls had windows.

Nevertheless, as unintimidating as a woman asking questions about construction was, women were an anomaly in this world of building with the exception of Daisy. Earlier in the summer, Joe and Dan were unloading the cabin logs from the semitruck that delivered them. Dan looped the cable around a log bundle, already packaged and wrapped in a mesh plastic cover, and from the cab of the boom truck, Joe worked the levers that swung the bundle up and off the semi and down to the ground.

"Should we pitch in and try to help?" I wondered aloud.

"Oh no, honey, that's men's work," Juanita admonished me.

Juanita was the chatty wife of the man from Colorado who delivered the cabin logs on his semi. As typical for a small-town Mormon woman, it took Juanita less than five minutes to get out news of some cousin's mission and a quote from Brigham—assuming that everyone understood these details of Mormon life. I told her that Daisy often worked right alongside her husband and could drive and operate virtually any kind of construction equipment or rig. Juanita proceeded to tell me of two couples she knew whose marriages were broken apart by a husband-wife construction project.

I switched the topic to wildflowers, since we were surrounded by them, and she went to get a pad of paper so I could write down names for her. I happily played naturalist, until my pupil started picking the subjects. Her husband, also less than useful in the off-loading, eyed the trees and asked me whether anyone timbered in here. I said it was private property nestled between Forest Service and BLM, so no, just some thinning for fire protection. That was a shame, he said, because they were such nice straight trees and were just going to waste. I didn't respond; certainly, the birds and mammals who lived among the trees wouldn't find them wasted, nor would the orchids and mushrooms that poked up through the duff and decaying logs.

Juanita had quickly found out that I was undertaking this cabin without a husband, which she found quite strange. She wasn't the only one who assumed that there was a partner in the background of my life. At the checkout in Home Depot, I proudly put my new DeWalt chop saw on the counter, only to have the young male clerk ask, "You buying that for your husband?" Other workers have had similar reactions, though some admired my solo journey.

The young driver of the truck from the Riverton lumberyard asked as he untied the stays on the load, "So, you alone up here?"

"Yep," I said. I stopped myself before I launched into my traditional spiel about how this had been my dream since childhood and how I decided I was tired of waiting (that is, for a man in my life) and decided to do it by myself. After a brief silence, I said, "You know, I don't feel alone really. I've got some great neighbors and lots of friends supporting me. And my brothers and dad are coming out later this summer to work. And, of course, the dog and cat," I joked.

"Yeah, you never feel alone with them," he said.

We carried down the hill a twelve-foot particle-board piece that would form the basement stairs—heavy and awkwardly long. As we walked back up to the truck, I asked, "Do you suppose we could manage two?" He turned his head, grinning, and said, "I'm sure you can handle it."

Several weeks later, the owner of the log-home company delivered roof trusses. The only time as General that I had to "kick some butt," as Scott would say, was regarding the late delivery of the trusses. Some of the orders for my kit had fallen through the cracks, and I nagged, raised my voice, and threatened nonpayment. In less than a week, the owner himself drove his truck up my driveway with the trusses on a trailer.

"You know," he said, "we've sold log kits to several women—couples—you know..." He didn't invoke the *L* word.

"But you're the first woman who's bought from us by herself, who's doing this alone. Good for you. You're brave to be doing this by yourself."

When I embarked on this, I didn't think of myself as brave, nor that this might be peculiar or foolish to attempt. But I heard the refrain a lot, how unusual this project was for a lone woman. I'm not sure if that said more about me, about women in general, or about how people seem to think that "a couple" is the only configuration possible for a woman to undertake such things.

〰〰〰

Of all the men I hired over the seven summers, there was only one I wouldn't hire again: Trevor, who did the concrete for the basement. My top choice was too busy for the job, and Trevor was available. He was nice enough, though a bit cocky.

When Joe examined the gaping hole in the west basement wall, he shook his head. "Did they forget to pour this?" An eight-foot span was open from the footers to the sky, from one corner past the location of the basement door and a large window.

"Trevor told me they had to leave it open—for the gravel and then for the cement for the floor," I said. From the look on Joe's face, I knew I'd been had.

"It's not that way on the blueprint, is it?" he pointed out. "Leaving it open was easier for him, maybe, like for troweling. But now we have to cut some big beams to put in here so it's as strong as the rest of the walls and then frame it all out." They had to charge extra for that.

When Trevor sent his final bill, it was double his original estimate and included an extra charge for work done without my knowledge or consent. Even though I told him I wanted Fred, the dirt guy, to haul and spread the pea gravel that would underlie the concrete, Trevor hired an expensive construction firm to haul it in for a thousand dollars, then tacked on an extra two hundred dollars for Trevor to sit in the basement hole and wait for it to arrive, a change in plans he never cleared with me. When I mailed the check, I enclosed a note explaining that I was not satisfied with his work and why I was withholding two hundred dollars for his basement sitting.

When the check arrived, Trevor called, fuming, and threatened to put a lien on my property. He said I had wanted the gaping hole in the basement wall. We went round and round, his voice crescendo-ing each time he responded, increasingly incoherent, sputtering, and full of rage.

I retold the saga at an impromptu happy hour that afternoon with neighbors. While it felt good to have them rush to my defense, this was exactly the kind of scenario I had feared: getting taken advantage of because I didn't know enough, couldn't head off such problems, and couldn't tell when I was being given a line. At least I found my voice with Trevor, which is more than I did with the half-a-drive-way guy.

~~~~~~

After watching men work that summer, the male-dominated part of construction made more sense to me—not just because of their physical strength, but from the joy and satisfaction these men had working with their bodies, tools, and machines to produce such practical and pleasing products. There was such ease and history in their practiced motions—working in large screws without predrilling a hole, freehand cutting a perfect half-circle, operating a scoop arm on a piece of heavy equipment like it was a natural extension of their own arms.

As a professor, I enjoy cerebral challenges and the respect given knowledge workers such as myself. But I miss the connection between thinking and doing that manual work demands, a true embodied labor that transforms what it touches. Joe burying large coated "sinkers" with just four or five hammer strikes—whang, whang, whang, whang—each strike ascending in pitch as the nail sunk deeper. Daisy ripping a board on the table saw, slow, even, exact. Harvey putting his weight into his drill with quick, sure motions. My brother Scott striking the power nailer to the board with quick taps, bap, bap, bap. It was all delicious to watch.

My young nephews have always been captivated by all manner of machines, but it was an attraction I didn't share—until the cement truck arrived. Because the cement truck couldn't easily (or safely) drive close to the basement walls, it slurried its gray mix to a second truck. The boom arm of this second truck was a flexible blue tube that stretched in a wide, tall arc down the hill and whose final length hung down above the basement floor, sweeping back and forth like a long blue trunk.

Standing at the dirt edge high above the basement was a rotund man, and suspended on a strap around his neck and propped on his belly was the remote control for the boom truck behind him. There was a joystick and several toggle switches, which he fingered to move the giant blue trunk through the basement and let loose, slow down, and stop the gray slurry according to hand signals from the workers in the basement. He was precise, but the look on his face wasn't somber—more like he was exceedingly entertained.

I asked him whether he had an Erector Set as a kid, which had a mechanical boom arm that could carry loads. "As a matter fact, I did," he said, as if he'd never made the connection.

～～～～

When I was in seventh grade, girls were required to take one semester of cooking and one of sewing, whereas boys had a semester of woodworking and one of auto mechanics. I was insanely jealous of the lathe-turned lamp bases my brothers brought home and could certainly have used instruction in auto mechanics. I already knew how to cook and sew, but the school said no, I couldn't take the boys' classes instead.

That dormant desire, coupled with watching men work with wood, was kindled the closer the cabin got to dry-in. By the end of my second summer, I would hang up my General Contractor hat and become an interior finisher and woodworker. So, I bought a saw, a sander, and a power nailer. I arrived at the lumberyard with my own gloves, measuring tape, and a decent vocabulary. My chest swelled a bit when a workman said "nice saw" when he spied my DeWalt. We all knew what a novice I was, and they could tell what immense respect I had for them.

Although the bulk of my general contracting occurred that second summer on the land, I continued to hire workers for various projects, especially for tasks beyond my skill levels. I had a new comfort and ease with workmen of every stripe, chitchatting and joking with them, and my anxiety about not knowing or getting taken advantage of for the most part disappeared. I trusted that if I did my homework and hired good people, and asked good questions at appropriate times, they would treat me fairly and do their best work. Most workmen seemed pretty accepting of me as "boss" or at least the client paying the bill.

My original goal as General Contractor was simple: to survive cabin construction and not get screwed in the process. How very low I set that bar and how much higher it was raised. The once foreign and frightening universe of men, machines, and materials was fascinating to me now, and it bust my buttons to be able to speak some of the language, or offer advice to friends and neighbors about insulation, etching a cement floor, or nailing up tongue and groove.

One Sunday, I hiked through the woods with Tobie to check out the fancy gargantuan house being built several ridges away for some corporate VP from back East. They had the plywood on the roof and the interior stud walls in. I walked through the three stories, looking at the way they installed the chiseled ceiling beams, guessing at the purpose of each room based on its shape, piping, and wiring. And I examined all the power tools, some of which were bigger and fancier versions of ones I now owned, and some whose functions stumped me.

As I was leaving, two men walked up the driveway—neighbors who were also there to check out the progress. We exchanged pleasantries and joked at what snoops we were.

"So why haven't they backfilled around the foundation yet?" I asked. "Shouldn't they do that after the basement walls were poured? They already have the tar up."

They told me the guy hired to dig the foundation dug it five feet too big. To simply shove dirt back in would be unstable, and it might not drain right.

"They could put in a French drain," I said.

"I know, they could—they probably should," one said. "But I guess they're waiting on the guy to deliver a load of crusher-run instead."

I said, "So that's why I always hear the boom truck over here—those poor guys are having to work as aerialists because they can't get close to the house."

We all just shook our heads.

EIGHT

How Hard Can It Be?

Scott warned me how gross and disgusting tarring the outside of the basement walls to waterproof them would be.

"Okay, thanks for the warning," I told him. "But hey, it's not rocket science—you're just slathering on some tar. How hard can it be?"

It was the end of my first summer on the land, and tarring would be my first real homestead task on the new cabin, which then consisted of footers and four new concrete walls. Okay, I could do this, I told myself, and I began asking questions and getting advice. Besides, there was no one listed in the yellow pages under *Tar.*

I bought a cheap pair of sweatpants and sweatshirt at a thrift store. I bought two five-gallon buckets of tar, gloves, and a paint roller. And on a brilliant-blue September day, I drew a crayon line on each wall (following the blueprint measurements) where the dirt would be backfilled against the basement walls—highest at the north and east walls, then sloping down at the south and west walls just below the windows and walk-out door at the southwest corner.

The first challenge was trying to warm up the tar, which the guy at the lumberyard and a neighbor said would make it easier to brush on. The only heating device I had was a little hot plate, which I connected with a fifty-foot extension cord to the temporary electric box by Dory. I balanced the heavy bucket on the wee plate and stirred it with a long wood stick. But the more the tar heated, the worse it got. I experimented with low temps, high temps, and smaller amounts, but by noon, the thickened tar blurped like the LaBrea tar pits and vented that pungent tar smell. By midafternoon the tar had hard lumps and a congealed consistency that was impossible to spread.

A second challenge was trying to move the tar-encrusted paint roller from one hand to the other. With my right hand, I pried my left gloved thumb from the roller, and it released with a sucking sound. Then I pulled the index finger from its neighbor, and so on, making sure that when the pinkie was set free, the roller didn't fall to the dirt. Then, reluctantly, I folded my right gloved hand around the black gooey roller, and it cemented into place. I sighed and wiped my forehead on a piece of my upper arm that appeared unspeckled.

When my friend Dennis drove over for dinner from his cabin near Pinedale (where I spent my sabbatical several years ago), I had changed my tar-coated clothes and attempted to wash up in Dory's little sink.

"Oh my," he said when he saw me. "God, what happened to you?"

My hair was wild and windblown and speckled with dots of tar, and my arms were covered with red welts where I had rubbed and picked off blobs of tar.

"Tarring happened," I said. "I didn't think it'd be this hard. Or gross."

After dinner, I called Joe and Daisy for advice.

"Put the tar bucket in a closed-up car," Daisy said. "When the sun hits it, it'll warm right up."

~~~~~

In 1905 when Helen Coburn from Carroll, Iowa, got off the train at Garland, Wyoming, her luggage included an umbrella, traveling bag, rifle, mandolin, golf clubs, and tennis racket. After two days on a stagecoach, she arrived in Worland (the closest settlement to her homestead property), which consisted of a few wood buildings and a handful of tents. Her golf clubs and tennis racket were a sure sign that Helen might have thought "How hard can it be?" to homestead in Wyoming. Such is the swash of a homesteader, full of bright, crisp hope—and delusions.

~~~~~

The tar-in-the-car system was a big improvement. I hoisted a new bucket into the truck and then scooped gobs into a smaller bucket to carry down into the pit. The system worked reasonably well, but by one in the afternoon I was running out of tar. As with most home projects, another trip to the hardware store was required.

The new brand I bought in Pinedale was thinner and a bit like rolling on molasses, but thank god it didn't require heating. The thin consistency was worse at filling the tiny air pockets on the surface of the cement, which required a second go-round after the paint roller with a paintbrush, poking and stabbing its bristles into the little holes. Up and down the ladder I went, maneuvering myself and bucket into position in the three-foot-wide ditch between the cement wall and the dirt wall. My arms ached and my wrists were stiff, requiring frequent, sticky changing-of-the-hands. The rubber gloves got heavier and blacker with coats of tar.

Like many hard, physical, repetitive tasks, tarring let my thoughts wander like rabbits. Each time I heard a rifle shot (it was the peak of deer season), my mind traveled from the dark tar to the deer. Crack! and I felt the warm impact of cold steel, pain, blood dribbling, a stagger or two, a stumble, a fall. When I heard a second shot follow the first, I pictured the deer running, leaping—maybe clear, maybe grazed, but free. Both deer and I were suffering, and I hoped at least one of us would escape.

As the afternoon sun peered into the pit and the temperatures rose, the tar fumes penetrated deep into my nostrils, my lungs, my brain, with an inescapable and sickening smell. I envisioned my entire body covered in warmed black-brown tar—movement frozen, senses assaulted, pores choked, suffocating, and the utter humiliation and inhumanity of such a cloak. And then, feathers, the final smothering insult, soft downy feathers as imprisoned as my body in the putrid and gummy goo. All afternoon, my head pounded and my temper flared, in a rage against tar.

When I arrived at Bob and Betty's for a shower, Bob (known for his off-color jokes) said, "We don't allow blacks in here." I wept and wept in the warm waters.

<hr />

When you're a single woman (and you lack money), sometimes you tackle things by yourself that you wish you hadn't. In St. Paul where I lived during graduate school, the heat and humidity of summer seemed to arrive all at once one day, so I decided to mount the window AC by myself. I struggled with the beast up the basement stairs, pausing every few steps to catch my breath and readjust my grip. I placed it in the open window and closed the top sash firmly on it. I was walking down the back steps to put a board under the unit's heavy back end when I heard it hit the landscape bricks below. At the repair shop, the man looked at the dented appliance and said with a grin, "Well, they look worse when they fall from the second story."

When standing at the edge of anything new—an exciting adventure or a necessary task—a certain amount of moxie and naïveté are useful. You can worry, fret, delay—or jump right off the diving board. You watch others springing off the board, splashing around and doing okay, and you think, "I could do that...How hard could it be?" Tarring a foundation? Looks simple enough. With the cabin, it was a combination of bravado and finances that drove me to give something a try, especially if my efforts were unlikely to permanently harm my body or the cabin.

〜〜〜〜

Meta Loomis was a Montana schoolteacher who convinced a fellow teacher to homestead on an adjoining parcel and share expenses, machinery, and "provide mutual protection"—not from physical danger but from loneliness. Meta, who said, "I don't seem to be made to live within doors," was eager to try her hand at farming and said, "I felt that I had every qualification for farming that a man has except the brute strength, and I argued that that was the cheapest commodity to hire." Their first winter the women "made sunbonnets and bedding rather than fancy work, and bought lumber and nails instead of dresses and hats." Their shacks were mere "box cars" with two small windows that cost $110 each. I have no doubt those dwellings felt as luxurious as little Dory.

〜〜〜〜

After tarring, the final task before the trench was backfilled was to lay the French drains. I never learned why they were French, but the concept was simple: lay perforated PVC pipe, connected at each corner, along the foundation so any water that collected there was channeled out and away and didn't seep into the basement or flake the concrete.

Log Homes Made Easy explained the process well but was vague on the exact positioning. I laid the pipes just outside the footings on the dirt, but questioned that and tried to picture how water would flow and drain. I went inside Dory and made some calls. Scott wasn't home so I called Dad, who thought they should go on top of the footer, next to the wall. A concrete guy agreed, and even suggested wiring up the pipe to the cement hangers if I needed a better grade for drainage. So I laid the pipes on the footers, connected the ends, and glued on the ninety-degree connectors to round the corners. Then I attached unperforated pipes on the downslope south and west ends to drain into the meadow.

I was celebrating my finished work with a beer when Daisy returned my call—no, the position was wrong. If they're on top of the footers, they encourage water to collect right next to the wall. I called Scott: she's right; they should be next to the footers, just a stitch lower, so water drains off the footer and onto the pipe. I had another beer and went to bed.

The next day was full of sawing, shoveling, and swearing. I had to build up the dirt next to the footer and compact it to make a pad for the pipe to sit on. Since the footers extended a good six inches out from the wall, when my lovely glued contraption was moved out and off the footers, each side was too short. Grumbling, I sawed off each glued corner and drove again to the lumberyard for more pipe and couplers. At least on this trip, a clerk said, "Don't forget to buy some hardware cloth for the open drainage ends." "Why?" I asked. He smiled, having spotted a novice, "So rodents don't move in."

Every cabin project had a learning curve of varying pitch and length, meaning that if I were to tackle a specific task a second time, I might zip along like a more experienced hack. French drains would

be straightforward—dare I say "easy"—a second time around, though
I doubt I'll ever install them again.

~~~~~~

Dory, of course, was a constant source of "How hard can it be?" thinking. The spring I bought her in Salt Lake, I noticed the water-stained
ceiling and headed to Home Depot for supplies. On a warm and sunny
day, I squeezed four tubes of silicone sealer over every joint and corner,
from the bottom skirt to the edges of the roof vents. I then slathered
on several gallons of white rubber roof coat, moving the ladder from
sidewalk to street as I worked from stern to stem. I finished the final
big section over the cab and backed myself over the roof edge, feeling
with my feet for the ladder. I held the paint bucket in one hand, and
with the other hand I grabbed what I thought was the railing on the
cab. It wasn't. It was a broom handle, and broom, paint bucket, and
I dropped down to the sidewalk, splat. Rubber roof coat flew everywhere: fence, tree trunk, plants, sidewalk, and me. I staggered to my
feet. My ankle smarted terrifically, and there was a long, deep sidewalk
burn on my right thigh. To this day, the outline of the rubber roof-
coat splat remains on the sidewalk, and a sizable indentation remains
on my thigh.

It became obvious from Dory's first summer on the meadow that
the caulk and rubber roof coat didn't plug up or stop much of anything. I switched to roof tar. It was black, stinky, and the consistency
of thick fudge frosting. I applied it with a spatula, and happily it was
far easier and less gross than the basement tar experience. While I
worked my way across the roof, a diminutive ruby-crowned kinglet
on a branch in the adjacent fir twitted and flitted about. He was quite
the nervous little thing but very curious about this human working at
tree level. I used the whole gallon, slathering places that hadn't even
thought about leaking yet. After it dried for a few days, I painted the

roof with a white waterproofing so the black tar didn't heat Dory like a can of baked beans.

One day, I turned on the kitchen faucet in Dory and nothing came out. I lifted the sofa seat up; the water tank had plenty of water. Must be a dead water pump. I called Daisy, who said Peter was in Rock Springs and could bring a new one up when he returned. It took me several days to work up the courage to tackle it. Things mechanical and things electrical have always felt beyond my abilities. Several times, I lifted the sofa seat and stared down at the wire and hoses, stared at the new pump in its box, then closed the seat and moved on to something else.

Eventually, I tired of pouring pitchers of water from the five-gallon container on the deck. I got some tools, propped up the sofa seat with a broom, and started pondering. At some point, I heard my father's voice saying, "Now think it through," urging me to reason, to weigh the options and alternatives, to problem solve. I chose the right piece of hose and stopped the water flow and attached one end of the new pump. Cool. Then I mimicked how the wires were attached to the old pump when I moved the wires to the new pump. I flipped on the electricity, the pump purred, I opened the faucet, and my god, water came out. I filled a big glass of water, drank it, and lay down for a nap.

Dory was the largest vehicle I'd ever driven, and I reasoned that if I could maneuver her, I could drive a moving van. A big van was necessary for procurement, for toting and hauling cabin materials from the city to this remote place. Half a dozen times I rented a big van, loaded it in Salt Lake, and drove it up to the cabin. The trucks were intimidating to drive, but I gained great empathy for the big rigs that go slowly up hills. Backing up flustered me, even with the oversize mirrors, and I have a dent in my SUV metal bumper to show for it; the rental truck was untouched. Plumbing items were a priority the first trip: bathtub, bathroom vanity and sink, toilets, faucets, and water heater. Another trip included the woodstove and associated pipe, tiles and cement board for under the woodstove, and a donated futon for my bed. I also learned a lot about turning radius; only one small fir tree was injured as a result.

～～～

In 1926 when Wisconsinite Madge McHugh spent her first night in a cabin on a relinquished homestead near Pinedale that she would attempt to prove up on, hoards of mice kept her awake all night. She said, "I was informed that it was no effort at all to 'chink' and 'daub' the place. Those were two words I learned to hate before my trials and tribulations were over.... Somehow I managed to spend several summers on my homestead. I chinked and daubed and I daubed and I chinked.... To this day, a mouse can send me up the wall."

～～～

By the end of my second summer, the cabin was at "dry-in" stage at last, snug with roof, windows, and doors. I ceremoniously walked down the hill from Dory carrying my belongings and began camping in the bare basement. I had until October and the snow flew to caulk and stain all those beautiful logs, as well as fill gaps and cracks, and cut and nail up outside window frames. I knew it was a big volume of work, but how hard could it be?

I drove up from Salt Lake every weekend I could spare to work this second job as cabin grunt, setting the alarm for 5:00 a.m. on Monday to drive four hours back to campus, bleary-eyed and exhausted. I appreciated the all-over tired and mushy feeling from a weekend of physical labor, but gladly returned to my cerebral job for rest and recovery.

As Madge learned, there's quite a difference between a dry shell and a tight shell. At some point during construction, mice explored the new cabin, moths spent the day in every dark orifice, and in the warmth of midday, large ants marched in through the corner joints. Joe told me that great stuff was the answer. Great Stuff was the name of a spray-in, expanding foam, dispensed from a can through a long, narrow plastic tube you attached, similar to the straw you use to dispense WD-40. In any gap too large for caulk, in went the foam—one kind for your basic gaps and a different formula for the inch-wide spaces around doors and windows that allowed for the wood to settle. Madge would have loved it.

I pulled on a pair of latex gloves and started on the corners around the deck low enough to reach without a ladder. When I pushed the button, yellow foam whooshed out, blurbing and growing into the crack. I removed my finger from the button, but foam kept oozing out, spilling down the log and dribbling on the deck. By the time I worked my way to the door, I was more practiced at judging the degree of expansion and when to quit dispensing. My gloves (and body) were sticky with yellow goo. When the stuff dried in a crack, it was as firm as a big bracket fungus on a tree trunk.

The ants preferred the gaps in the butt-and-pass corner joints, whereas the moths seemed to gain access in any fissure bigger than a paper clip. I found their black-brown bodies huddled against the wood and gently pushed them out with a screwdriver so they weren't sealed in a foam tomb. I vacuumed up the dead moths and mouse turds, hoping that any reappearance would make it easier to detect their access points.

One evening I encountered a bat upstairs—very cute, with dark-brown ears and a creamy head and chest—that was very stubborn about leaving. I opened the doors and used my arms and a broom to encourage him out an open door, but after flying around a bit, he kept perching right above the open door, observing me. I left him, assuming he would find a way out as he had a way in (he did). My guess was that he entered through the fascia boards on one end of the attic, which needed a great deal of caulking.

My prior experience with caulk was dispensing some from a little tube along the top of the bathtub in Salt Lake; the result was ugly but functional. The amount of equipment supplied with the log kit should have been a big clue that caulking was a big job: two five-gallon buckets of caulk, a three-foot-long metal refillable caulk gun, and a fancy "follow plate" to transfer caulk from bucket to gun.

The weekend I began caulking was warm and breezy, the smell of dry leaves in the air, and I approached this new task with remarkable good cheer. The follow plate was a rubber-rimmed metal cover that fitted snugly inside the big bucket of tan caulk. In the plate's center was a threaded hole to screw on the caulk gun barrel.

I quickly learned that filling the gun wasn't meant to be a one-person operation because it required simultaneously pushing down on the follow plate while gradually pulling up the gun's handle. I tried a couple of positions and techniques but no caulk moved. Finally, not seeing another way to go about this, I climbed into the caulk bucket and balanced my feet on top of the follow plate—which did indeed put downward pressure on it—while I pulled the handle up with both hands to fill the barrel. This method certainly wasn't featured in the instruction manual.

I began caulking in the same place as I did the Great Stuff, the corner nearest the main door. I squeezed the trigger, and caulk squiggled and wiggled along the log edge, growing from thin to thick and back to thin. The line looked as though a child had been playing with a frosting decorator. I changed locations to a less visible place, under the deck by the basement. Just until I perfected my technique, I thought.

The heavy metal gun was more than half my height and took my fully extended grip to squeeze the trigger. Whoever designed it presumed that large men with large hands would be doing the caulking.

As the day wore on, my arms ached from holding the gun up high and away from my body. I stopped to massage my hands, cramped and frozen into position around the trigger, gazing out over the meadow, reminding myself why I was here.

By late afternoon when the air began to cool, I had quarts and quarts of practice and could sometimes lay a pretty straight and even bead of caulk, especially when the surface was smooth like along the window edge. But invariably the weight of the massive gun or the angle or my tiring muscles kicked in, and the bead squiggled and curled and globbed. On a cement edge or log edge, I had to smooth and press at least part of the sloppy line into the crack.

When I called her that evening for suggestions, Daisy said to put on a latex glove and dip the index finger in rubbing alcohol and then smooth the bead. I tried this technique the next morning, but it seemed to work only once when the glove was brand-new. As a one-person operation, I also had to keep switching from caulking to smoothing, so it was tricky taking the gloves off without making all matters worse. By the end of the day, I abandoned it and just smoothed with a dirty naked finger and rubbed the excess on T-shirt rags. The lines I laid still looked amateurish.

The hardest place to caulk—which of course happened to be the place most in need of it—was the high roof end opposite the deck, which was covered with half-round fascia boards between the highest log and the attic. I borrowed Bob's extension ladder and climbed to the tip-top. I held the caulk gun out from my body with one arm and held onto the ladder with the other. I was extremely grateful that the first fall frost meant no mosquitoes or horse flies buzzed around me seeking blood and flesh while I perilously balanced up there.

By the end of my second full weekend of caulking, the gun started malfunctioning. The brake kept sticking, so caulk streamed out when I wasn't dispensing, and something was screwed up at the push head

that moved caulk through the barrel to the nozzle. But the biggest
frustration was that I was no better at caulking than I was five gallons ago and doubted that I would ever be able to lay a perfect, even
bead. Nevertheless, before the caulk gun died and my body wearied
of a thousand trips up and down the ladder that left gray aluminum
bruises on my legs from pressing and balancing against the rungs, I
managed to plug the major bat access holes and, if lucky, the mouse
and moth holes.

In that second weekend of caulking, I alternated caulking with
a new task because my arms and hands were so sore and I needed
to punish a different body part. The outside window trim was fairly
simple compared to the inside trim and sills. The outside frames called
for straight cuts, not mitered at a ninety-degree angle, so water didn't
seep down between trim and window. Just cut it and nail it up, so how
hard could that be?

I started with the basement windows, the least-visible ones. I measured numerous times, then drew a line against a T-square, placed
one knee on the board, and directed my little handheld circular saw
across. The cuts seemed hesitant, uneven, of slightly varying width,
and I got only marginally better with practice. With the advice of both
my brothers, on my next trip to Salt Lake I bought a fabulous tabletop
"chop saw" that made straight and mitered cuts.

When I told Dennis of the purchase, he said, "If you get any more
power tools, I'll marry you," a comment all the more touching
and sweet when it comes from a gay man.

The new saw made downright gorgeous saw cuts. And the more
I hammered up window trim, the better I got (unlike caulking),
which was very satisfying. My aim became so much more true; I left
fewer and fewer dings on the surrounding wood and could sink the
nail with fewer and fewer strikes. The trim gave such a nice finished
look that it looked like it might really be a cabin someday. Still, my

arms got so sore from pounding that it hurt to raise them or brush my hair. My calves felt like cement from climbing the ladder countless times.

With each trip up to the cabin, the temperatures cooled. I arrived in mid-September after a week of snow to glorious fall weather. Bundled in the morning, but wearing shorts by noon. The aspen leaves were the yellow-orange of farm-fresh egg yolks. Flowers lingered by the meadow edges. Elk bugled in the evening, though the call sounded to me more like a strange, high-pitched grunt and trumpet and not a bugle at all. Sometimes I heard the great gray owl. They were good reminders that despite the work and bruises and blood and aching muscles and all the money I was spending, this place charmed me. The shift in seasons also made it apparent that the window was closing on my work and I needed to get as much stain-sealer as possible onto the exterior logs.

Florence Blake left her bank job in Chicago to homestead in Wyoming in 1920. In considering a dwelling, she wrote:

> Thinking to be on the safe side, I had purchased in Chicago a portable garage, nine by twelve feet. It was just the size of our living room rug at home.... It could easily be assembled by a woman. Or so I was told by the affable old man who sold it to me. A generous number of nuts, bolts, and screws had been included to prove his point, and to provide complications for the "putter-upper." ... Lucky for me I did not take that elderly salesman's advice and try to put the thing up alone. It took three husky men all that day to assemble it.

I had a little pump sprayer that I used to stain my fence in Salt Lake, so I had good reason to think, how hard could it be? True, but the project was an entire cabin, not a little fence.

The weather held in late September, and I began with a frenzy, taping and covering windows and doors with plastic. On the first long wall on the north side, where the ground was flat and I could reach the top logs with just a step stool, the spraying began well. I swept my arm back and forth, leaving a nice coat of warm reddish-brown stain-sealer that smelled pungent but not too much so. Then the tank ran dry. I stirred the five-gallon bucket and refilled the tank. Soon, empty again. Then, the nozzle clogged. Then empty again. By lunchtime I had part of one wall done.

The next day I moved on to the two walls that required climbing to the tip-top of the twenty-foot extension ladder. I'm not afraid of heights per se, but I don't rock climb or skydive, either. Because the cabin was built into a hillside, the ground along these two walls sloped, so I positioned a triangle-shaped piece of wood under one ladder foot so the ladder wouldn't slide once positioned against the cabin.

When I applied the foam and caulk to these walls, I used one hand to hold onto the ladder and the other hand to dispense foam or caulk. But spraying required two hands, one to hang onto the tank and one to hold the spray nozzle. All I could do was lay my body as close as possible against the ladder and clutch with my feet. Each time I climbed and moved the ladder, I contemplated various unlucky scenarios concerning ladder and me. I retrieved the portable phone from the cabin, sealed it in a plastic bag, and parked it below the ladder. At least if I fell, perhaps I could crawl to the phone.

As is typical for Wyoming, the wind picked up in the afternoon. And with just the slightest breeze, stain went EVERYWHERE. The first day I didn't really fret about it because the instructions on the big bucket said "cleans up easily with soap and water." It was warm, so I wore shorts, an old T-shirt, no hat.

After six hours of staining, I was a speckled mess and I drove to Bondurant to get a shower. I walked up to the counter to pay for my shower, and people turned and stared. A cowboy near the door still in his chaps and Stetson looked me up and down and said, "Somebody's been workin'!" After the shower and much scrubbing, my arms and legs still looked like they had oversize liver spots. I couldn't comb through my hair for several days. The next day I covered up.

By mid-October, only two of the four sides were stained, and I crossed my fingers that the other two sides would winter well.

~~~~~~

The bulk of my cabin laboring took place in that frenzied second fall, as well as my fourth summer when I turned to the inside finish work. By then, my friends were well acquainted with my infamous phrase and the optimism and determination from which it sprang. So when I told Donna about a project Dad and I would tackle in summer number five, she laughed, shook her head, and said, "How hard could it be, right?"

This project was a cement patio outside the basement door. For years I'd covered the dirt there with OSB waferboard, which attracted carpenter ants and encouraged the chipmunks to tunnel under it, which encouraged Tobie to dig after them. So, we would make a little wood frame, mix cement with water, pour it in, and level it. How hard is that?

At the lumberyard, the man looked at my little SUV and asked, "Ain't you got a bigger rig?" On the spot, we reduced by half the size of the patio; even then, the SUV bottomed out with a worrisome scrape at every bump in the drive home.

I borrowed Joe and Daisy's small electric cement mixer—much better than mixing in a wheelbarrow—and wheeled the mixer down the path to the basement door. I was in charge of mixing, not wanting my then eighty-one-year-old father to lift the fifty-pound bags of deadweight up to mixer and pour. (Why don't mattresses or bags of cement have handles, for goodness' sake?)

After stalling the little motor a few times, I learned the correct amount of water to add initially, and how much more to spray in with the hose to get the right consistency. When a batch was sufficiently mixed, I pulled the handle and the mixture sloshed into the wheelbarrow, which I wheeled over and dumped in the wood frame, where Dad leveled and worked it. My back and arms felt the strain after two bags. And there were many, many, many more bags to go.

When the final corner was leveled and we carved in our initials, I was coated in sweat and layer upon layer of chalky dust and dried cement, 100 percent filthy and exhausted. Thinking that I could use some visual documentation to remind myself in future cases, I went inside, made a cardboard sign, and posed for the camera in my dirty and sapped state: it read, "How hard can it be?!?"

NINE

The Dry Doe

I fell with such a crash that Tobie came trotting back up the road to investigate. I lay on the gravel, gasping. She sniffed my torso and nosed my face, waiting for me to rise and resume our walk back down the road to the cabin. As I struggled to sit up, she gave me several encouraging licks.

The road near the ridge had patches of ice, some small, some extending across the road, typical for mid-May. It was our third day of the third summer, and we ventured out after lunch for some exercise and exploration.

I arrived bursting with energy and enthusiasm, charged for a summer of splendid hikes and hard, physical labor, the kind that makes you a bit rubbery, aching for a hot bath and a beer, ready to fall into bed like an exhausted puppy. This was the summer I would lay the wood floor, tile the tub-shower and bathroom floor, sand and stain the walls and ceilings, and triumphantly move upstairs from the cold cement cave in the basement that was my temporary residence. I dreamed of having a septic tank and hot water in the bathroom by summer's end.

I thought my left foot was firmly planted on the gravel when my right foot touched the spot of ice, but it shot out so quickly that the planted foot couldn't stop the momentum. I landed flat on my back and butt, my forearms bent backward to brace myself. As I raised myself, my upper right arm had a strong, flat ache.

By dinnertime, the pain in my right arm and shoulder was too intense to hold an onion while I chopped it. Over the weekend, the pain got worse instead of better, a rather constant, dull, painful throb, no matter the number of ibuprofen I inhaled. After some gentle chiding from my sister-in-law that weekend, I went to the clinic in Pinedale on Monday and waited for hours to see a physician's assistant who guessed that I might have a tear in my rotator cuff. She recommended stronger painkillers, no activity, and, if it wasn't better in ten to fourteen days, getting an MRI in Salt Lake. She said typing was okay (I had a deadline for my first book), but even that hurt like hell.

That night I lay in bed trying to get comfortable, contemplating the consequences of this injury to my summer. The best position was on my back, but I needed several pillows to lift pressure off the right shoulder. While I lay in the cold, quiet dark, I thought about a conversation a few days before the semester's end with a young student who came into my office and proudly announced she was getting married to Chris, a pleasant but rather dim young man she always sat next to in class.

"My, well, congratulations," I said. "That's great. But I gotta ask—what about grad school?"

Our previous meeting concerned recommendations for master's programs; she was one of the brightest and most articulate undergraduates I'd had for quite some time.

"Oh, I'm going to wait a year or two, until after the wedding and everything," she said.

I wanted to believe her, but I'd seen this scenario before, and there was a good chance she'd be pregnant soon—and done with school. For these young Utah students, especially the Mormon ones, getting married seemed as easy and uncomplicated as falling off a log. When I was an undergraduate in the 1970s, it was rare to see a fellow student with a wedding ring, and even rarer to meet one with kids. Now, when I looked out across my classroom, many students wore rings, and each semester there were missed classes and exams because of births. What happened to feminism, I wondered, to bold independence and choices for women, to waiting for marriage and children? But here, cultural expectations held that a young woman's two most important monikers were wife and mother—and if she was Mormon, she wouldn't get into the highest levels of heaven without them.

I shifted the pillows again and pulled the blanket and sleeping bag closer around my chin. The basement was cold. I was injured and alone and feeling teary. This wasn't my plan, single and childless at forty-nine. Being a professor wasn't the original plan either, though I was happy with that outcome. And the cabin—that dream was about forty years old.

But it was the single and alone part that occupied the still, dark night. I already envisioned my self-reliance slipping out the basement door, and without that freewheeling cuss for company, the summer looked positively empty. When you've been single as long as I have, it's tempting to mistake self-reliance for company; it helps the days echo with activity and not just your own footsteps. Sometimes that seems easier; there's familiarity and comfort in my own companionship, so much so that in the weighing of it—should I stay home and read, or try to find a movie or dinner date?—the former is the less demanding path.

⌇⌇⌇⌇⌇

Two weeks later in Salt Lake, I tried to lie perfectly still in a very narrow tube for forty-five minutes amid extremely loud and rhythmic pulses. I wish I'd been warned and even tranquilized before my body was slid into that tube for the MRI; I get claustrophobic even when caught midway removing a sweater over my head. As I lay in the narrow tunnel, my heart was racing, and it was all I could do to avoid a full-blown panic.

The next day my doctor pulled up the MRI report on the computer screen in the exam room.

"Oh," she said. "Ohhhh…Ummm…Not good." I asked her to print me a copy.

"FINDINGS:…a near complete tear of the subscapularis tendon with only a few deep fibers of the most inferior extent of the tendon remaining attached to the lesser tuberosity. The long head of the biceps is torn and apparently retracted into the upper arm. A small portion of the proximal stump remains.…There is a complete rupture of the middle glenohumeral ligament. There is marked periosteal stripping along the anterior glenoid as a result of the subscapularis injury.…"

With all the stumps, tears, and ruptures, I marveled that my arm wasn't flopping around more. Sadly, this wasn't just a little tear in the rotator cuff that the tendons moved through, but two major tendons themselves were torn.

I drove back to the cabin (grateful for my automatic transmission) and walked around the cabin shell, taking note of work not finished last fall—graying logs on two walls that needed staining and cracks still not caulked—and where the carpenter ants ate right through the spray-in foam filler. Inside, each room was dusty and bare, and the particle-board flooring echoed when I walked from room to room. It was hard to face that it would remain this way all summer. The basement was cold enough to cloud and thicken the olive oil in my little camp kitchen.

Surgery was scheduled for July 1; the surgeon said waiting longer was a bad idea because a torn tendon was like a rubber band: the longer you waited, the harder it was to restretch and reattach it. I felt somehow betrayed by my body, worried that this was the beginning of some big downhill slide. In six months I would turn fifty.

~~~~~~

In high school, everyone thought I'd be the first to marry. Michael and I dated for almost five years, through high school and into college, and we presumed we would marry—that is, until he became an evangelical Christian and told me I had to first accept Christ as my savior and accept that he would always love Christ more than he loved me. I eventually fled his proselytizing by transferring universities, where I took classes in environmental studies and soon worked as a seasonal naturalist in Olympic National Park. (I later heard through my mom's bridge club that Michael and his evangelical wife had nine children. Whew.)

My ex Nate and I took scores of great outdoor trips. Conflict was pathologically absent in our relationship, so much so that the dog growled when our voices raised, unaccustomed to the strangers in the room. I continued my quest to please him and lost myself in the process. After a stalemate on the issue of children (he was adamantly opposed), he became stony and silent and slipped further downstream. In an unusual act of defiance and independence, I cut my long hair (which he loved) into a short bob when I flew to the Midwest for my brother's wedding. He met me at the airport when I returned, surprised, but he never said a word. Two months later, he had rented a house for himself before he told me he was leaving.

When Nate left after almost four years together (and soon married my former best friend), I fell into college teaching and then headed to graduate school and a new academic career. In Salt Lake, Paul professed his love three weeks after we met. He was a warm and funny man, and we became inseparable. It didn't last. He grew silent (what IS that with men?), and specters from his past rose from the rubble and he inexplicably departed; soon, I got tenure and then bought the land. Remarkable, really, that after the breakup of each of these three major loves—at least after the blue crying jags and crises of self-confidence—my life took major, positive shifts.

With other relationships, the timing was inexplicably off, like two turning sprockets whose cogs didn't quite engage. There was a sweet, geeky computer guy who trembled when he kissed me, but I met him fresh from the wounds of my ex. A few men, similarly, were newly divorced and had no sense of who they were or what they wanted from me, except to heal. Three men left girlfriends for me, but three strikes, the girlfriends eventually won them all back. A couple of men said they liked independent women, but then bristled when I did something or went somewhere without them. And of course, I bristled at men who wanted to control me or mold me into their version of what they wanted a woman to be. Recently, a man I dated for several months put a breakup note in my mailbox the day after I said it'd be nice if we could sometimes talk about things deeper than the day-to-day stuff.

My last therapist told me that I needed to be needier. I laughed; in my twenties, "Needy" was my middle name. I worked so hard to please a man that as long as he loved (or wanted) me, that was enough. I depended on him for my happiness, my confidence, my very sense of myself—so much so that when he left, I felt like an empty shell. I set out to learn how to fill it up myself.

By the time I entered graduate school at thirty-two, I had learned I was okay on my own and could be more discerning. I wanted someone to respect me—my thoughts, feelings, intelligence, my ambitions. Someone to make me laugh and whom I would never tire talking with. Someone who was kind and warm, not the strong, silent type nor overly macho. My grandmother said I was being too picky; I said I deserved to have all that. Some single friends have essentially given up the search, thrown in the towel, saying the good men are all married, gay, or crazy. I believed there was another love or two in my life, but I wasn't coupling for the sake of being half a couple.

Through the years, I've witnessed friends embroiled in bad marriages, or settling back unhappily in mediocre marriages. At times, I envied their having a built-in date or travel partner ("Yeah, but he doesn't like to travel") or sex mate ("You know the last time we had sex?") and especially a partner to share things with, to laugh with, to partake in the load ("That'd be nice, wouldn't it?"). Happy marriages seemed few and far between.

At the same time, some married friends envied my solitude and possessed an overrated sense of what it's like to be single. "You've got it great," one said. "You get the whole bed, can eat what you want, and you don't have kids to cart around. God, sometimes I daydream about being single..."

"Being single isn't just about having alone time," I told her. "It's like the difference between a day hike and a solo backpack." It's a metaphor I've employed several times to help people understand.

When being single is like a day hike, it's idyllic. For one hour or five hours, you have peace and solitude and luxuriate in your own thoughts, totally uninterrupted. You hike at your own pace and stop when you want. It's quiet and you hear wind in the trees, birds chipping, and you come back refreshed.

But when living single stretches from one year into the next, it's like a long solo backpack. You shoulder all the weight, and you can't divide the burden of big items like the stove or tent. You are solely responsible for navigating, which is okay when the trail is clear and obvious, but hard when you encounter obstacles and there's no one who shares the stakes. The view from the peak is magnificent, but there's no one to ooh and ahh with, or to laugh with when dinner is spilled in the dirt. When you're tired or hurting, there's no one to lean your body against and listen to his breathing and heartbeat as assurance that life thumps on and you share the same air with another.

〰〰〰

After shoulder surgery, I spent two blistering weeks in Salt Lake sleeping fitfully while propped up in the recliner, trying to adjust to my helplessness. The sheer frustration of not being able to do something simple with one hand—open a letter, close a bag of pretzels, dress myself—made me feel like a two-year-old, always on the edge of a tantrum. My right arm was immobilized in a sling, so I wore the same top for several days straight, even to bed. A bra was out of the question. I swore like a sailor trying to put up my car's windshield shade with one hand.

Needing and asking for help put a smart dent in my do-it-myself persona, a persona suited to building a solitary life in the woods, but that couldn't help me tie my shoes one-handed. Some friends came to the rescue. Dennis brought me a pepper grinder that you squeezed with one hand. Donna brought me one-handed teeth flossers. Natalie washed my hair and shaved my left armpit. I learned to hold a beer bottle between my feet to open it.

After a few weeks, I called Dad and said I wanted to go to the cabin. He already had a plane ticket to Wyoming for late July, but we'd put the trip on hold after the surgery.

"Are you sure it's not too soon? Will you be all right up there by yourself after I leave?"

"If I've gotta rest and recuperate, I'd much rather be at the cabin. The neighbors will help me if I need it—a few have already offered to shop for me and haul my water. It certainly would be more healing there than in this smoggy place."

Bless him, he acquiesced, changed his ticket to Salt Lake, and drove me up to the cabin, where he hauled water jugs, stained the deck, and washed the dishes. It was hot and the horseflies were hungry for flesh.

~~~~~

When I was a teenager, Dad decided that I should not leave home before I knew how to change the oil in the car and clean the spark plugs in the lawnmower. At the time I didn't own either a car or a lawnmower, but that wasn't the point. He wanted to make sure I could do things, all by myself, even if foreign and most often done by men. Perhaps it was a recognition of my independent and adventuresome nature. Perhaps self-sufficiency was second nature to children of the Depression, like my parents. When I was in college, Mom and Dad would inquire about school and classes, but rarely about my love life; I wasn't sure why, but it left me with the impression that school performance and career were more important (at least then) than a partner.

As was true of most of my childhood friends' parents, my parents had a traditional gender-role marriage. Dad was the wage earner and worked in the yard and did house maintenance; Mom raised three children and fed, clothed, and took care of the lot of us. Her age, her generation, her genes—all contributed to this loyal and nurturing woman who loved her children fiercely and completely and poured so much energy and devotion into them.

By the 1970s, surrounded by the feminist movement, Mom asked me whether I thought she should have had a career. As my brothers and I got older, she had turned her college textile experience into handwoven and stylish women's clothing, but she was easily wounded by art critics whose judging methods she called "whimsical." She also became self-conscious about not bringing money into the family coffers.

Years after she died, I found a feature article on Mom and her weaving printed in the little local newspaper. She told the reporter, "With the world now there are things that make you feel that being a person at home is really just a dumb and lazy thing to do. I find that distressing. A beautifully run home with an interesting person is wonderful—instead of two tired, desperate people trying to get ahead. I don't consider myself submissive but making someone happy, making a nice place to live, is a nice thing to do."

Mom indeed worked to make her husband and children happy, which involved incredible self-sacrifice and serving others at the expense of herself. That wasn't something I could see myself doing, though it's exactly what I fell into with my ex. The statistics show that women don't benefit from marriage the way men do; married men live longer, are richer, excel at their careers, and are happier than single men. But married women do not live longer than single ones, and they earn less, are significantly less healthy, and are more likely to suffer from depression.

Yet marriage remains the normative destiny for a young woman in Utah. Self-sufficiency is sadly not a quality found in many of my female students; a great many can't even cook. I once asked a large auditorium of students how many knew how to check the oil level in their cars; only a few hands went up, all male. A professor friend was coordinating a field trip of her nature-writing class to a city park, and one female confessed that she needed a ride because—though she had a car, knew how to drive, and knew where the park was—she was too afraid of getting lost.

~~~~~~

By early August, several rain-filled thunderstorms mushroomed over the mountains and quelled the heat momentarily. It felt like summer was flowing through my hands, and I couldn't seem to close my fingers around it, couldn't hold it tight and feel its light and coolness. I felt sentenced to my basement cave, reading magazines and books from the library, walking outside only on flat surfaces like the driveway. With my right arm still slinged, my balance walking in the woods was precarious.

I woke at three one night, my nightshirt drenched in sweat and unable to fall back asleep. It wasn't just the pain and meds from surgery; these were bona fide hot flashes because they'd also been striking in the daytime. When my plumber Bill installed the shower fixture into the wall that week, he said that the "stop" was missing from the box of hardware, a piece that kept the handle from spinning hot to cold, one way and then the other. I seemed to have lost my own stop, and my thermostat (for no apparent reason) turned up several notches until sweat broke out on my forehead, chin, and chest, and then just as suddenly spun the other way. I also had lost the regulator for my menstrual cycles, which disappeared for a couple of months, only to return with a bloody vengeance and soak bedclothes and perturb sleep.

Besides blood, sweat, and yes, tears, my body bore other signs of its metamorphosis. The skin on my legs was drying to a less supple parchment. When I saw this dry, crinkled skin on other women, I had always assumed they didn't use good lotion. Dimples appeared on my upper thighs. I'd always been proud of my strong, thin legs—legs that literally had stopped men in the grocery store to stare and stammer, "Wow, you've got great legs." My hands bore more lines, and beneath my chin the skin sagged slightly. The five pounds I put on ten years ago when Mom died had nudged into ten. I gladly subverted the gray when it crept into the part in my hair with #5 Coffee Bean dye. Though everyone told

me I didn't look forty-nine (I was carded in liquor stores until almost
forty), my body increasingly revealed that it was.

~~~~~

Emma Peterson was in her mid-fifties when she moved from Omaha
to eastern Wyoming to homestead in 1919. She was widowed twice,
was childless, and wanted to make a fresh start. She was unusual in that
most single women homesteaders were in their twenties, and photos
showed the fresh-faced, smiling young things in front of their shacks.
A significant number of these women had some kind of professional
training; many were schoolteachers who found that teaching at a rural
school during the winter months when homesteaders weren't required
to remain on the 'stead was a good way to earn an income and to hire
work done. Other women were physicians, nurses, accountants, post-
mistresses, secretaries, even phone operators, photographers, and res-
taurateurs. They tended to marry at a much later age—twenty-seven
compared to twenty-two for the general population.

I was surprised to read that some people criticized the single-
women homesteaders, saying they weren't real farmers because they
hired farmwork done, or that they lacked commitment and treated
time on their homesteads as "extended vacations." I kept reading; it
turns out that a lot of homesteading men also hired hands to break
their sod and plant crops. One study found that 94 percent of women
homesteaders oversaw all the operation of their land (sound like General Contractors to me) and contributed both domestic work and a
great deal of outdoor work as well. When I read about Mildred Belle
Hunt rising at 4:30 to plant nine hundred hills of spuds, pulling mus-
tard and tumbleweeds out of the wheat, and fixing pasture fence, it
hardly sounded like a vacation.

What struck me most about these women—whether they
loved their homesteading experience or loathed it—was that they

understood it provided a chance at capital accumulation and economic independence that was unequaled in any other occupation then available to women. Regardless of whether they stayed until the end of their lives (single or married) or leased or sold the homestead the moment they got the deed, landownership was an economic boon. Even those who chose the commutation clause of the Homestead Act (meaning they lived on their 'stead for just six months and then purchased it outright for $1.25 an acre) put themselves legions ahead economically. I wonder in which of their shoes I would have fit and how I would have negotiated the power difference between men and women a century ago, a difference that makes today's considerable inequality (in income alone) seem minute.

In graduate school, one of the most memorable books I read was *Women and Economics,* published in 1898 by Charlotte Perkins Gilman. She studied the economic relations between men and women as a factor in "social evolution," concluding that until women possessed economic independence, women's lives and futures would remain utterly dependent on their "sexual assets" to please men so they'd bring home the bread. Gilman said women could gain economic independence through either "outside" work or having their domestic work properly valued and rewarded. She called for household work (like mopping the floor, I mused) to be shared equally. And she declared that there should be no difference in the clothes worn by little girls and boys and that so-called tomboys were the "perfect humans." Charlotte must have been a shocking and prescient social thinker in her day—far more radical in her writing and living than this single woman tomboy building a cabin.

~~~~~~

In the lengthening shadows of late August, four mule deer cavorted in the lower meadow. One was smaller, probably a yearling. A young spike buck and a doe rubbed necks, then hopped and sidestepped each other playfully. An older doe stood to one side and watched; her rear haunches were still molting a bit, and it looked as though she were wearing a ratty couch throw. Tobie was on the deck with me, amazingly quiet but alert.

I read in a magazine about the older "dry doe." A Paiute Indian woman said that the dry doe was easy to spot—the way her color had changed, how she had a different look. This doe could no longer reproduce and she acted differently. Her place in the herd was as an elder matriarch and she helped take care of the young deer. The Paiute woman said this ritual teaches Indian women to follow nature and follow their own changes as they leave their childbearing years. She said, "It teaches us about life-cycles and keeps us ever-present in nature."

I watched the dry doe, trying to discern her role in this little herd. Mostly, the foursome just grazed on the drying grasses. Occasionally, each popped its head up to listen, paused its chewing, cocked an ear, and turned a head, before returning for another mouthful. The doe looked older, but it was hard to see whether she behaved or was treated differently. But then, I hadn't watched deer like this and wasn't sure what to look for.

〰〰〰

Over Labor Day weekend, Sara and her girls were coming from Minnesota. Sara and I met when I was in graduate school and became—and remained over the distance and decades—the closest of friends; she was the sister I never had, and to her two toddlers I was Auntie Julia. I was so excited to show her the land and cabin for the first time, though disappointed that there was no bedroom, kitchen, or bathroom for them.

"Oh you, don't worry about it," she said on the phone before they left. "We're used to roughing it, remember?"

Sara and I had taken canoe trips through the Boundary Waters in Minnesota, and the year I moved to Salt Lake, we backpacked in the Wind Rivers.

"I know," I said. "I just thought this place would be so much more finished this summer."

"I know you're disappointed and this summer has been hard for you, but it doesn't matter to us what's finished—it really doesn't. We just want to be with you and see this incredible place. We can't wait. The girls are so excited."

"I can't wait either. The girls look so much bigger in the last photos. And I'm crossing my fingers that water is hooked up to the basement utility sink by the time you get here."

The girls, who arrived with plenty of activity books and a couple of DVDs, didn't mind the basement camping, though they weren't all that keen on being outside, either. The younger one especially didn't like the bugs.

When I was in graduate school in my thirties, I talked to Sara about having a child on my own. My clock was ticking to be sure, but I still wasn't sure I had a strong mommy gene. I didn't long to hold infants presented to me and was relieved to hand them back when they started bawling. I always believed that I would meet a man who really wanted kids, and then, okay, I'd have some, trusting that the rearing wouldn't be put entirely in my lap (which for many women, past and present, it was). But motherhood alone? I wasn't convinced I had the patience or selflessness to become a mom without a dad.

Sara also struggled about having kids, though for a different reason. Years ago en route to a backpack in southern Utah, Sara and I stopped at a well-known psychic's house, who told Sara that she had two girls chasing her. She was thrilled; she had always wanted kids but had spent years trying to convince her husband that parenthood would not be the same as what he grew up with. It finally happened, two sweet little redheads two years apart, Claire and then Erin.

Sara and I sat at the table in the basement drinking tea while the girls played with their dolls on the sofa bed. New crayon drawings adorned my fridge, Claire's of a nearby lake and Erin's of flowers and mountains. I had just finished reading several books to them (one of my favorite auntie activities), one girl on each side, their sweet, warm breath on my arms. Even when we read books they'd heard dozens of times, they had questions, saw new things in the drawings, anticipated the next page and helped turn it.

Over tea, Sara and I were deep in conversation but kept getting sidetracked with a steady stream of interruptions. "Mom, Erin's touching me." "She won't share. It's my turn." "Claire, stop it!" "Mom!" Then tears. Sara was present for their needs, though not hoveringly so, and her voice never escalated or showed exasperation in the face of theirs. I marveled at her patience, and it exhausted me. Eventually, I couldn't complete thoughts in my head before another upset veered me off in another direction.

When I babysat for neighbors' kids in my teens, the whining and crying outbursts and squabbling over minor infractions really set me on edge. It was just typical kid behavior, but it set me off, and it still did. It was constant, relentless, depleting. My brother Jim, who loves being a father, said the requests, the wants, the needs of his two boys were sometimes like a ping-ping-ping in the center of his forehead. Even though the opportunity to be a mother never arrived, I always doubted my ability to do it well.

On their last night in the cabin, the girls played happily on the basement rug while Sara chopped vegetables for dinner. Claire got up and ran over to her, excited to tell her something. Sara reached down and stroked her hand over Claire's hair and cheek while she listened, and smiled adoringly. There was such love in that gaze it made me ache.

~~~~~

By late September, more deer came to graze in the meadow, usually in feeding groups of four or five. At first, all were does and fawns, who were bigger now with fading spots. I tried to spot the dry does, to watch for clues of their new place in the herd, but was never sure of my identification. By October, a buck sometimes joined the females, his tending herd, especially if a doe or two were in estrus. Fall was really the only time the males had much to do with the females and were seen with them. Male mule deer did not contribute in the slightest to rearing offspring. As the deer moved through the grass, clouds of grasshoppers rose in front of them, clacking, their bright-orange underwings flashing in the angled sun.

Though deer primarily pair up to mate, some animals have stronger pairings and equally shared duties toward young. The naturalist in me knew that the animal world shows as much variability in these activities as humans. Sandhill cranes mate for life and share the brooding and rearing of their colts. Beavers are usually monogamous and mate for life, but this occurs infrequently because members of a pair typically are of different ages. Coyotes show great variation; some live singly, others in mated pairs, and some in packs. Deer mice have two to four litters per year; males may stay briefly with females after mating, but mice are pretty solitary except in cold weather. The mating of brown-headed cowbirds varies from monogamy to a mixture of monogamy and polygyny to total promiscuity. A female cowbird lays about forty eggs a year—all in the nest of another bird to brood and feed—though only two or three eggs each year become adults.

Since I reared no brood of my own, I wonder about my role in the herd, especially toward young ones. I babysit on occasion for the kids across the street or friends, and for years I volunteered each month for a kids' literacy program at the library. But most of my contact with young people is through my students.

From all the years I spent in college, I remember only a couple of encouraging female professors. They were greatly outnumbered by men (even in my graduate program). My department now is easily half women professors. Some students come to my office for advice and counsel—about class, about career, sometimes about life. I dispense Kleenex when needed, even serve tea. But students rely on e-mail contact mostly these days, and I'm often left to ponder the effect or impact I've had. I've gotten a few cards, a poem once, a jar of homemade chutney, and hugs, but mostly they pass through my classes by the hundreds, and they leave, and I never see or hear from them again. Like every teacher, I hope a snippet of material that students grasp during a semester contributes to their lives beyond. I am accustomed to our semester-long dance—of dependence, then interdependence as we learn from each other, and finally independence as we go our separate ways—but nevertheless, I feel both gratified and estranged when it ends.

As hard as it was to put my independent self on the shelf this summer, I learned lessons. I am proud of my half-century journey to stand on my own two feet, responsible for my own happiness as well as my bank account. But the arm that was slinged and held tight to my body was a constant reminder that arms are designed to be held out and open to others. Too much solitude and self-reliance wraps me up too tightly. When my inner dialogue tumbles round and round inside, a talk with a friend quickly opens the door and puts the thoughts out to pasture. Depending on others—family, friends, neighbors—actually bolsters independence far more directly than I imagined.

While watching the deer this summer, I thought about young Paiute women learning about life cycles in nature and in human lives. I thought about Sara, my mom, a host of girlfriends, and how all women must negotiate self and others in a way that men generally do not. All women dance this dance: when to follow and when to lead, how to support others without losing sight of themselves. The steps change over time and with circumstance—children, partners, injury, economics, and luck of the draw. The key is to be versatile and learn to dance both parts, letting neither define you wholly.

~~~~~

An occasional complication of shoulder surgery such as mine was "frozen shoulder," and mine was indeed frozen. The surgeon didn't want my reattached subscapularis tendon to pull apart so had me wear a sling for the first month, but the resulting inactivity meant I couldn't lift my right arm straight up or rotate it very far backward from the elbow. That autumn back in Salt Lake I began four months of painful physical therapy, including a month of home sessions in "the rack," a device that stretched my shoulder up and back and with a dial that I moved every few days to pull it more. It reminded me of getting braces tightened.

In the middle of the final month in the rack, I turned fifty. I eschewed a party of any kind, though I let Dennis and Natalie take me out to dinner. In January, I tried Internet dating, once again.

My girlfriends—and a book so encouragingly titled *Love in 90 Days*—suggested I have a "glam" photo shoot. I needed a professional photo for work-related things anyway, I thought. The photographer was chubby, heavily made up with bouffant, overdyed blonde hair, and she wore a baby-doll short black dress. She gushed when I told her I needed a photo for Internet dating—as well as work. "Ooh, I met my hubby that way! Oh, you'll just love it!" As soon as I got home, I washed off all the makeup, which felt suffocating.

I sent Dad and Jim some photos inside a valentine; Dad disliked them and Jim wasn't crazy about them. "They make you look fake," Dad said. "I like the way you look naturally." Curiously, my girlfriends thought they were great.

A divorced man in Salt Lake read my online profile and sent me an e-mail. In his photo he had graying hair and a mustache, and he wore a black turtleneck and gray slacks and leaned against a high balcony railing. He wrote: "Lovely profile and great smile. I'm wondering what a beautiful woman like you is doing single."

I laughed and shook my head. What she is doing is a helluva lot.

TEN

Riding the New Wild West

The grassy field behind the Pinedale grocery store was rimmed with square white canvas tents, their front flaps pulled back to reveal the goods inside. Children gathered in front of a man dressed in buckskin who readied a small canon. "10, 9, 8...," he counted, and the kids watched with rapt attention, each with a foot planted slightly forward in anticipation. After 3, 2, 1, a compact "boom," and a puff of gray smoke, candy shot forward in a wide splay and the children launched, weaving around each other to pluck prizes from the grass.

"Wow," I said to a woman in a long gingham dress standing just outside her tent, watching the shoot.

"Yep, that's my husband. He always likes to do this for the kids. Shoots it several times a day."

I had traveled to Pinedale on a Friday for my weekly grocery-library-hardware-dump-etc. trip, but also to experience the beginning of the annual Green River Rendezvous Days, always the second weekend in July. The series of events honors—and in a sense reenacts—the historic summer gatherings along the Green River by fur trappers, traders, and American Indians. Some activities take place at the Museum of the Mountain Man up the hill by the clinic. This grassy field was Trader's Row, a replica of a fur traders' marketplace, for trading was the primary purpose of the Rendezvous.

In the dozen or so tents were men in buckskin pants and vests with cotton shirts, and one with a coonskin cap. Most of the women wore long cotton calico dresses or skirts. Their wares were pottery and woven baskets, glass beads and wooden boxes, belt buckles and beaded jewelry, period clothing and hats, and in virtually every tent animal skins. By color and size, I made out the bodies of beaver, fox, coyote, mink, and bison; there were others I could not distinguish, though I did not ask. I had never seen more animal skins in one location in my life. Some pelts, like the coyotes, had the sunken and dried face and feet still attached. I felt slightly sick.

I bought a black-and-tan woven basket (from Africa) for the woman watering my Salt Lake house plants this summer and a small, square blue-pine jewelry box for a friend's birthday.

~~~~~~

Even though I've lived in the West most of my adult life, I am still somewhat surprised by the attachment to the "Wild West" past and how its myths and icons live on in the new West. We can't seem to let the old West go—not westerners, not easterners, not Europeans, and not Hollywood.

As a kid, I learned in black-and-white from the *Lone Ranger, Rin Tin Tin, Gunsmoke,* and *Roy Rogers* shows (and an occasional western with John Wayne) that in the West you encounter a rattler and a mountain lion every day and dispatch them both. Coyotes howl every night. Red-tailed hawks scream constantly overhead and great-horned owls hoot around every campfire. (And those campfires never have smoke, just yellow flames and bright-red embers.) There are as many bad men and bandits as good men, yet the good ones prevail. Cattle are a source of bickering and headache, though somehow necessary for survival. Water is always worth fighting over. When riding the range, one has to be careful about mirages and poisoned water holes, and of course all those bad men popping out from behind boulders with six-shooters blazing. Women come in two varieties: the barroom floozy and the devoted, long-suffering, hardworking ranch wife or school-marm. Guns and horses are the most essential tools a person possesses. And Injuns are primarily bad and warmongering, but on occasion, one helps the white man and speaks pretty good pidgin English. Holly-wood's West plays with us, makes us feel as if we know this place, have seen it before, and know what comes next.

From residing in the West for three decades, I've discovered (in ways that are comforting and intoxicating to me) that the two Wests have enough sameness to recognize the old in the new. Red-tails do soar over much of the West and you sometimes hear them call, as you can the hoot of great-horned owls (though they prefer the woods to the sagebrush plains where the movies put them). And coyotes still course the plains and foothills (despite centuries-old government-sponsored eradication campaigns), though some summers I hear them hardly at all. Cougars still reside here (though I have seen just three in three decades), and rattlesnakes still rattle, though in much fewer numbers and not at this high elevation. Water is still scarce and still worth fighting over (though scarcity is relative if you consider all the bluegrass lawns and irrigated alfalfa fields in desert climes), and a changing climate has upped the stakes. And although the landscape has filled in and been peopled over the past two hundred years, wide-open spaces remain. Public lands constitute the biggest slice in western states' pies, and you can walk or ride for hours and feel like John Wayne might be just around the bend. Even driving on the interstate, you get the sense of space and sparsity in signs proclaiming "No Services" and the poetic (if not prophetic) "Exit Only, No Return."

The people in the new West encounter the familiar flavorings of the old West: its dust and dryness, pine and sage, extremes of weather and light, and friendly casualness and love of land and lifestyle. But who these westerners are and what they do have been pushed and pulled into quite a different century. Devotion to place in the face of adversity is a balancing act, then and now.

In my slim phone book that covers most of the county, there are pages and pages of livestock brands. The brands let you look up an animal's ownership in case it wanders onto your property and serves to discourage rustling, which has made a comeback in some western states. Although ranching has a big stamp on Wyoming's land and its soul, it doesn't play a big role in the state economy. Ranchers struggle to break even on cattle and sheep and to grow crops in dry, short, unpredictable seasons. Yet cattle continue to hold a great deal of power and sway when it comes to land-use decisions.

Over the past century, ranch life has become highly mechanized with trucks, ATVs, and heavy machinery, but you still see horses saddled for pleasure and men (and some women) atop their mounts driving cattle along the highway in sunshine or hail. Many westerners still have guns, often displayed in pickup gun racks, though they are used mostly for hunting, not shooting bandits. You're more likely to see a cell phone hanging from a belt than a gun.

What drives the Cowboy State's economy now is oil, natural gas, coal, and tourism. Mining has attracted nonwesterners to commix with the natives and has brought money, the perennial blessing and curse. Small towns like Pinedale expand their library and build a recreation center with the added revenue, but struggle with the boom's effects on infrastructure, housing, traffic, and crime. This once-sleepy town at the edge of the Winds now has winter ozone pollution worse than Los Angeles from all the gas drilling. Boom-and-bust makes it tricky to hang on to the prosperous middle ground.

At the dawn of the last century, my great-grandfather John Henry Corbett manufactured bricks from the gray-brown soils of eastern Washington. On my mother's side, my grandfather, Oscar Lienkaemper, worked in an orchard during the Depression in a little town on that same dry side of the state. My roots in the West are at ease in soils that grew apples and cherries, soil that was stirred into clay to bake bricks to build the West. Now, I belong to the new West: I live in a city (like four-fifths of westerners) and have a second home in rural Wyoming where I'm a part-time resident. I am more connected to the land by passion and preference, not occupation.

During my summers in Wyoming, these two Wests rub awkwardly against each other, like root on stone in a test of survival, material, and resources. As a homesteader in the new West, I seek purchase on the shifting grounds, seek to understand their folded and fractured surfaces. As a naturalist, I want to ensure that the iconic West of electric-blue skies, tranquil spaces, and healthy forests and plains endures. My desire to reconcile my place in these Wests led me back to the Rendezvous.

~~~~~~~

On Saturday morning, I drove back to Pinedale and found a place on the curb about midway through the route of the Rendezvous Days parade. The parade trekked through the heart of town, a state highway whose traffic was diverted down side streets. Tobie panted in the warm sun, happy to be surrounded by all the people and smells but not thrilled with the heat. We watched kids scan up and down the street, hoping to spot some action, and listened to the chitchat of folks in lawn chairs with Stetsons or shade umbrellas.

Pinedale has thus far escaped much of the yuppification of Jackson Hole or Moab. One excellent restaurant with fresh, healthy, and eclectic offerings closed after years of struggle, leaving steak houses and Mexican and Chinese restaurants. There is a small organic food store, which is empty of customers each time I go in. On the highway into town is a hut on wheels that sells espresso. The sole big grocery store sports mounted heads of game animals on the walls. It's a telling factoid of this new West that the town has a dozen real-estate offices.

The first parade participants to pass by were typical of any parade in America: the mayor and sheriff in convertibles supplied by the local Dodge dealership, the fire truck, a couple of politicians, and the high school marching band. Interspersed were a few entries with a more western flavor: the rodeo queen and her attendants on their horses with cowgirl hats and sashes, Smokey Bear and Woodsy Owl on a US Forest Service truck throwing candy to the crowd, and state game-and-fish wardens on horseback (with guns).

The Rendezvous portions of the parade were easy to spot: lots of horses and canvas-covered wagons and people dressed in buckskins and fur-trimmed caps and carrying guns. There was one float of "floozies," meant to look the barroom type with feather boas and satin velveteen dresses. A handful of "Indians" strode by, clad in buckskin pants and sleeveless dresses, their faces coated with red-brown paint, their light hair covered by black pig-tailed wigs. Groups of trappers—called mountain men in this festival—carried strings of animal pelts slung over their shoulders.

Before the parade, I parked Tobie and the car in the shade and walked to the library to check out the official website of Rendezvous

Days: "Since 1936, residents of scenic Sublette County in western Wyoming have united in July to re-enact events of the fur trade era of the 1820s–1840s that opened up the American West to trade and settlement. Rugged trappers and explorers like Jim Bridger, Kit Carson, Jedediah Smith and John C. Fremont carved their legends in this historic region."

Just six rendezvous were held in this location, the first in 1833, and each lasted anywhere from a few days to several months, with men bartering and selling skins, pelts, guns, trinkets, and provisions for the coming winter—and partying in a big way. There were a lot of references to barrels of whiskey and rum and the never-ending flow of alcohol. The website listed current activities at the Museum of the Mountain Man, where men in costumes gave presentations and demonstrations of skills from this "romantic era": mountain-man firearms, clothes, tools, beaver trapping, and how animal skins were brain-tanned by mountain men.

Other websites filled in some of the blanks about the Indians. The Shoshone who traded with the whites were forced onto reservations about thirty years after the rendezvous. The Northern Arapaho and the Eastern Shoshone, thanks to the skillful negotiations and foresight of Chief Washakie, went to the three-million-acre Wind River Reservation east of Pinedale in 1868. Other bands of Shoshone and Bannock were sent to the Fort Hall Reservation in eastern Idaho, a large high-desert site that was greatly reduced in size after the treaty was signed, and the Indians were forced to cede the prime real estate of Pocatello and Lava Hot Springs. The Shoshone and Arapaho would no doubt commemorate the annual rendezvous differently.

History has long been told through the eyes of the conquerors, who can never do justice to the stories of the conquered. But I am still disturbed by the rosy-eyed retelling. The West they're replaying never existed, not like this: the heroic young mountain man loping across an empty plain, always and forever triumphant in his battle against nature, opening and taming the West through selfless sacrifice, through Manifest Destiny. But the plains weren't empty; they were occupied by hundreds of Indian tribes for thousands of years. If the trappers hadn't opened the West, some other conquering for-profit venture would have.

A curious quality of history is that it's hard (if not impossible) to see when you're living it. In the midst of the fur-trapping heyday from 1820 to 1840, it was no doubt hard for an individual trapper to see the changes he was creating, both to the habitat and for generations of humans to come. Even by the midcentury, it was unimaginable to think that an animal as big and plentiful as bison would be virtually extinct by 1900, or that beavers would never bounce back.

~~~~~

Most every guest at my cabin has enjoyed an evening walk down to the nearby pond that hugs the Forest Service boundary for a chance to see the beavers. We lather up with bug repellent, gather binoculars, and descend the steep path. The beaver lodge lies on the opposite bank. An earthen levee built by the landowner across a small creek created a large pond and precludes any upstream dam maintenance by the beavers but performs a similar function, backing up water and slowing it, creating a marshy habitat for frogs, nesting birds and ducks, and moose. The beavers cut saplings and feed in the willows on the pond's upstream and downstream ends, hauling out at the same places on the banks and wearing a bare, muddy trail. My nieces giggle and bounce on their toes when a beaver crosses the pond to slap! its tail at us.

By most estimates, North America had at least sixty million beavers before European settlement; after a century of heavy trapping, only ten thousand remained, a fraction of which were in the West. Beavers made a slight comeback from that nadir but faced a lot of obstacles.

The most momentous one is that the landscapes created by beaver engineering have not existed for more than a century and are beyond the memories of us all. When I hike, I see quickly flowing water and riffled creeks and rivers—not the slow-moving, shallow streams with wide and marshy channels brought to you by beavers. A languorous creek holds the water into late summer, keeping the valley moist and creating rich habitat. A quick-moving creek empties its spring runoff in just weeks, leaving a valley dry and warm for the remaining weeks of summer. Even the now swift-moving Green River was likely a languorous labyrinth of beaver-braided streams. All for men's black top hats made of beaver "felt."

Near the end of the parade, there was a block-long gap in the lineup, so I stood up from the curb to stretch and turned slowly in a circle, viewing the flat expanse around Pinedale. I crossed two small rivers driving into town, and it was easy to imagine their waters slowing and filling this entire basin, dotted with beaver dens. The degree to which conquering forever changed this landscape and its inhabitants was profound. It was hard for me to lionize these mountain men and celebrate their actions, to join in the party that was Rendezvous.

~~~~~~

On the way back to my car after the parade ended, I saw a couple emerge from a shop with a large shopping bag and a brand-spanking-new cowboy hat.

"Oh Herb," she said, grabbing her husband's arm. "We forgot to ask the salesgirl."

I pegged her accent as New Jersey or thereabouts. Her husband saw me looking at them and said, "Perhaps this little lady might know."

They wanted to see a cattle drive.

"You know," she said, "where the cowboys on their horses steer the cows." Her bejeweled hand wove left and right. "We wanted to shoot some video for our grandson, and we thought we'd see those drives all over the place."

I explained that much of that took place a couple of months ago when cattle were driven to their summer range. Besides, I said with a smile, there were no cattle during the original Green River rendezvous. She looked at me blankly.

"That's okay, honey," she said. "Tomorrow we're going to Yellowstone. They'll probably have one up there."

Years ago I was asked the cattle-drive question when I worked as a park naturalist. European and Japanese visitors in particular would seek out the Wild West artifacts they had seen in dubbed westerns: cowboys and Indians, rocky spires and distant peaks, rattlesnakes (alive or on the menu), and cattle drives. Places like the shop these tourists patronized capitalized on those myths and memories, yet cleverly catered to both tourists and real live cowboys. It carried Carhartt jeans for the working man (and woman), but also rusty souvenir horseshoes for twenty dollars each and candy resembling moose droppings.

Some westerners believe tourism is our salvation, for it creates jobs as well as incentives to preserve our scenic places and public lands. However, lots of those jobs are low-paying service types, such as maids and clerks in chain hotels whose profits travel elsewhere. If tourism truly connected travelers with nature and place and the natives who live in the new West, I might be more enthusiastic. Instead, it often reinforces old myths and grand expectations like empty roads, peopleless vistas, and abundant wild adventure. A recent ad campaign for Wyoming's national parks pictured the "wild, wild, wildlife" of bison, moose, and yes, jackalopes. It urged folks to "leave your nature tapes at home and just roll down your window."

After the parade my interest in Rendezvous Days was flagging, but my Wyoming neighbor Janet urged me to go to the pageant on Sunday afternoon, the crowning event of the festival.

"If you've never been, you should really see it," she said. I asked why she liked it.

"It's really moving," she said. "It's such a community event, and the whole community really comes together for it and participates in it." And what about the topic, I asked.

"Well, it was an amazing time, an amazing history," she said.

The pageant was at the county rodeo grounds on a plateau above the main part of town. I parked on the grassy area full of large pickup trucks and walked to the bleachers. The upper sections, covered by a shade cloth, were already fairly full, so I sat in the second row near the middle. The aluminum benches had little space for feet and legs, and a guy behind me with a big belly, cowboy hat, plaid shirt, and tight jeans struggled politely to keep his knees out of my back.

The stage was a grassy oval about the size of a football field, ringed by a waist-high round iron rail. At the far side, a tall, rough wooden-slated fence with a high tower resembled a stockade. Above and beyond the stage rose the Wind River Mountains, and thin, high clouds graced the blue-blue sky. It was a warm July day and the only dark clouds hung well to the south. As I watched people arrive, the announcer gave instructions to the entire cast, assembled in front of five tepees for an official group photo, trappers next to Indians. Attendees leaned against the iron rail to take their own unofficial photos.

I read through the souvenir program and the special supplement to the Pinedale weekly newspaper headlined, "The Green River Rendezvous: An Ongoing History." The program made sure to mention that no government representatives took part in the early fur explorations, but it was the fur industry, the trapper, and the missionary who "opened the gates of the west." "Their hardship have [*sic*] never been surpassed and their courage and fortitude seldom equaled," the program said. I chuckled, noting that the sentiment toward the government is indeed ongoing. When it comes to the government, people hate the "forest," but love their favorite "trees." Westerners tend to bristle at the amount of federal public land and generalized government "control," but welcome federal dollars for water development, grazing and mining subsidies, highways, education, and economic development.

〰〰〰

When I worked for the Bureau of Land Management in the early 1980s, many of our constituents wore a sense of entitlement about the West and believed they deserved a big piece of the resource pie. It was the height of the rush to privatize federal public lands led by Interior Secretary James Watt, a movement symbolized by the Sagebrush Rebellion. It was a rough balancing act, executing our role as resource guardians while bending to political winds. The battles between public and private that boiled then still simmer now and occasionally bubble over.

But over the past thirty years, the constituency of public land management has changed. The Pinedale BLM office is busiest with oil and gas permits, not grazing leases or wildlife management. And sometimes, ranchers and hunters come together with conservation groups to protest the ever-expanding push to drill in new wild places. Private ranches have been sold and divided into ranchettes, second homes dot the edges of waterways and forests, and part-timers like me have moved in.

As a part-time resident, I also carry a sense of entitlement and expectations of what the new West means and what its land is good for and how it should be treated. I love the land as a naturalist, enjoying deer in my meadow, clean air delivered by the wind, and silence that makes my ears hum. I'd vote for sage grouse over oil and gas, and antelope migration instead of new hotels. But I don't need to make a living from this land. I don't commute from my cabin when it's twenty degrees below or scrape out a living here; I come for the summer when life is easier in Wyoming.

~~~~~~

A few minutes before one, the announcer, perched in the rodeo announcer's box above the bleachers, welcomed us to the Seventy-Fifth Annual Rendezvous Pageant. He then read extensive obituaries (which chronicled jobs, residences, and ex-wives) for three past pageant participants, while a costumed actor crossed the grassy arena from left to right. I surmised that this was the character the deceased once played. The announcer then thanked a number of local sponsors and donors.

The program listed the pageant in five scenes, the first of which included a "prelude to history" and a pipe-lighting ceremony. By costumes, I could easily discern Indians and white men, though I had trouble spotting the individuals discussed by the announcer. At times, when the announcer began a story about a specific mountain man and a buckskin-wearing man rode his horse toward the stands, I could put the two together, but I often later lost that guy in the crowd of two dozen white men with specific parts. The women were easier with only four named parts, though one was not given a name, just "Harris' Bride." The program listed an additional thirty-two men as part of "trapper camp."

The various scenes with the trappers and explorers played out in front of the bleachers and to the right in "trapper camp," where the white men hung out in front of one tepee and a skin-covered lean-to. Up the hill directly behind the trapper camp sat a large RV parked in front of a very large frame house under construction.

On the left side of the field were five tepees, each decorated with different designs and symbols, representing the Indian encampment. The fairest-skinned encampment residents wore red-brown face paint. Women in buckskin dresses and black wigs with pigtails busied themselves with infants and a variety of props: skins, hide-covered big drums, baskets, and antlers. Indian children wrestled, tossed things to one another, and chatted. Indian men seemed to arrive and leave the encampment on horseback, and both men and horses were painted with brightly colored stripes and symbols.

None of the actors spoke. When the announcer talked about a pipe shared between Indian and trapper, three men sat midfield passing a pipe. When he announced that a fur trading company arrived, a horse-drawn wagon entered the field from an opening in the oval rink, either stage left or stage right. (The stockade fence along the back acted as a curtain behind which horses, men, and wagons could remain hidden until their scenes.) Instead of voiced lines, there were sometimes hand gestures or an action to accompany the script, such as when mountain man Jim Bridger attempted to steal an Indian "bride" while a young Indian "warrior" tried to stop him.

Sometimes the announcer used a different voice for a character; when he did so for Jim Bridger, it sounded like Elvis. The mountain men were referred to as hard-riding, brave, fearless, and superb scouts, while Indians were called shy and roaming. The program said the Shoshone "were stout, well formed, active men. They were cheerful, and fond of gambling and amusement. They were also expert marksmen and good riders. Their squaws were said to be excellent housekeepers and mothers."

When a story began about the adventures of Kit Carson, his character rode his horse back and forth along the iron rail near the bleachers while his story was read. The program described Carson as "a rare combination of dauntless courage, true nobility of mind and generous

impulse, tempered with discretion and sound sense." During one narration, a character made his horse back up, which drew scattered
applause. There was a lot of whooping from men on the field.

The announcer's voice was so loud that I stuffed wads of tissues
in my ears, which helped only a little. As I watched the horses and
men move about the field, my mind wandered away from the history
narration. My attention sometimes returned when the sound-track
switched, from the drum and chants representing the Shoshone to
the same bluegrass fiddle tune (representing everything non-Indian)
played over and over.

The man in the row in front of me was rubbing his mother's shoulders, and I joked that I could use some of that myself. He lived in Philadelphia now but grew up in Pinedale.

"Yeah, I wanted my wife and sons to see this. We went every year
when I was growing up," he said. "It's kinda Hollywood maybe, but it
brings back good memories."

"Why did you leave Pinedale?" I asked.

"Work. It's hard to make a living here unless you're a cowboy or an
oilman."

<hr />

The West allows only a few to live in concert with the land, earning
a living in and from it. Accepted on its own terms, the West is not an
easy place to love—or live. All of us, visitors and residents, hold tight
to a belief in the durability and never-ending-ness of our open spaces,
which makes us a hopeful but deluded people. We desire freedom
and the wide-open spaces to express it in, and creature comforts surrounded by the stark and beautiful lack of them.

As a woman, I don't feel there was much place for me in the old
Wild West. As a naturalist more interested in communing with than
conquering nature, even less so. No amount of revisionist history

will change that. But I do feel I have a place in this new West and
its future.

The Green River Rendezvous is indeed a spirited community event,
but it was hard for me to see it as more than a rewrite to forgive us our
sins, to pardon our ancestors. The true lessons from the mountain-
man days are so important and vital to the new West—making a living
but not destroying the very resources that support your existence, and
making a home but not at the expense of others who preceded you—
and we could learn much from them. New westerners must negotiate
the slippery surfaces of old and new, to balance rugged individualism
and collective survival of land and livelihood.

~~~~~~

In the middle of scene 4, the dark clouds I'd been watching build
behind our backs arrived at the rodeo grounds. With the first few
light raindrops, dozens of spectators left the stands. This part of the
scene was titled "The Dude," and some guy was riding back and forth
on his horse, but I wasn't paying much attention to what he was
doing or why he was called the Dude. The rain got a bit steadier
and I pulled my raincoat from my pack. More feet clanged down
the aluminum bleacher steps. The family in front of me pulled on
sweatshirts, others raised umbrellas, and even more headed quickly
toward their trucks on the grassy field. The announcer kept narrat-
ing "The Dude."

Then, a burst of hail rained down at a sharp angle from the dark
cloud, pinging loudly on the bleachers, announcer's box, iron railing, and tepees. The actors tried to stay in character but stole glances
up toward the announcer's box (which was silent), looking for signs
as to whether the pageant of the Rendezvous would continue. The
actors looked at each other, at the emptying stands, at the box on
high. The pellets eased for a moment, then gathered momentum. The

microphone switched back on with a click and the announcer said, "It's time for the pony dance."

The man from Philadelphia turned and said, "You gotta stay for this—it's the best part."

Nine young women in buckskin entered the field riding bareback and began to weave in a pattern of figure eights, shying their faces from the pellets of hail, working their knees, and holding tight to the reins to stay atop their slick, slick ponies.

ELEVEN

What Happens at the Cabin

MAY

A dark gray mass with tints of purple and green was all I saw in the rearview mirror. A storm was chasing me as I zipped north through Wyoming along the two-lane blacktop, past sagebrush plains, sheep turned out to forage, and scattered bands of antelope. No billboards, just static on the radio. In front of me, thunderheads roiled and mushroomed, issuing small, intense curtains of rain along the horizon that glowed in the afternoon sun. At times, the pavement steamed off recent rains, leaving shiny, thin puddles in the rumble strips at the side of the highway. In late-afternoon light, the bluffs along the Green River, layered rock in pastels of dark pink, pale green and yellow, glowed and rippled like ribbon candy.

As usual when I first pushed northward again from the city to the cabin, my eyes soaked in the scenes and soaked up the smells, happy to see familiar bluffs and rivers after a seven-month absence, but my mind carried city baggage. This time, it was some nasty politics at work, a leaking roof, and a kitchen cabinet that fell off the wall, seriously denting the microwave on the way down.

I know the drive well: ninety minutes on the interstate, two and a half hours on two-lane, and the final twenty minutes on gravel—a meaningful progression to smaller and slower roads. I have pegged the cheapest gas, the city park with a river for the dog, and reliable caffeine carriers. Latitude ticked north, 40.7 to 43.1.

Just past Big Piney, the Wind River Mountains cleared the horizon, white and glistening, and I smiled. Kaya slept under my seat, having wandered and meowed for the first hour. Tobie tilted her head so her nose reached the top of the cracked window, charting our olfactory journey. The car was packed: a big cooler of provisions, power tools, clothes, dog and cat food, DVDs and books, laptop and file folders, camera and binoculars. When we turned up the steep gravel drive, Tobie was beside herself. When the cabin came into view, I saw the usual bank of snow along the north wall where it slides off the roof and hardens into a little ice field, and it just looked comforting and welcoming somehow. After zooming around the meadow at full speed in happy, wide circles, Tobie plopped on top of the snow pile where she snatched mouthfuls between grins.

I carried Kaya to the cabin, cooing and kissing her, then filled her litter box and food bowl. The cool, dim cabin smelled piney and soothing. I raised some blinds; dead flies littered the sill. I switched on the electricity and emptied the cooler contents into the humming refrigerator.

Each year as the cabin became more finished, my time there slipped into a comfortable pattern of watching the seasons advance. The shoulder surgery in my third summer slowed all the finish work upstairs, so it was late in the fourth summer when I moved upstairs from the cold basement cave and had a place to shower and lay my head, though I still cooked on a campstove. There were still projects (and probably always would be), but each summer now possessed such pleasurable familiarity. I witnessed the remnant snow and ice melt each May, followed by the long, liquid stretch of summer, and finally October's first flakes and fallen leaves heralding winter's return.

〜〜〜〜〜

"Come on, Tobie, let's take a walk," I said. "We'll unpack and turn on the water later."

The woods and meadow were wet and snow-pocked, so we walked down the driveway and then the empty road. Bluebells cheerfully nodded in the sunniest slope near the drive. The tree trunks were dark and wet, their needles washed of road dust. Tobie trotted left and right, sniffing, sometimes returning briefly to me, as if in thanks for our return. To the north called a hermit thrush, its silvery tones hanging in the late-afternoon air. Depending on my mood, its song is either soothing and enchanting, or it's the most mournful and melancholy lament I've ever heard. In the distance, cows bawled on Forest Service land, already loosed for the summer. Sprinkles speckled my cheeks. It was a walk of no great significance; it was a walk of profound normality.

I left the road and climbed up the snow-speckled ridge to walk a rough perimeter of my land. I took stock of what transpired over the winter. The beetles continued to march through the lodgepoles, with dozens more trees now sporting red needles. A massive Douglas fir at the northwest corner had toppled dramatically, its trunk rotten, taking several smaller trees with it. During our champagne celebration here after I signed the papers for the property, Camille took a picture of me standing next to this stately tree. Now there was a massive hole where its roots once splayed, and a dirt clod the size of a large melon dangled from one thin root. On the southeast corner, I found tail feathers and the wing joints of a grouse. Tobie ate a few mouthfuls of feathers and I pocketed several. When we walked to the dry meadow on the adjacent property, both of us heard a crack. We caught a glimpse of a cow moose heading down the steep hillside to the marsh.

〰〰〰

I am accustomed to this transition, city to cabin, my annual May per-egrination. I left a city that was so full—of noise, thick air, machinery and cars, people and buildings—never dark, never quiet. I heard the thump bump thump of car stereos, morning rush hour on the inter-state, sirens, and every time I ventured into my yard the yapping of the neighbor's dogs. The week I left, I submitted semester grades, turned on the sprinkler system, packed up office and kitchen, turned onto the interstate entrance ramp, and hit the gas.

My annual migration is not well understood by some of my acquaintances and elicits the same questions each spring. "You're leav-ing for the entire summer?" a colleague asked me in the mail room. "And what do you *do* up there? Don't you get bored?" a staff member asked me in the hall.

Migration is not oft practiced by our country's white culture—bound as we are to property and year-round jobs—but it was prac-ticed centuries ago by Indians not tied by land "ownership." Like many species of birds and large animals, the Eastern Shoshone picked up their belongings in spring and moved to cooler locales where they dug camas bulbs, fished, and gathered berries, plants, and roots. In today's parlance, theirs was a light footprint, for they ate locally and seasonally, minimized heating and cooling costs by migrating, and utilized local materials (willows and grasses for grass lodges). When they gained horses through trade with other tribes, they also hunted buffalo and used their hides for new portable dwellings, tepees. When winter reduced their available foods, they journeyed south.

I migrate not to emulate Indians, though I much admire the sensibility of their journey and in adjusting to changing seasons and conditions rather than fighting them. If modern heating-and-cooling temperatures are any guide, humans are most comfortable in sixty-five- to seventy-five-degree temperatures. That's close to the average daytime summer temperatures on my land. If I didn't journey to this cooler clime, in the heat of Salt Lake I would wilt, sweat constantly, and retreat to air-conditioned buildings, my energy sapped, my brain thick and slow. My body has always pulled me toward cool habitats.

〰〰〰

Within three hours of our arrival, two gray jays hopped along the porch railing, spying in the windows. What a sweet little greeting party, hailing my return. I scooped a handful of dry cat food and walked onto the deck.

"Hello, little guys. Were you waiting for me?" I asked. One bird took several two-footed hops toward me, with a soft chirp and chur. I assumed it was the same pair I said good-bye to last October, but I could never be sure. At first, they were cautious, but it was obvious they remembered our routine. One jay looked at me with dark eyes, then hopped from the railing onto the thumb of my cupped palm, pecked up two pellets, and swallowed them. The jay was light on my hand, its delicate black feet and talons clinging gently. He glanced at me, and stuffed several more pellets into his gullet until he could barely close his beak. Then off he flew to a nearby fir to cache his stash. The other jay hopped onto my hand and followed the same routine. The first jay flew back across the meadow with fast and graceful swoops, landed on the porch rail, and hop, hop onto my hand. When the pair had exhausted the pellets, they each hopped once more onto my empty palm, cocked their heads up to my face, then glanced back at the empty hand. One pecked gently at a fold in my palm.

"Sorry guys, that's all for now," I said, and off they flew.

~~~~~

At sunrise on my first morning, I awoke to a loud rapping on the cabin. I was disoriented—wait, I'm not in Salt Lake—and then heard the rapping again. Tobie rushed to the window and put her paws on the sill. We saw a bird fly away, a series of deep dips in its flight and a flash of white on the wings, a flicker. Suspicious, I put on my slippers and walked outside. High up the wall outside my bedroom under the roof edge were three holes, flicker-size holes. He had bored through the fascia boards (above the log wall) into the attic, trying to create enticing nesting sites to attract a mate. Though they migrate, flickers arrive very early to set up shop.

"Damn you," I cursed and shook my head. "No female's going to choose these for nests!" After breakfast, I climbed the tall extension ladder and tacked a square of wire hardware cloth over each hole and sprayed in expanding foam to keep out the bees.

By the end of the first week, I felt settled. I'd unpacked, vacuumed up flies, popped in window screens, set out the deck chairs and hung the roll-up deck shades, and hung the birdbaths and bird-feeders. I hung the hummingbird feeder as well, though I knew they probably wouldn't arrive until the weather warmed and more flowers bloomed. Within hours, chickadees flew to the feeders with a soft purr of their wings, and then nuthatches with their muttering conversations. Next, the juncos, soft and plump, were on the ground beneath the feeder cleaning up, flying to and fro with a tik-tik-tik. The following day, pine siskins and Cassin's finches had joined the queue, waiting on branches near the feeders for an open spot.

In the first week, I saw a large dark owl glide across the meadow against the setting sun, but in the glare couldn't be sure if it was a great gray or great horned. By the time I arrive at the cabin, owl households are feeding chicks, having mated and defended territory as early as February. And Mouse Meadow had food to spare.

〰〰〰

By Memorial Day, the ice pile under the north eaves had melted, much to Tobie's disappointment. Other neighbors had completed their migrations—Bob and Betty and Janet and Mark from Florida, two from Michigan, four from Arizona, and several from Utah—and little flocks arranged social gatherings, drinks there, a dinner here, a hike out there.

I awoke that holiday to the first hint of daylight and birdsong after a night of deep, long sleep and whimsical dreams. I lay there watching the sky gain color, and Kaya came to curl under my arm; Tobie arose, stretched and yawned, and joined us in bed, lying long at my side. Every muscle, tendon, and nerve in my face was soft and relaxed. In just two weeks, I had begun to pull my wheels out of their accustomed ruts and steer them over fresh ground.

I took my morning coffee onto the deck and curled up in a chair. Below the meadow in the wetlands, the spring chorus frogs were creaking, their voices carried up to me on the lightest of breezes. Tiny frogs and light wind, those were the only sounds. One of the starkest contrasts from city to cabin is the noise; when I arrive here my ears fairly roar with the enormous silence, as strange as that sounds. Here, each sound seemed to have its own place and moment, discernible from the sound next to it, blending with the sound above it—frogs, breeze, and overhead a raven providing a bass note. It was such uncomplicated music, easy to follow and feel lulled into a quiet of my own. And in these woods, I remembered what space felt like—around my body, around my dwelling, above me. I saw no roads, no structures, no people, and there was room to breathe, to see, to contemplate. This day had no plan, no list, no schedule. Bit by bit, it emerged like a new flower in sunlight. It was a welcome surrender to a place that cradles me as one of its own.

One final piece of magic traveled through the air while I nursed my coffee, the warble of a pair of sandhill cranes from the wetland opposite the little frogs. Like the owls, they too set up their menage long before I arrived.

~~~~~

JUNE

The month began with two weeks of rain and a spit of snow. Although TV weathercasters tell us that rain will "ruin our weekend," in the woods, weather just is, and I adjust accordingly. The weather doesn't give a damn what I'd prefer on any particular day, but I can count on a fairly consistent forecast for most of the summer: partly cloudy with a chance of afternoon mountain showers.

I built a fire in the woodstove and watched the woods from my office window, waiting for a break in the clouds to take a walk. I wrote reviews of journal articles, edited a master's thesis, and worked through a tall stack of journals and magazines. Like most professors I'm not paid in the summer, but I am hardly "off" and do most of my research and writing then. But the work slips easily into a day at the cabin, tucked between walks, cooking a pot of soup, chatting with a neighbor.

When I tell my students that American Indians labored roughly three to four hours a day, their mouths fall open. We wonder together how this could be. We conclude that when you require only the basic elements for survival and not consumer goods, a car, and a bank account, your day opens up.

If cabin workdays are any guide, my brain seems to operate most efficiently for about four hours—Indian style, I think—though it often keeps ticking away after I leave my laptop. When one dry, warm day turned into two in a row, I left my office to sand and restain the little landing and stairs on the east side of the cabin. When I washed the paintbrush in soap and hot water, I realized I had "solved" a puzzled piece of writing I'd been struggling with. It was as though the rhythmic strokes of the brush loosened enough small stones in my edifice to get the pieces moving again.

One June evening when the rains had ceased, I sat on the porch with Tobie, gazing at the dense stars and Milky Way, waiting for the moon to rise. I knew the moon was close to full (something I seemed to lose track of in the city), but I suddenly realized I had no idea what day of the week it was. I tried to reconstruct the past several days, but those blurred as well. The Monday-to-Friday cycle had indeed disappeared, and a Saturday had no more significance than a Tuesday. I went inside and looked at my daily vitamin container with the seven little compartments; it was Wednesday. I laughed, and went back outside to wait for the moon.

~~~~~~

"Wow, wish I had a resting heart rate like that," said the nurse as she bent over my chart to write it down. My heart rate wasn't a number that ever stood out for me—high or low—so I asked her what it was. Fifty-two, she said. I was at the Pinedale clinic, I was in pain, and I had been waiting more than two hours to see a doctor, yet my heart rate was 52. Last time I was at the doctor's in Salt Lake, it was 72.

A resting heart rate is indicative not just of physical fitness, but of a body and soul at peace. This was where my heart was happy, surrounded by the rustle of leaves and the scolding of squirrels. I wasn't in the lap of luxury here, yet I resided in the relaxed bosom of it.

Until I experienced what happens to me at the cabin, I wonder if I ever truly let go of all those stressors in relationships, work, and the negotiations of daily life. My colleagues, my students, my friends—most all of us seem to carry (if not invite) stress in our lives, trying to cram too much into the day, to work too many hours, to zoom about like bees all abuzz. For me, it shows up in teeth grinding, an occasionally anxious stomach or inability to sleep, and tightness in my shoulders and lower back. Between the constant stimuli of the city and my job, my body gets stuck in fight-or-flight mode, ready, slightly on edge.

When I was in my twenties, I played the weekend warrior, tromping away with friends for a quick backpack or a ski into a yurt. These quick vacations (and some longer ones) were full of adrenaline and thrills, and I returned spent with snapshots and sometimes souvenirs. It fitted both my age and the modern-day notion that "leisure" must be full and busy, and inextricably tied to consumer goods. It's taken me decades (and this cabin) to learn that true leisure, like Aristotle said, is self-sufficient and not tied to goods or nonstop stimuli; true leisure is a mental attitude of nonactivity and inner calm, of silence.

Leisure is not about being busy, but about letting things happen.

Thoreau strove for this kind of leisure in a form of walking he called "sauntering," whose goal he said was to reach "a holy or sacred space in mind or spirit." Such walking required no destination or time frame, yet was capable of connecting us to the natural world and our natural selves.

My walks in June are limited to low-lying areas, generally closer to the cabin, until the higher peaks and alpine areas melt in July. In early June, Janet and I hiked a section of Forest Service land just behind a neighbor's place.

Janet was my most regular hiking partner, though in recent years her trips to Florida to care for her aging mother put a dent in our adventures. When I lived in Dory, Janet came walking up my drive to meet her new neighbor, and I immediately liked her enthusiasm, her quick laugh, her droll humor. When we walked the network of roads and trails among our neighbors, Janet knew the names and stories of all the residents; I knew the names and stories of all the flowers and birds. She always wore showy earrings (even hiking) that dangled below her brown curly hair. We had happy hours on the deck and sometimes joined each other for treks to town. She made me laugh, worried about my love life, and checked in like a mother hen.

After we climbed the fence, we walked a faint two-track into an open area of sagebrush, willowy draws, and aspen- and conifer-covered knolls. Snow lingered in low, shaded spots (to Tobie's delight). Spreading out from the melting snow lay matted brown grasses, and out farther, buttercups poked their yellow heads through. The progression from spring to summer was a slow one at this elevation, and the presence of sun in one place made leaves and flowers burst forth, while right next to it in dark moistness lay the browns and whites of winter.

We followed a dirt track up a ridge and then curved along its southern side. We stopped for a swig of water and I said to Janet, "What's that over there?" It was a pair of elk antlers, lying side by side as though he lowered his head and they gently fell to the ground. We posed for pictures, holding the antlers out from our temples. After sandwiches (which always tasted so much better while hiking), I said to Janet, "You know, we should probably keep looking around for antlers—you never know when..." I squealed, for just to my left lay an even bigger elk antler, a six-point, on the bank of the stream. Until that hike, I had never stumbled upon a fresh "shed."

In mid-June, I saw the first sign of deer fawns—diminutive tracks in the dust—when Tobie and I hiked up the gravel road early one morning. I was admiring the impossibly tiny prints next to the mother's tracks when I looked up and saw a doe. "Oh, there you are," I said, one hand on the dog's collar. She eyed me for a few moments, then turned to the road edge, huffed, and bounded up the road, followed by two fawns. We tried to creep around the next bend—the hillside was so steep that I thought they might be staying on the road—and did indeed catch sight of them through the trees. One fawn trotted up to its mother and they touched noses, then continued up the road, leaving tracks of tiny hooves for us to follow.

A few days later when I readied myself for a longer hike up a nearby peak, I spied a cow moose in the meadow. Her frame was sleek and rounded, her pelt dark and shining, largely finished with her spring molt. I watched for a while, thinking maybe I should delay my departure. Then she turned and walked to the meadow's edge...followed by a calf! The little one had been standing behind a small fir in the meadow, and I didn't see it. It was so sweet looking and a much lighter shade of brown than its mother. I loitered, drinking my coffee, and sure enough, in about twenty minutes, mama reappeared, but she browsed right near the meadow edge and kept the young one out of view.

Creatures that continue to elude my view of them are the spring chorus frogs that creak-croak so sweetly from spring to midsummer at the pond and other marshy areas. I walked down to the pond two evenings in June (sans dog) to get acquainted, to put a picture with the voices. I heard them as I approached and slowly crept closer. All went silent. I stood still, and soon they began croaking again. I scanned with my binoculars but couldn't spot so much as a pillowing throat pouch. Were they that small and camouflaged? Frustrated, I tossed a pebble into the pond. Silence. No splashes, no movement. Smart little frogs. If I can't see them, neither can predators.

Each year, my curiosity grows for a host of other harder-to-observe creatures here: salamanders, snakes, and the various mice and voles in the meadow. I've thought about borrowing a live trap to place in the meadow to see these residents up close. There are also butterflies, moths, and insects to identify, not to mention all the tiny creatures below the surface in the soil. With familiarity comes a whole lot more questions. Such bottomlessness to my education gives me great joy, like there are an infinite number of boxes yet to open, and with each one I get closer to becoming an insider in my own world.

On June 21, two dozen neighbors came to celebrate the longest day of the year, the summer solstice, an annual tradition I began my second summer on the deck of the unfinished cabin that has grown each year as I get to know more of my neighbors. My little cabin hummed with happy conversation that spilled forth onto the deck. We compared winters and plans for summer guests and cabin projects. I made a Creole-spiced cold cucumber soup and grilled a whole salmon, and they filled in around the edges with canapés, salads, and pies. As the sun descended, blazing into the kitchen and lighting our faces, the silhouette of the mountains grew dark and precise as a knife edge. Guests lingered, waiting to watch the sun sink on this longest day, slipping down just past the notch in the river canyon that separated the Gros Ventres from the Wyoming Range. Pinks and golds lingered in the sky as they walked to their cars, glad to have so greeted the summer, though for me, one-third of my summer was already gone.

~~~~~

JULY

I was drinking coffee on the deck, and my book kept sliding down into my lap as I was distracted by all the activity. Sandhill cranes called from the wetlands and yellow warblers sang in the aspens. The chickadees were busily flying to and from their nest box with offerings, and the dog and cat were sitting in the sun like contented Buddhas. On a large limb of a Douglas fir, a black-headed grosbeak fed its newly fledged chick. The chick shimmied its wings and tail and thrust its thick black beak to its parent, gaping wide. The parent obliged. Each spring, I've noted the arrival of these colorful birds, seen the courtship behavior, watched them fly to birdbath and feeder, and then one day they are gone—migrating south before me. But this was the first time I witnessed the progeny.

In the meadow, the first green growth of yarrow, sticky geranium, cinquefoil, and balsamroot that filled it in June were giving way to a sweet succession of new wildflowers: a carpet of blue flax between cabin and aspens, spikes of scarlet gilia, blue penstemon, sweet white bedstraw, and violet lupine, soon to be followed by the delicate cups of sego lilies and tall pink spires of sweetvetch. The bunchgrasses—rye, bluebunch, gramma, brome—waved in the breeze, cupping and supporting the flowers sprouting among them. In the woods beyond, fairy slipper orchids and heart-leaf arnica had ceded to purple stalks of silky phacelia and sunflowers.

Each breeze that passed the porch and lifted the boughs of the firs north of the cabin released a cloud of yellow pollen. Each day, golden dust lay on my windshield and pooled on pond surfaces. The firs' pollen sacs looked like tight little clusters of purple grapes just a few weeks ago, but they had quickly dried and released their flaxen powder.

There is something intensely grounding about methodically noting the progression of a season, not by the calendar but by patterns of growth and activity. I take such comfort from knowing this place deeply, of learning its cycles and characters and feeling a small part of them.

A guest speaker in my class last spring talked about his research on the restorative powers of nature. I knew some of this research, including the well-known study that found that hospital patients with a view of a tree (instead of a building) healed faster—amazing, just seeing a tree! Other studies have discovered that time spent in a wild place decreases your heart rate and respiration, turns off the flight-or-fight response, and helps physiologically de-stress you.

The guest speaker focused on how being in nature can also restore your ability to pay attention. He said if you're in a city, stuff requires and demands your focused attention, and that gets really tiring. But in nature, the various intriguing stimuli—clouds drifting by, rippling water, a chipmunk scurrying—modestly grab your attention involuntarily in a bottom-up kind of way. You don't have to work to pay attention in nature; it's just interesting and catches your attention without a whole lot of effort, which feels good and is restful. Because a natural setting gradually unfolds before you, it allows that focused working-to-pay-attention part a chance to relax and replenish. He told us about one experiment that had people walk in nature and then take a bunch of cognitive tests; the nature walkers performed better on the tests than people who walked downtown.

Lucky, lucky me. In the height of this mountain midsummer, I feel as tall and as supple as the meadow grasses, as happy and engaged as the busy birds, and utterly comfortable with the rhythms of the day. I have shed my snake skin, molted my winter pelt, restored my marrow.

One warm late afternoon, I was chopping onions and garlic and listening to the evening news on the radio. I had no newspaper up here (which I thought would be hard for a journalism professor), but I bought a high-powered FM radio and could get two excellent public radio stations. As I lay the garlic cloves on their sides and pressed them with the flat of the knife to loose their skins, the reporters recited a familiar litany: bombs and violence and destruction, political battles, corruption in business, religion, even sports. I turned off the radio and went outside with my glass of wine. From my little perch on the mountainside, it all seemed like insanity taking place somewhere in a world far, far away and different from my own.

During my first two summers here without a radio, the only thing I felt I missed, frankly, was what famous people had died. The rest I quickly caught up with in the fall, rather like jumping back into the plot line of a soap opera. Professionally, it felt a bit like I was cheating, not keeping up with the top stories, though I had numerous magazines that kept me up on all the depressing environmental news. But each summer, the daily headlines fell into a big basket of things I once believed were very important, but simply didn't matter.

As I sat on the deck with my wine and marveled at the peacefulness of the newsless world, I noticed what else no longer mattered at the cabin. I was wearing the same shorts and top I had for three days, no earrings, no mascara, my long hair pulled back messily with a big clip. There was a line of dirt on my ankles above where my hiking socks hit. I wasn't a "high-maintenance" female to begin with, but physical appearance nevertheless consumed a lot of my energy back in the city, a busy-making activity that I gladly put several notches lower on the list of things that matter.

~~~~~

Sara and the girls were arriving in mid-July for a week (one of four sets of company this summer), so after breakfast I headed to Pinedale for my weekly trip. As I turned onto the highway and got the car up to sixty-five, it felt like I was in a rocket as the ground zipped by at a dizzying pace. I hadn't been in a car for several days and had grown accustomed to the ground traveling past me at foot speed. It was the same sensation I remembered when I got into a car after a weeklong backpack.

Along the highway in the broad valley of sagebrush I spied small bands of antelope, some with springy little fawns testing their legs in little sprints. Two red-tailed hawks sat three power poles apart, watching the ground. A few miles later I saw a male marsh hawk coursing the field, tilting his body first one way and then the other. When I approached the field with the wet springs and sinks, I was glad the traffic was thin so I could slow and watch for sandhill cranes. Two stood probing the mud with their bills, and yes, followed by a small reddish chick! Past the junction, I did a double take—yes, a male moose, how lucky is that, standing near the braided river. Though this trip takes almost an hour, it still ranks as the most pleasant commute to town imaginable.

First stop was the dump (actually, a trash-transfer station), and the cashier gave Tobie a dog biscuit when I handed her my dollar. I returned a book and videos at the library, dropped off my recycling, and made quick stops at the liquor store and hardware store before I parked at the grocery store.

If credit card companies ever monitor this kind of stuff, they might wonder about the weekly flurry of activity on my card, followed by six days of silence. This half-day trip is the only time all week I feel like a consumer, and even then, it's hardly the consumer experience in a city the size of Salt Lake. Here, there's not one billboard en route or in town, my forwarded mail doesn't include the advertising fliers and junk mail, and there's no television in my cabin and no commercial radio on my set stations. That means for almost two months, I haven't heard that I'm not sexy enough or young enough, that my home is full of germs, and that I'm not feeding friends and family the right processed foods. For all intents and purposes, I have disappeared as a demographic object for marketers: highly educated fiftysomething SINK (single income no kids) with green purchasing patterns. I am oblivious to the latest and greatest goods I'm not supposed to be able to live without.

My students are amazed when I tell them the average person is exposed to about three thousand advertisements a day. They ask, how on earth is that possible? Then we add them up—on mass media of all kinds, ads on billboards and buses and benches and buildings, and of course all the ads on clothing. There aren't enough eyeballs in Pinedale to make most advertising economically feasible, for which I am most grateful. It allows me to revert from consumer in the marketplace to citizen of the woods.

As I carried groceries into the cabin, three gray jays appeared on the porch rail. When I returned with cat food pellets, two jays flew straight to my hand, but the third hung back shyly. It had dark feathers around its eyes and a backside that was much darker gray, not an individual I had seen before. When he finally flew to my hand, he pecked at my finger instead of the pellet in my palm. Then he hopped over to another jay, gaped open its pink gullet, and rapidly called, feed me! The gray jays had brought junior to learn how to panhandle.

~~~~~~

AUGUST

I was lying in the hammock reading a book when the phone rang. It was Betty calling to invite me to happy hour, and to complain.

"We haven't seen anything all week," she grumbled.

Betty was one of several neighbors who seemed to judge the quality of their summer in the woods by the large mammals they've seen.

"Last month we saw the fox several times, and we had moose every week, and even that elk, but now, nothing," she said.

"Betty, it's hot; it's the height of summer. We always see fewer animals now," I said.

"I know, I know." But she was still disappointed.

Bob and Betty's land was a regular highway for mammals, a ridge with wetlands downhill on either side. They always saw far more animals than I did. Although both our properties were nestled between swaths of public land and provided a good variety of habitats, animal sightings are remarkably unpredictable and infrequent. One of the first things I do upon rising is scan the meadows around the cabin but see something perhaps once every thirty times. Smaller mammals, of course, are predictable and ever present. Uinta ground squirrels begin tunnel repair and expansion as soon as the snow melts, and chipmunks and squirrels are likewise busy and noticeable.

But I don't mind the rarity of the larger mammals, as long as I know they're there and occasionally stumble upon signs of them. Just that morning I walked into a patch of air heavy with the scent of large mammals—deer, moose, or elk—arising perhaps from urine, perhaps from hair sloughed from their coats, their breath, their hooves and hanging in the thick, still air of early morning. I imagined that I had entered a wild stable and was standing among them. Recently on an evening walk through the woods, Tobie and I came upon a broad matted bed made in tall grass and fresh moose droppings nearby. Then we smelled the musky scent marking of a red fox and saw a black bear's paw print in the dust along the road.

When I returned from happy hour, I took my dinner out on the deck. Tobie sat at my feet, sniffing the air. She stood suddenly and barked once. At the bottom of the meadow was a fox, sleek and dashing with his bottlebrush tail dipped in black. The fox must have sensed that the dog was contained on the porch and not a threat, for while we watched, the fox backed up to a shrub and either sprayed or shat on it, then bounded across the meadow like a ribbon of water. He then thought better of his path, reversed, sassily trotted back across the grass, and disappeared into the woods from which he emerged. The foxes were thriving that year, and no ducklings had survived at the pond. I decided not to tell Betty about the fox until her luck had changed.

~~~~~~

After a light rain the night before, the tall pile of gravel (waiting to be spread) looked like a mound of candy, the nuggets of granite and quartz sparkling with red, white, green, and black shiny faces. With each shovelful, several pieces twinkled up at me, and it was all I could do to transfer the load to the wheelbarrow without bending down to select a few treasures. Already, the butt ends of the log walls held dozens of pieces I found too colorful to resist and had parked there for safekeeping. When the first load of driveway gravel was delivered years ago, it was mostly rounded rocks of sandstone and other sedimentary conglomerations, not these colorful metamorphic gems.

I had only a few days to spread gravel—along the path to the house, under the deck outside the basement, and along the drip zones from the metal roof—before I had to return to Salt Lake for the start of fall semester. Mid-August always seemed far too early for "fall" anything. I took Dad to the airport the day before, and it was time to tackle my remaining chores.

By midmorning, the bandanna wrapped around my forehead was heavy with sweat, and my arms were slightly rubbery from the exertion. I wheeled the barrow back up the hill, removed my work gloves, and took several long draws from the water bottle parked under the eaves. I sat on the porch steps with Tobie, who was happy for this outdoor project.

The meadow grasses were tipped with pollen and seeds, and some clumps in the sunniest areas were entirely brown and dried. A thick spread of sunflowers and harebells ringed the shaded edges near the aspens. A chorus of buzzing and snapping grasshoppers filled the meadow. Above the porch against the cerulean sky, dozens of swallows coursed the air for insects, accompanied by the buzzy-zip calls of a few nighthawks that were active in early morning. I heard a yellow-rumped warbler singing in the fir trees and saw a red-naped sapsucker hopping up an aspen trunk. What a nice break room, I thought.

Our historical notions of manual labor are that the lower classes did such work, while the upper classes had money or professions and were largely removed from sweat and dirt under the fingernails. Modern professions, divided into blue- and white-collar, continue to segregate labor of the body and of the mind, but to me the ideal job would be a glorious integration of the two. There is honest reward in hard, sweaty work, something connected to earth and environ—even in moving a pile of gravel from one place to another.

~~~~~

SEPTEMBER

From the deck, it sounded like someone was throwing rocks at trees or breaking sticks. Tobie cocked her head, convinced that strangers were walking through our woods. It was the squirrels harvesting nuts, severing the still-tight new cones from their branches and dropping them with percussive bonks and clatters onto limbs and deadfall below.

Tobie and I drove up to the cabin for an extended Labor Day weekend. The aspens had only a hint of color, but it seemed as though we left in one season and returned in another. The heat had abated, the nights cooled, the sun more angled and briefer in its daily appearance.

After a morning hike with Janet, I graded some papers and edited a manuscript. But I had trouble staying inside and at my desk. I found myself walking around outside, moseying down the driveway, ambling through the meadow. For twenty minutes, I watched a tall mound of Formica ants, mesmerized. I was trying to drink in this place, to swallow these sights and memorize these sounds, to capture the way my shoulders felt and how deeply I was breathing.

Last year for my birthday, a friend gave me a plaque: "What Happens at the Cabin, *Stays* at the Cabin!" I know what the gag intends and how it's supposed to be funny. But I couldn't bring myself to hang it up, because it was unfortunately too true. Somehow, I have never been able to sustain and maintain "what happens at the cabin" when I'm back in the city during the school year. The city closes in; my anxiety rises. Work stress accumulates on my body like layers of old clothes. I zone out in front of the TV for escape; I sleep fitfully. I've tried numerous times to close my eyes and visualize myself in the meadow. I've leafed through my photo albums to revisit summer memories. But I never really return. The winter is long. But as soon as the valley gets a fresh wind that hints of warmth instead of thin coldness, then I know I'll make it until May, and I can begin to remember what will happen, once again, at the cabin.

Tobie and I returned for a quick weekend in late September to aspen leaves that glowed like they were lit from within. Their leaves collected into colorful, crunchy confetti on the trails. Each evening, we sat bundled on the dark porch, waiting for elk to bugle and grunt from the distant ridge. It was hunting season, so Janet and I donned our orange vests and hats for a short loop hike, and I put a red bandanna around Tobie's neck. Each morning I built a fire, but by noon I could eat lunch on the south side of the deck. By late afternoon, I could open the windows briefly to bring the crisp, warm scent of earth and leaves into the cabin.

~~~~~~

OCTOBER

The trails through the woods were littered with fresh ungulate droppings, dark and shiny. The animals were moving around, for the most part free of their summering human neighbors. Frost coated the leaves and branches on the trail, from which rose a rich, dense smell of frost and decay and animals. On several rocks was the scat of cats and mustelids, marking boundaries of the new season. Coyote scat crossed the driveway. The meadow was brown and bloomless, its dry stalks clattering like bones when we walked through.

The weeklong university fall break in mid-October is a leisurely and bittersweet last visit, sometimes cut short by early deep snows. Each day I took frequent and slow walks through the dry meadow. I read magazines, finished a novel. From the depths of the freezer, I pulled small, shriveled packages of frozen vegetables and from the fridge the last carrots and cabbage, and added them all to the last onion and several wrinkled potatoes for a large pot of soup.

Slowly over several days, I visited each closet, each cupboard and drawer, and decided what stayed and what got packed into duffels. Closing up the cabin was a familiar list of tasks, and try as I might to approach it willingly and lightly, it was a somber undertaking. Remove window screens (which I learned the hard way that the owls shred in winter). Put deck chairs in basement and bring in doormats. Bring in bird feeders and -baths, rain gauge and thermometer. Drain water heater. Turn off well pump and drain pressure tank. Drain all pipes and pour antifreeze in toilets and drains. Lower blinds. Load remaining fridge and freezer contents into the cooler and prop open the door. Turn off the circuit breaker in the electrical box.

When I checked the final items off the list, the afternoon was well under way. The sky turned grayer and darker with each satchel I loaded in the car, and the temperature dropped and the winds strengthened. Tobie lay in the backseat, head on her paws, resigned to the inevitable. As we descended the driveway and turned up the road, big wet snowflakes the size of quarters hit the windshield and dissolved like big tears. I tried my best to think of spring.

TWELVE

A Finger of Owls

I awoke in darkness to the smell of smoke blowing in through open windows. There is no smell as disconcerting and discomposing of sleep when you live in the woods in a wooden structure. Winter mountain snows this year were paltry, and we pinned our hopes on raucous spring storms that never came. Now in June of my fifth summer, a fire in full fury burned in record heat and rock-bottom humidity about fourteen miles south of my cabin. In what was typically the lushest month, the meadow grass was browning, holding on, quickly trying to make seed. The midday sun cast a rosy-orange glow on every surface. Smoky sunsets smoldered across the horizon. Bits of ash floated by the windows, resembling small gray bugs, flitting up, floating down, briefly up, then again down.

Officials tell us to get used to this—a warming, burning West. My neighbors and I realize that fires are an expected risk—though never a welcome one—for the privilege of living in the woods. But we never bargained for a drastically and abnormally warming planet. The warming temperatures, in addition to shrinking snowpack and soil moisture, have created severe stress for the trees and good homes for beetles: pine beetle, spruce beetle, fir beetle. They burrow through bark and lay eggs that feast when they hatch. Within a year, the needles start to turn red-brown, and by the next year, the entire tree is clothed in red, like a torch ready to burn. An added consequence of warming temps is that some beetle species now complete their life cycle in one year rather than two, essentially doubling their population.

Though I have lived here just five summers, I know the symphony of Wyoming summer—when the aspen leaf out, when I spy the first western tanager, when the spring peepers fall silent, when the sandhill cranes fly south. It's painful to imagine this music and its choreography changed. Already, pikas, those sweet-faced rodents who squeak from alpine rock fields at passing hikers, are on the brink; there is no cooler, higher elevation for them to seek. How stingingly poignant that all the creatures whose lives we will irrevocably alter will not be conscious of the source of their destruction. I'm partly grateful for their oblivion, partly ashamed. But I fear most for my favorite resident bird.

~~~~~

Bwweak! Sher-reecht! The call came from the western edge of the meadow. Shortly, another call to the south. Sheek! Sher-reecht! A strange, enchanting call—a bit like a pika or unfamiliar rodent but far too loud. It was my first summer on the land and I was eating lunch outside in the warm, angled sun of late September, aspen leaves of butterscotch falling, warming on the ground. The call from the meadow repeated, high-pitched, insistent, and strong. A large, dark form gracefully—and utterly silently—glided past me. An owl. Nothing flies without disturbing air or feathers like an owl. It landed on a bare branch in a fir. A second owl flew near and perched in sunlight. A third owl called behind me, and after several minutes of round-robin calling owl-style, it joined the other two.

The field markings said "great gray"—large body, no visible ear tufts, a lovely round facial pattern, a mix of brown and gray—but the strange call didn't fit. I had heard great grays during the black of night, the monotone *whoo, hoo, hoo, hoo, hoo,* low and deep, declining in strength at the end. No embellishment, and certainly never at midday.

"Bweak! Sher-reecht!" "Juvenile great gray owl." A CD of bird calls solved the mystery. The tallest North American owl with the longest wingspan (almost five feet), though it weighs only half as much as a great horned. Lemon-yellow eyes in a facial disk of concentric circles, a black-and-white bow tie beneath the chin. Calls at night, but often hunts at dawn and dusk. Young cared for by female until four or five months old, when they begin to disperse. I had witnessed the owl equivalent of teenagers cruising the 'hood.

The range map of great gray owls colors a large swath of Canada and other frozen lands. For the southernmost reaches of their range, a slender finger arcs down the spine of the Cascades and Sierra Nevada, and a thumb curves down into western Wyoming, through Yellowstone and slightly beyond, pointing to exactly where I summer each year. Delicate fingers of owls.

I come from a family of owlers. In his youth in the Yakima valley of eastern Washington, my father had a saw-whet owl in addition to his trained prairie falcons. One winter while tromping through the creek valley near our Iowa childhood home, my older brother found a great horned owl frozen solid at the base of a tree, perhaps from starvation and frigid temps. He carried it home and convinced my parents to stuff it. It sat on top of the piano and served as the silent critic when I practiced.

During graduate school, I volunteered as a naturalist for the Raptor Center at the University of Minnesota so I could see, hear, and best of all touch owls. My charges couldn't be rehabilitated and returned to the wilds, whether from tangles with cars and wires or injury from assailants of unknown origin. I held on a gloved fist diminutive screech owls lighter than Nerf balls and the magnificent feathered spitfires, great horned owls. When I'd take an owl to a classroom or senior center, it felt not like holding a bird, but a wild spirit, a personality. On my gloved fist, the great horned owls would clack their bills, hiss, rock from foot to foot, and occasionally hoot. Their taloned grasp was intense; for added measure, they would nip at my glove with formidable beaks. It was as if my demands in broad daylight were an insult, an affront to their very owlness. The barred owls—similar in size and markings to spotted owls though far more common—were less intimidating and much lighter though impressive in size. One barred would close his giant chocolate-brown eyes when I smoothed the feathers on his crown, yet he too would hiss, clack, and promptly ignore me when returned to his flight pen. It was a gift to get close to those owls; it was another gift that the distance between us never closed. I never forgot they were owls.

At the cabin, I haven't encountered juvenile great grays again in the five years since, just adults. Once or twice on a summer evening walk through the woods, I get a sense of one perched and watching, and turn to witness its silent swoop through the pines. *Strix nebulosa,* an owl appropriately nebulous in its presence, and from the Latin *nebulosus,* meaning "misty" or "foggy." A phantom of the North that even experienced birders struggle to spot. At night, I fight sleep to listen to its somber lullaby, measured and unhurried, though sleep is the very entity it elicits. Once at sunrise, I watched one dive into the rodent-pocked meadow below the cabin, but come up empty-taloned. The owls seem unalarmed by or at least mildly tolerant of my presence and conversations with them. On a cloudy morning in early fall, I crept fairly close to a great gray with my camera; it ruffled and roused its feathers, the sign of a relaxed bird, or at least a bird that thinks I merit little attention. All the neighbors compare sightings, glad to hear of its presence somewhere near, announcing "I saw the owl yesterday" as though there is just one species that really counts. I've searched the surrounding woods, looking up for a scraggly stick nest at the top of a broken snag and looking down for large pellet castings, but have found neither.

For many people who live in the woods, it's the large mammals that signify the place and whose images grace their cabin walls. Deer, elk, bear, moose. I celebrate those encounters—a bull elk snorting across the meadow during mating season, a curious moose staring in the basement window and sending the cat hissing upstairs. But it's the great gray owls that most thrill me, that personify wild enigma and elegant ferocity.

It's my enchantment and love for these elusive winged creatures that make the vision of the slender finger of owls pulling up, retreating north, all the more terrifying. Biologists have documented that centuries-old patterns of migrations and bird habits are changing, morphing in response to a warming world, often moving north or upward in elevation and altering the timing and ultimate destination. Robins are returning to herald spring two to three weeks earlier. Many warbler species are flying an average of sixty-five miles farther north. And one of the most vulnerable ecosystems in a warming country is the alpine meadows of the Rocky Mountains.

My ties to this mountain are emotional, spiritual, even intensely physical; I have never loved a habitat like this one. I suspect that owl ties are similarly felt. If fire took my cabin and woods, I would mourn profoundly, deeply. But compared to the owls, my options are many. Great gray owls don't pack their feathered bags and migrate, moving little if at all between winter and summer. In a fairly contained hunting ground, they catch mice, gophers, voles, and rabbits year-round, locating prey under the snowpack using auditory clues alone. They are perfectly adapted to boreal forests near open meadows where they have a principal role in a chorus of players and seasons. Meadow and mouse, ground squirrel and grass, fir and aspen, snow and wind. Other worlds are not now in their genes.

~~~~~~

The smoke was thick again today, harsh on the throat and eyes, obscuring everything beyond the bottom of the meadow. Like living in an ashtray. My neighbors have their escape bags packed and placed at the door, along with car keys and pet carriers. I have resisted—either from denial or from hope—for what I could grab wouldn't be what's really valuable.

I tried to bring sleep by listening for owls, but heard only the breezes crescendo, turning the aspen leaves on their stems. The dirge gathers momentum: the greenhouse gases that spurred the warming are worsening the fires that are contributing more and more gases, and the breezes carry gas and ash up and up and north, warming the sea ice. As sleep finally came, I envisioned wisps of wind, contrails of gas swirling over sagebrush plains, drawing up grouse feathers, tumbleweed seeds, and the dust of antelope dung. Ever northward they drifted, mingling ash with pine pollen, cottonwood fluff, and the down of new birds. Dancing north, ever north, ferrying owls on their wings, higher, higher, higher.

THIRTEEN

"Are You *an Environmentalist?"*

"So, are *you* an environmentalist?" Peter asked.

We had been chatting in vague terms about some environmental issue while working, he drilling a hole for a dowel between two courses of logs and I shoveling dirt. Anywhere else, I wouldn't have hesitated an answer. But we were in the woods, surrounded by high-elevation conifers and sagebrush meadows, nestled between parcels of federal lands, far from town. He didn't look up from his drill, and I kept my eyes on the earth beneath my shovel.

"Depends on what you mean by that," I said, and instantly felt ashamed at my avoidance.

Peter was a pleasant guy, probably in his thirties, and most of his questions for me had to do with the cabin he was building for me. I knew bits about him, like he moved here from Green River, was in a custody battle for his kids, and that he worked some with his parents, Joe and Daisy. But generally, he kept his cards close to his chest (though I was pretty sure of the hand he held), and he no doubt had guessed what I was holding as well.

~~~~~~

A few years ago at the university, I conducted six focus groups with professionals who communicated about natural resources for a living. I wanted to learn about the challenges faced by the state wildlife agency, the mayor's office, activist groups, federal resource managers, and environmental consultants when they endeavored to get their messages across to the general public. What they taught me were the dirty little words that they "try to talk around": *environmentalist, environmentalism,* and *environment.* The participants said they avoid using these words like the proverbial plague and preferred euphemisms: a *conservationist* or *passionate person* to denote an *environmentalist,* and *open space* or *viewshed* instead of *environment.* These professionals had devoted their working lives to protecting the stuff of the earth, yet *e*-words were bad, too emotional. They said that *e*-words were often barriers to critical thought by their audiences and affected the ability to attend to their messages.

They didn't attach their *e*-word avoidance solely to the rural West, though they felt it was more pronounced here. The participants had grown up in four different countries, and many had lived in various parts of this one. A former Californian said *environmentalist* wasn't a bad word there, but a former South Carolinian said it was negative in that state. "Why?" we probed. "Why is *environmentalist* a dirty word?" People think that environmentalists chain themselves up to trees, a county health official said. A state public information officer had been told to stay away from all the *e*-words when the 2002 Olympics came to Salt Lake City. Even some of my undergraduate students in Salt Lake think of violent ecoterrorists and "extremists" when they hear that *e*-word *environmentalist*.

A similar negative stereotyping took place decades ago over the word *feminist*. Now when I ask my students to visualize a feminist, they see a woman who is loud, angry, dowdy, and—my favorite— hairy. A strategy used by a recent women's march on Washington, DC, had women wearing T-shirts proclaiming, "This is What a *Feminist* Looks Like," but the word hasn't been so reclaimed in the public's eye. I am proud to be a feminist, but then again I'm not asked to defend and justify all things done and said by feminist women. That's what it felt like Peter's question was asking me to do for environmentalists.

~~~~~

In this part of Wyoming, where cattle outnumber people three to one, environmentalists are seen as the ones filing lawsuits and holding up good resource management. They are perceived as being against every- thing, as making things worse instead of better. They make a conve- nient and easy scapegoat to point at and say, "It's their fault." In most cases, it was a whole mess of people's fault.

But I get it. I am uncomfortable with holier-than-thou environ- mentalists who seem to think that because they are participating in the good fight, they are free from sin and somehow not personally impli- cated in environmental problems. They hate logging, but use paper prodigiously in all its forms. They detest mining, but use its products in all their electronic gadgets. They put lots of miles on big SUVs to go hike in the woods with the latest and greatest consumer toys. They are, indeed, full of contradictions—like the rest of us.

I'm far more comfortable proclaiming myself a "naturalist," and I gladly accept the stereotype of a bookish woman with big binoculars hanging around her neck and a field guide in her hand, who's sticking her nose, her hands, and her heart into every nook or cranny where a fascinating spectacle of nature might be found. A naturalist seems such a pure lover and learner of nature and its phenomena, seemingly divorced from the political. Of course, that's false; a naturalist's passion and valuation of nature puts her in direct conflict with those not so enamored and those attaching distinctly different systems of value to the nonhuman. Nevertheless, I proudly identify with my naturalist label.

A few summers ago, I overheard a conversation about environmentalists in a coffee shop among a group of hat-and-boot-wearing older men. The sentiments and stereotypes were what you might expect: a bunch of city folk butting in other people's business, against progress, wolf lovers. After a pause in the conversation, one man stroked his chin and said, "Ya know, they just don't git the Wyoming way a' life."

Given their manner of dress, I took that to mean ranching and farming, though that's a way of life for only a small percentage of the state's population. Still, it's the identity of the Cowboy State, and the cowboy is what you see on the license plates and in gift shops. Tradition stands strong even when economics don't.

There's a myth in both the country and the city that if you own a piece of land, you'll take good care of it. Maybe you will, maybe you won't. And ownership is what some ranchers feel about the federal lands on which they hold grazing leases. I remember from my BLM days ranchers who padlocked gates that crossed public roads or who added range "improvements" on public lands without permission. Some grazing leases date back decades and have been passed through generations, so a sense of ownership is understandable. I get pretty possessive about the land adjacent to my cabin; some of it's private (but unoccupied) and some of it's public, but I hike on it and feel protective of it like it were my own. Hence, a rancher doesn't take kindly to the government or some environmentalist criticizing what he does on "his" land. Except it's not his land; it's the American public's.

Yet despite all our differences, in some ways I feel closer to many Wyomingites than I do my fellow Salt Lakers. On the surface that doesn't make sense: I'm an avid hiker who eschews guns and motorized vehicles, likes coyotes and sage grouse, and doesn't eat meat. Our politics are miles apart. But I know that most residents in my part of this wide-open state—whether they are ranchers, outfitters, or hardware-store clerks—love this land and have the roots to show for it. (You don't stay in Wyoming for city perks or the weather, after all.) We share experiences of this place, like the golden light of a frosty spring morning when larks flit among the sage tops, singing forth the sun. We know the sting of horizontal snow that freezes your eyelids shut, borne on winds that invite madness. We know that ranchers and farmers, struggling to eke out an existence, possess horse smarts and land smarts that a transplanted oil and gas worker will never have. I git the hard honesty of the Wyoming way of life, but "the environment" figures in my beliefs in a might different way.

~~~~~

"The damn environmentalists drove all the lumber mills outta business. The nearest mill is Belgrade, Montana, and the only person who'd make money on that deal'd be the truck driver," Ted scoffed.

I had asked Ted if he was going to sell the beetle-killed trees he was felling for me to a lumber mill. The beetles stained the lodgepole wood, which sold as a lovely patterned "blue pine," and the local lumberyard often ran short of it.

I liked Ted and his soft-spoken and gentle manner, which seemed out of character for a logger. He was a slight guy with a long, full beard flecked light brown, blonde, and gray, and he wore a Deadwood T-shirt.

"Now Ted," I teased him, "don't go blaming and stereotyping all those environmentalists. You know there's more to it than that."

"I know, I know," he said. "I'm an environmentalist too, ya know."

I grinned. In the right context, it's funny how this dirty little word morphs into a rather benign label, one that public opinion pollsters find widespread support for, one that even Presidents Reagan and Bush Sr. proclaimed they were. *E*-words can also be veritable cash cows for savvy marketers.

Ted and I agreed that it was indeed stupid and just not right to have no local lumber mills, especially in the midst of a beetle-kill epidemic. We lived in the woods, we used wood and paper, and local people deserved to make a living from the woods. Depending on the diameter of my logs, Ted said my logs were destined only for firewood or buck-and-pole fence rails.

I told Ted about my time working on the Olympic Peninsula. He and the other logger looked at each other with a knowing gleam, and grins spread across their faces.

"I know," I said, "really big trees, right?"

"We can't help it—we're loggers!" Ted said.

They agreed that the skinny cosmetic strips of trees that logging companies in the Northwest left along highways to supposedly hide the clear-cuts behind them were a joke.

I admit that I was surprised at the impact of the week of logging—drag trails through the meadow, piles of red-needled slash in the forest, the soil in the loading area powdery and devoid of vegetation. Logging was logging, even though the team of horses that they used to drag the logs through the forest was logging-light and left far fewer long-term scars. In a few areas along drag trails, Ted used the Bobcat to gather slash for large burn piles, which he would snowmobile in to burn the following winter. But he was reluctant to drive the tractor any deeper into the woods and off the drag trails "because you'll kill the baby trees in there."

During the years I worked at Olympic National Park, the logging industry was facing tough times. When we walked into the coffee shop in Forks in our park uniforms, heads turned, eyes dressed us up and down, conversations hushed. The park was off-limits to logging, of course, and we were generally viewed as the enemy. The town lived and breathed logging and relied on timber sales on Forest Service land just outside the park and a good amount of private land as well. One summer I went to the logging festival in Forks with a boyfriend and watched men fast-stepping on massive logs rolling on a pond and men racing to the top of a tall tree with boot cleats and a waist strap. Contestants probably had to practice log rolling and tree climbing on weekends, for logging was so highly mechanized.

Historian Richard White wrote about a bumper sticker he once spied in Forks that read, "Are You an Environmentalist or Do You Work for a Living?" He argued that environmentalists are often quick to condemn "work in nature" as destructive and bad. It's also true that environmentalists are more likely to have so-called white-collar jobs and come to the woods to "play" instead of work. However, the environmental consequences of white-collar work are no less serious—just disguised and less apparent. His conclusion: environmentalists would do well to consider all types of work, blue and white, for their impacts on nature.

The controversy over spotted owls came after I left Olympic National Park for Idaho, but I read news stories about owls nailed to trees, about a park ranger I once knew who was beaten up, and about protesters sitting in and spiking trees, which angered and endangered the loggers. That featherweight creature was bearing the burden of an industry so economically catawampus that enormous old-growth trees were loaded onto freighters bound for Japan to become toilet paper, while local mills were going out of business.

The owls bore the brunt of the conflict because of the Endangered Species Act. This act was perhaps the most controversial environmental law ever passed because it went beyond conservation or preservation; it said that all creatures (and plants) deserved to exist and not be extirpated regardless of whether they were useful to humans. Many people just can't go that far, can't understand how a creature could be valued and deserving of protection just because it is. In Wyoming, that includes grizzlies and wolves and perhaps soon sage grouse.

Animals "listed" under the act are held up high as examples of trouble, separate from the landscapes in which they live. It's ironic really, because it's the broader ecosystem that's in trouble, the ecosystem that has lost its ability to support its family of creatures, but we aren't moved enough by "just" a troubled landscape. It's also ironic that we seem to picture the trouble as out there somewhere and easily divorced from daily activities like taking a shower and eating lunch. And the crowning irony: we humans are *in* that family of creatures and that landscape, just as much as the fruits of that landscape are in the shower and on the table.

The separation (if not divorce) of our daily lives from the land was centuries in the making. In the northwest corner of Wyoming is Yellowstone National Park, the first national park, established in 1872. Its founders decided that the area's protection necessitated removing the indigenous people from their ancestral land before it could be proclaimed pristine, "untouched" nature. As much as I love national parks and forests and wilderness with a capital *W,* their designation sets us up to think that ideal nature is quite apart from our daily lives and frankly is better off without us. And if "real" nature is out there somewhere, what exists around us every day isn't as real or valuable or worth protecting. It gives us permission to foul the nest, if you will.

To this day, some environmentalists consider their work to be "saving nature from people." That's a simple statement with a fair bit of truth to it. Humans seem hardwired to focus on the short term and unable to say "let's not" or "let it be," unable to leave unharmed the parts of the natural world that need it or deserve it. But here's my take: the real work is to save people *with* nature. That means accepting our membership in the greater family of nature with gratitude and profound humility. Whether we acknowledge it or not, our membership provides the very foundation of our corporeal existence. To me, that is the greatest "family value."

~~~~~~~

Peter and all the Lamberts are handy and talented folks, building houses and finishing interiors, making log furniture and cabinets, even welding. On a couple of occasions, Peter's sisters and their husbands pitched in on a project or two at my cabin while visiting the area. Hunting was a tradition in the family, and Joe and Daisy's living room was full of mounted animal heads. Joe knew the surrounding mountains well and gave me advice about hiking trails and places to visit. Everyone had an ATV and seemed as comfortable on them as bikes, even the little kids. Like so many rural residents, the Lamberts loved their natural surroundings, but it seemed a different love than mine.

Many years ago, I compared rural and urban newspapers' coverage of wildlife for my master's thesis. I found far more differences than you might think, the biggest being that the theme of wildlife news stories in urban papers was largely "stewardship," while the rural papers' stories were "utilitarian." It made sense; urban areas are often centers of government, and an important government charge is wildlife management. Urbanites also are physically more distant from wildlife, except for the backyard squirrels and wildlife in city parks, and their jobs are less connected to them. In rural communities, residents are closer to wildlife and given the land-based employment there, are more likely to interact with them as part of daily work. A rural landowner might view a fox as a threat (such as to chickens), while a city dweller might think only "what a beautiful fox." I see such sentiments in my part of rural Wyoming, where animals are valued for their utility and scorned according to their threat.

Around here, part of the utility of wild animals is as meat for the table. If someone eats meat, hunting is an honest way to obtain it, a personal connection and reckoning with the animal that provided it. And success in hunting requires knowledge and experience with animal tracks and scat, vocalizations, and habits like daily movements and bedding sites.

When I lived in eastern Idaho, the meat I ate was wild game, like venison that my ex hunted. I had given up cow and other domestic meats because the wild tasted so much better, was easier for me to digest, and didn't have all the antibiotics and hormones. But when he left, my venison source was gone, and meat just left my diet.

There was an ideological component to my meatless decision as well. When I left the BLM, having edited numerous grazing environmental impact statements and having spent years tromping around the desert, range, and forests of my district, I decided that cows had too dang much power in the West, drove far too many resource decisions, and degraded too much public land. Despite all those powerful western traditions and myths, most of its rangeland just isn't productive. One particular factoid stuck in my head: you could take all the cows off all the public lands in the West and put them on the skinny little highway medians in the East, and they'd get the same amount of forage. That's not to say there aren't some very good and sustainable examples of cattle ranching in the West. There are some ranches (and neighboring allotments) in western Wyoming where the grass is tall and thick and where wildlife flourishes alongside the cattle. As the popularity of grass-fed beef grows (particularly among city folk), I hope those ranches flourish and avoid selling out to subdivisions.

If I ate beef, a cow that roamed free on the sagebrush plains eating its preferred diet of grass and browse would seem a more humane choice, as opposed to one raised in a crowded, disease-prone feedlot.

But even most of those range cows are "finished" on corn in those feedlots, a feed that creates great digestive problems in the animals over time. For me, each scenario has big environmental consequences, and both involve eating higher on the food chain than one needs to.

I dread when someone asks me, "Why don't you eat red meat?" almost as much as being asked, "Are you an environmentalist?" They both take far too long to explain and require negotiating a whole lot of stereotypes. I am an anomaly in a Cow-boy state.

Regardless of my diet, where I get tripped up is how large mammals—deer, cattle, and other hoofed beasts—dramatically tilt the "stewardship" of western landscapes. It relegates the vast majority of creatures to the less-than status of "nongame" and reinforces a backward war on predators. Biologists have found time and again that tinkering with ecosystems to produce more ungulates produces a lopsided and ill-functioning family of flora and fauna.

~~~~~~

Over the past decade, my Wyoming county has granted one building permit after another in a historical pronghorn antelope migration route. Although these animals have journeyed these same routes for centuries and centuries, in the words of one planning commission member, "The antelope can just adapt."

Years ago I was helping with a spring range survey for the BLM when I almost stepped on an antelope fawn. Its small tawny body lay curled between the sagebrush, its nose touching its hind legs; it was like stumbling onto a pot of gold. Its eyes were open, but it looked straight ahead, unblinking, frozen. Given that fawns are able to run with their mothers shortly after birth, it must have been just hours old. I took a picture and quickly moved away; on a rise to the east stood a pronghorn, watching.

When I see antelope on my weekly drive to Pinedale or on hikes in the rolling sage lands, I'm always struck with how ancient and exotic these animals look. It's for good reason: *Antilocapra americana* is the sole survivor of a taxonomic family that has existed on our continent for more than eighteen million years and is more closely related to the giraffe than to any other present-day species. The thick tan-and-white stripes on their chests and sheathed horns make them impossible to confuse with any other mammal. And they are unequaled when it comes to speed, aided by a heart that's double-size and a windpipe that's vacuum-hose size. In early summer when I spy little fawns frolicking in unorganized wind sprints, as if having just discovered they can run, I feel so lucky to live among them.

When pronghorn reach the Pinedale area on their seasonal migrations, they face extensive gas drilling fields, troublesome highway crossings, and several subdivisions. Development has blocked six of eight historical migration corridors and pinched one remaining corridor to just a half-mile wide near Trappers Point, west of town. Unfriendly fencing is another impediment; their thin legs are built for running, not jumping. A smooth bottom wire that allows them to crawl under is their best chance of clearing a fence.

There's a quote that I often put on my class syllabi from historian Kirkpatrick Sale: "In its attitude to the land, and the creatures thereof, a culture reveals the truest part of its soul."

If we humans truly are the more intelligent species, why can't *we* be the ones to adapt, to move our developments over and allow these ancient antelope room to pass? We clearly have the capacity, but seem to lack the magnanimity. I do not accept the customary attitude that our actions need no restraints and that other creatures deserve no accommodation or respect.

My beliefs no doubt have been schooled by a naturalist's passion for the whole kit-and-caboodle of nature. Once you get enthralled by a newt and a flower and a marsh, it doesn't matter whether they (individually or collectively) lack an obvious instrumental use or function to you. Even if you try, the water, fish, newt, flower, marsh, and antelope are not easily divorced from one another—or from humans. I care about that newt and the health of its habitat, whether said newt benefits me or not, and yes, even if its well-being means some restrictions on my behavior. Its health and success and mine are woven into the same fabric.

Each semester I introduce my students to an environmental ideology that's less human centered and dominating. "Ecocentrism" recognizes humans as interdependent players in natural systems that have great intrinsic value. Ecocentrism calls for us to be more humble in the face of Earth systems beyond human ken and control. My students like it; they know it's a tough sell. *Ecocentrism* may be another *e*-word, but it better describes how I understand my place in the world and why the other-than-human world feels like part of my body, like an extension of my very limbs.

~~~~~~

A common piece of the "Wyoming way a' life" is a loathing of predators—not just fear, but full-blown hatred. A bumper sticker on some county pickups reads, "Wolves: Government Sponsored Terrorists." If I were running sheep or cattle on grazing land, I might hold a similar sentiment about predators eating my profits. I might forget that even though the sheep were mine, the land that produced their summer forage was not. I might forget that the so-called killing frenzies wolves and coyotes are accused of pale in comparison to the killing frenzies we have wrought on them. To me, predators are part of that broad view of marsh and mountain meadow interacting with mouse and elk and wolf—less popular members of the family perhaps, but members just the same.

I've seen only three blacks bears in all my summers here, and it was probably a black bear that hauled my little hibachi from under my little motor home and licked the grill clean during my first summer. I like black bears, and I know they are basically nonaggressive omnivores that avoid humans. Many years ago in Olympic National Park, I frequently encountered black bears; once I leaned against my pack for almost an hour watching one rip apart rotten logs and suck out the ants and grubs. Once I came between a sow and cub, and the mamma bear sent the cub up a tree and then huffed and bluff-charged me.

One of the local bears I saw was in a BLM drainage thick with spruces where I was hiking; it eyed me and Tobie through the branches, then turned and walked back uphill. I learned the next summer that a hunter shot a black bear in the same drainage that spring, a female. He had placed bait (basically dead smelly stuff) to lure the bear in the open. The spring bear hunt, which can leave cubs abandoned and doomed, is to me one of the most nonsporting hunts ever created. Bear hunting is primarily about the trophy. Many years ago, I tried a piece of bear meat at a wild-game potluck in Idaho and learned why many hunters don't eat it; it was greasy and strongly gamey.

Most all of my neighbors enjoy our infrequent black bear sightings, that is, except for Nora and Mack. They have lived in a trailer for four or five summers east of my cabin while making small stabs at building something. I was walking the gravel road by their encampment one morning with Tobie when Nora yelled out to me, "There's two bears right up there! You'd better watch out!"

I turned around and walked back toward her; I'd been fuming about their place silently and needed to say something. Nora walked past the big Ford pickup toward me, her spatula held high in her right hand like a flag. Nora was cooking bacon outside again. She didn't seem to recognize me, though we had a similar conversation several summers before.

"Yes, I know there are some black bears around this summer—several neighbors have seen them," I said.

"Yeah, we been here three weeks and been seein' 'em all the time. You shouldn't be out here walking with your dog."

They had been there less than two weeks. I said, "Oh, I'm fine with black bears—as long as they don't associate getting food from humans, they really want nothing to do with you. But you know, I gotta say, when I walk past your place, I put my dog on a leash now because she keeps finding things to eat in there."

"You mean my bird feeders. Well, it's my neighborhood and I can do what I want," she snapped.

I paused, trying not to bite my tongue too severely. "Well, actually, not just the bird feeders. There's also the cracked corn spread on the ground. And bacon grease that my dog found. And dirty Styrofoam plates. You know, Game and Fish recommends…"

"Yeah, yeah, Game and Fish's already been here… Ya know, a bear killed a calf over there"—she gestured east with her spatula—"and now they set up a trap for him, right over there. So you really shouldn't be walking around like that."

She was confusing a calf killed by a grizzly near the Winds the previous month, which I ignored. "All I'm saying is that we like our black bears, and I'm concerned that they might get habituated by the food they get here."

"Well, why don't you tell that to our neighbor over there?" she sneered. "His place is a mess, worse than ours, that's for sure," and she walked away. That neighbor had construction debris scattered about but no food.

Although Nora told me that Game and Fish had given them a permit to shoot the "problem bear," Game and Fish had done no such thing. Nevertheless, Nora told me proudly, "They said we can keep the skin, too." A neighbor later told me she saw Nora walking the road with a shotgun.

When Peter asked me, "Are *you* an environmentalist?" he probably knew darn well I was "one of them" and perhaps just wanted to hear my defense of all things environmental. I wish I could say that my reply was compelling and persuasive, but in truth I diverted the conversation and it went no further.

The conversation nevertheless continues in my head. Over the years, I've debated abandoning the *e*-word, even tried to come up with a different word. I am secure in my love and affection for the natural world and my interdependent place in it, but moving beyond the stereotyped perceptions seems arduous.

And I remain conflicted with "environmentalism" itself. Most large, national environmental groups seem to think that warring over nature in courtrooms and Congress is somehow more effective than loving the natural world and helping others do the same. I get that, especially when bulldozers lower their blades for new subdivisions and energy extraction turns landscapes into moonscapes, and I'm glad environmental groups react and speak up. But focusing on these destructive end points cuts the tangible tethers to the oversize lifestyles that spawned them. The "need" we think we have for more space, more energy, and more stuff means more wells drilled, more forests cut, more prairies lost to warehouse stores and strip malls. There is far more "nature" welded into our I-gadgets and woven throughout our walk-in closets than there is in nature preserves.

Some environmental groups have even shied away from uttering the words *climate change,* thinking them too controversial and preferring a focus on *clean energy.* It's a moot point. Climate change looms as the panoptic environmental issue of all time, but it's more accurately the symptom of our larger relationship with the other-than-human world. To me, the work of environmentalism necessitates a "getting right with the earth" in the same way that people talk of "getting right with God."

I sincerely believe that my Wyoming neighbors share the love of this wild place and the conviction that its treasures should remain so. And that deserves some form of coming together, of hiking boots and cowboy boots around the table sharing a cuppa and talking about the Wyoming way of life we want.

So the next time someone asks me, "Are *you* an environmentalist?" I'm gonna smile and say, "Yes, well, sort of—have you got a minute?"

FOURTEEN

A Crush on Cranes

I was muttering about the cow pies lining the creek and the muddy bog created by the ATVs, when the pair of cranes rose from the small bench above the trail, alarmed at our approach. As they lifted their large bodies with a slow and steady beat of wavering wings, they warbled, the call of one sandhill crane slightly touching and overlapping the call of the other. The calls were quickly followed by a response from the steep hillside opposite the creek, an echo. Call and response, call and response, the calls full and tremulous and loud, the echoed responses slightly truncated and softer. Tobie and I paused midstep, to listen and watch the wide and graceful birds, their long necks and legs stretched fore and aft, as they slowly flapped downstream.

When they banked right and flew out of sight, I was still smiling. The cows and mud machines faded and all was right with my world.

I had gotten close to cranes that day, birds that have always been like a wild salve to my soul. Their ancient sound, their grace and beauty, touched me to my core.

Every single time I hear cranes warbling from the cabin or while hiking, I stop, smile, sigh, and melt back a little into myself. The warble isn't a fine trill like a warbler or thrush, but a strong and somewhat pleading call—audible up to a mile away—that clatters and trumpets and fills the air. Utterly unique, indescribable, unforgettable. Early in the morning, their calls float up to the cabin from the wet marshes below, strong, clear, solemn. It's like getting a kiss to launch my day.

My fascination with sandhill cranes began after a couple of close encounters. But it wasn't until I summered at the cabin, where I saw and heard cranes often and sometimes encountered them hiking, that my fascination developed into a love affair, an obsession even, for these winged wights.

~~~~~~

My first very personal encounter was in early March at a small state wildlife refuge in eastern Idaho, probably twenty-five years ago. I rounded a large hummock, the brisk spring wind bending the grasses horizontal and whistling about my ears, and there it was, perhaps thirty feet from me, this massive bird, head turned away from me, body bent forward to probe the ground with its formidable long bill. It walked slowly forward on its thin legs, crooked at the knees, followed by its lovely feathered bustle ruffling in the breeze. The wind must have muffled my approach. I sucked in my breath, shocked at this impressive creature in front of me. The crane then turned, unfurled its massive wings, and warbled into the air on a gust of wind.

Back in the truck, I found it in my bird book: *Grus canadensis,* sandhill crane. Adult gray overall, with dull red skin on the crown and lores; whitish chin, cheek, and upper throat; blackish primaries. More than three feet long, with a wingspan more than six feet.

~~~~~

My crush on cranes led my friend Mary Ellen and me to drive to Nebraska one spring break weekend during graduate school in Minnesota to witness the sandhill crane migration along the Platte River, the site of the greatest crane assembly on earth, where no fewer than ten thousand cranes can be sighted at once. I had met Mary Ellen while folk dancing, a gentle, sweet soul with soft blonde hair who worked in the schools with troubled children. We soon learned of our common love of birds and took several birding excursions to nearby parks and rivers. While drinking red wine one winter night in her tiny apartment, we excitedly hatched our plan to visit the Platte.

We did our homework before we left and reserved spaces in several different blinds, in addition to booking a room at the Motel 6. For our first evening, we parked and walked through sparse woods about an hour before sunset. The blind was a multistory wood structure with viewing holes cut at different elevations and angles. We chose a spot on the second level and hung our jackets on a hook. Soon the blind filled up and we hushed our tones and waited. The river beyond shimmered and sparkled silver in the late sun. "There's one," someone whispered loudly, and each pair of binoculars lifted to find the first crane.

The cranes came to roost in the shallow river corridor each night, with safety provided by wide-open vistas and by the large numbers. The name *sandhill* was derived from their preference for night roosting among the shifting sandbars that lie among the braids of a stream channel, something the Platte had in abundance (though greatly reduced nowadays by irrigation and dams).

The first dozen cranes trickled in, landing in the water with soft splashes, dancing to a halt, flapping their great wings dramatically.

Soon the trickle became a torrent and the sky was full of gray bodies and slender appendages, descending and lighting on the river. They had spent the day in adjacent open fields, feasting on leftover grains, tubers, leaves, and whatever small invertebrates and vertebrates their probing bills discovered, feasting to gather strength for the remainder of the considerable migration that lay ahead.

As the cranes massed in the riverbed, the warbling and cackling crescendoed, like the final forte movement of a symphony. Occasionally, the music faded, calmed, only to commence and accelerando to a deafening chorus. The noise saturated the wooden shack; Mary Ellen and I grinned at each other, and I mouthed, "Wow!"

When the evening grew too dark to use our binoculars, we leaned against the wooden walls and listened. When the night was totally dark, the music from the river softened and groups of birders got up to leave, flashlights scanning the floor and wall hooks for belongings. Happy and exhausted, we walked down the dark path to our car.

At the motel, we toasted ourselves with a glass of wine and went to bed, setting the alarm for 4:30 a.m. The same rules for our morning blind applied in reverse: we were to arrive at the blind in total darkness and wait for light. We followed the directions to a small graveled parking area and stumbled down the path. This blind was a small and old shack, with an odor of rotting wood and dampness, but it was our shack alone. We waited in the darkness, dozing fitfully while we leaned against the worn boards, checking a watch with a flashlight.

It's an interesting sensation, waiting in a dark and foreign location that is eerily quiet and you can only imagine what you'll awake to. We said "I think I hear something" several times before we actually did. The quality of the light as it transmogrified from night to dawn— from a black without depth through seemingly infinite hues of gray— was such that painters and poets struggle to capture. Only when the grays had fully progressed did the sky absorb any color and show any hint of blue. As each gray lightened ever so slightly, we became aware of movements, of forms. Hundreds upon hundreds of gray forms were unveiled in the soft light, crane upon crane upon crane standing in a broad bend in the river.

Gradually, the cranes awoke in their watery beds. A squawk here, a trumpet there, a rattling clatter over there. It gathered and built and began. But this time, in addition to witnessing an orchestra, we viewed an unparalleled ballet. Dancing is important to sandhill cranes for courtship, especially among young birds that haven't yet bred. Individuals leaped in the air, wings spread, flapping. Pairs took synchronized dips and bows and swung their long, thin bills and heads side to side. Leaping, flapping, springing from the water and scattering droplets like shiny coins. Through binoculars, we saw some cranes pick up pebbles or pieces of plants and toss them in the air. Crane confetti. The dancing seemed to be contagious, and spread from a pair here to dozens more over there.

Our arms ached from holding binoculars on this breakfast ballet. We'd rest, close our eyes to soak in the music, then watch some more. Then the cranes began lifting up from the river, first a pair, then a dozen, then a hundred, singing choruses of departure as they flew to the fields for feasting. Author Peter Matthiessen quoted an observer of this crane departure who said, "Then, with this great hurrah, they went up and were gone. It felt like they'd ripped my heart out and taken it with them."

~~~~~~

When I spotted my first sandhill in Wyoming more than a dozen years ago, I had flown out near the end of graduate school to backpack in the Wind Rivers with a girlfriend. We were driving home on the dusty road, spent and dirty, when I spied two cranes, but they were rusty red, not gray, which baffled me. I learned that in some parts of the West there is enough ferrous in the soil that when sandhills preen with a muddy bill, the feathers stain to a rusty iron color. Toddling after the two cranes were two fuzzy strawberry-blond chicks, called "colts." All four were just off the gravel road in a wet meadow, probing for snails and such, the young following their parents. We stopped the car and glassed them for a good long while, transforming ourselves from tired and grumpy to giddy and joyful, just like that.

Now at the cabin, it's a rare summer day when I don't hear the rusty cranes warbling in early morning or evening. It's also rare not to spy them when I drive to Pinedale; I now rate my weekly trip by the number of cranes spotted, such as "it was a five-crane trip." Passengers have stiffened slightly at my birding at sixty-five miles per hour, but as one commented, "I was dubious, but you're really good at this!" By now, I've pegged their most likely locations, where I look for the mounded rust-colored hump of a crane feeding, or the sweep of the long neck and legs of a crane walking.

A friend once asked me why I love these cranes so. "They live large," I said. "That's one reason." For this bird, there is no hiding in the tall reeds, no camouflage in the treetops, no coming out under cover of darkness. They want to stand out and be seen; as a bird that feeds on the ground, it's part of their defensive strategy to have a 360-degree view. Standing tall in the middle of an open field, proudly wearing their red crown, they boisterously call "Here I am!" In a Cree Indian tale, when Eagle refused to carry Rabbit to the moon, Crane undertook the task, for which it was rewarded with a beautiful red crown.

On the way to Pinedale, there's a bend in the road where the Green River braids itself in the distance. I had seen a sandhill sitting on a nest the year before, so I pulled to the side of the highway one June day and got out my binoculars. The nest was still there—bits of vegetation forming a simple platform in a marshy area that formed a moat of sorts to discourage nest predators—but cranes rarely reuse nests.

Then on the far side of the moat, I spied two sandhills walking stately through the bogs. Their steps reminded me of when a ballerina puts each foot forward with such overstated emphasis, bringing attention to that leg, that foot, that deliberate placement and movement. It's a forward motion that's all about the leg, not the body. And what lovely legs they have.

I kept adjusting my eyes as the trucks flashed by between me and the far field—a streak and roar of blue past my binocular lens, then a longer and louder wash of steel gray from a semi. Amazingly, the birds paid no attention. This pair was rusty red only on the curved feathers of the bustles, with gray on the upper bodies. At times, they cocked their bodies upright and tall, thin as fun-house mirrors. And then, a still-fuzzy chick! Its head appeared above the bog grasses, then disappeared entirely, then rose again to reveal more baby body. It stumbled through the thickets, launching itself forward but sometimes propelling itself beak first to the ground on what seemed to be new legs and awkward balance. Upon righting itself, it flapped its tiny wing stubs with vigor. Then, a second chick appeared above the nape of meadow, and together they tumbled after their parents.

When sandhill chicks are born, they are covered with down but leave the nest within hours of hatching, following their parents on foot. As with other baby birds I've seen, even after they begin to feed themselves, this pair continued to solicit food from their parents. Within two to four months, sandhill chicks have fledged and flown and will migrate with their parents south and then north the following spring. These were the youngest sandhills I'd seen, and I watched until my arms and eyes grew weary. Cars and trucks and semis raced by—whoosh, whiz, neeooorrmmm—oblivious to the bog babies.

~~~~~~~

One of my favorites hikes right from the cabin is a loop that begins by walking up the road, then down another, then up to Forest Service land, and down to a pond just below my cabin. Before Tobie and I descended to the pond, I glassed the area to check for moose and other critters below. Two Canada geese led their goslings at the upstream end of the pond. To avoid those and the beaver lodge (which Tobie became fascinated with the summer before), we started to descend slightly east of where we normally did. Partway down, I stopped to glass a pair of birds (gray jays, I discovered) in a dead fir. Then, I heard a familiar but truncated warble—of what, a sandhill? That was very unlikely way up high in the dense sagebrush, so perhaps a goose? No, I know that warble; it was a sandhill, and it was close.

I called Tobie and thank god she came; we'd had several recent cases of "selective listening" when it came to chasing cars. I put her on the leash and scanned the hill below with my binoculars. Nothing. I decided to make the descent even more easterly, just in case.

We had progressed about ten yards downhill through the thick brush when a crane warbled manically, this time behind us. It was moving laboriously through the sage, its wings partially extended and brushing noisily against the bushes. My first thought was, oh my god, Tobie had hurt it. When Tobie saw the large, noisy figure, she lunged at the leash and starting whining. I made her sit and watched the bird through the glasses. The crane didn't appear visibly hurt, though I'd never seen one crash through thick brush like this.

As I watched it, the crane pulled its wings in tight to its body, turned its scarlet-tipped head toward us, opened its long beak, and scolded a brassy warble in our direction. Then with a barely percep- tible movement of its wings, the appendages turned into kites, and the bird hung in the breeze about five feet off the ground and steered itself to a spot a bit lower on the hillside and considerably closer to us.

No pirouette was executed more powerfully and full of grace. Wow. Whew. Let's get out of here.

We continued our descent, but suddenly the crane was in front of us, walking quickly through the sage, its head pulsing forward as it strutted directly toward us. Our escape route was just cut off, or at least was fully occupied. The crane turned toward us, beak leading the way. At almost four feet tall, a six- to seven-foot wingspan, and with a long, sharp bill, this bird could do some damage. (I read once that a researcher witnessed one crane attack and kill another; a necropsy revealed that the cause of death was a lethal stab wound in the back of the head!) I sat down in the midst of some large sagebrush and pulled Tobie down with me. The crane continued past, trumpeting loudly.

Were we near a nest, I wondered? Perhaps the noisy dragging through the sage was the crane version of the broken-wing routine—that powerful parental instinct, "Here, take me—spare my young." I didn't know what to do, and I couldn't read the crane's signals—were we heading away from the nest or toward it? I knew we couldn't stay crouched in the bush for its nervous machinations would just continue. We needed to leave as soon as we could find an escape route.

I stood up, quickly scanning for the crane's location. Tobie strained on her leash, easterly but now uphill. I hissed, "Stop it!" She whined and tugged and panted; in the direction of her exertion, about twenty yards away, was a second crane, noisily maneuvering through the dense brush. With every fiber in her canine body, Tobie longed to pursue this "wounded" creature. No treat nor enticement nor command could persuade her otherwise; only the choke chain now fully in choke position stopped her from taking action. As she strained and panted, I felt the intensity of her quest. Golden retrievers were bred to hunt birds.

I plopped down again in the sage to pant a bit myself. I was surrounded by mad cranes who were instinctually doing a good job of intimidating me, making me think that attack was imminent. Their large, loud display was ominous enough to send my heart racing and to feel afraid of a bird I once thought entirely regal, and harmless. The dog remained passionate in her pulling, and we crashed through the sagebrush, flopping inelegantly down the hillside.

The second crane then took flight, making a wide, graceful, and seemingly unhurried loop around the wetland and pond, landing finally above the rushes at the water's edge. The first crane continued calling unabated, but our path down remained clear for now. As we descended, the first crane joined the other at the water's edge, still strutting, jutting out their beaks, and clattering. Only when we crossed the narrow berm at the top of the pond and disappeared into the trees did the cranes fall silent. My heart was still pounding, and Tobie, resigned that pursuit of "injured" birds would not happen today, turned her interest to smelling hoof prints in the mud.

I later read in my Sibley guide to bird behavior that sandhill cranes engage in a variety of "aggressive behaviors" to defend breeding territories or feeding areas. Our run-in with the cranes may have had nothing to do with a nest, but instead a sense that the hillside and pond was their territory to defend. That realization just made me love them more, knowing that these elegant and beautiful birds were also so powerful and bold.

~~~~~~~

There are so many birds that I like and enjoy at the cabin: the brilliant red and yellow western tanagers that set up house every summer, the gray jays who hop along the porch rail unabashedly looking for handouts, the acrobatic aerial antics of the hummingbirds, and of course great gray owls. Flushing a family of grouse around the meadow edges lets me know they successfully brooded, and I never know who's more startled, grouse or girl. But it's the sandhills that thrill and touch me most and best represent my summer in Wyoming. When a fellow I'd been dating told me that he hunted sandhills and they tasted good, my crush on cranes won out over him.

I splurged on one bit of "art" in my modest cabin: a stained-glass window, facing west and transforming the afternoon sun into a colorful display. When I met with the designer to talk about the window, I told her about my attachment for this region, about first hearing the "wind river" sound while backpacking many years ago, about the view from the cabin, and about the cranes. And there it is in the window, a crane feather, rusty red and gray-blue, floating on the wind above the peaks.

～～～

One March I was hiking in the Salt Lake foothills, trying to spot the first signs of spring. I stopped walking because I heard something, something out of place but familiar. I waited. And there it was again— a sandhill crane! And then another, its rejoinder slightly higher—the female's call—overlapping and echoing the male. They seemed to be on the wing, just out of sight, their call buffeted about by the stiff breeze, but the warble bounded off knobs and bounced off knolls, and down to me. Indian tribes revered the crane and its oratorical talents, and called it the Echo Maker.

They were migrating north, their spring journey more urgent than their return in fall. They were flying thousands of miles, some to Wyoming, anxious to arrive, feed, build nests, and rear young. I imagined them socializing and fattening up before the journey, then lifting off a few hours after sunrise when the thermals developed. I heard bird expert David Sibley speak once, and he said if you lay on your back and scanned the skies with binoculars on a clear spring day, you would see the specks of hundreds, perhaps thousands, of migrating birds. A sandhill flies with its mate from the previous season, and they teach the route to their offspring. Sometimes they join a V formation of other sandhills, gliding, flying up to a thousand feet high, and traveling up to five hundred miles in nine or ten hours. All the way back down the trail, I pictured these cranes landing in the wet seeps along the highway where I see them each summer, the snow still melting, the nights cold. It gave me joy, knowing they would set up house before I joined them in May.

Though they have made this journey for millennia and I just a half-dozen years, it's a migration that we share. We both await spring. They precede me, lead me, pull me north, so I too can feed deeply, build my nest, begin anew. In both Salt Lake and the cabin, I keep a small vase of crane feathers up high on the bookcase, safe from the cat, feathers in various states of gray with touches of rusty red. I've found the feathers while hiking over the summers, some on my land. It's my altar, my homage to cranes and the seasonal journey we have in common.

~~~~~~

In my sixth summer, I read a book that filled in the final missing piece of my crush on sandhill cranes. In *Birds of Heaven,* Peter Matthiessen described his pilgrimage to see the world's crane species. Of the various species of cranes worldwide, it's the sandhill crane, he noted, that shares distinctive traits with every other crane species on earth, which strengthens its status as the "ancient one." Indeed, the oldest fossil of a creature still living in its present form is that of a sandhill crane—nine million years old—found in, yes, Wyoming. Matthiessen wrote of watching sandhill cranes from a blind on the Platte River, saying, "It moves me (for strange reasons I cannot fathom) that the elegant creature rising in companies from the bars of the Platte on this March morning is the most ancient of all birds, the oldest living bird species on earth."

I've long struggled to describe that something, that quality in their rattling, echoing cry that strikes my heart like no other. Now I know:

that cry conveys primordial wisdom and omniscience, a voice so full of opera that each refrain carries all the emotions and struggles and joys of crane-kind. For nine millennia, sandhills have graced Wyoming skies. Their warbles have been witnessed by uplifting mountains, receding glaciers, roving Indians, and now me. This ancient voice touches something in me that I'd have to call my wild—an essence deep within that instantly reminds me that my roots are in the earth, the soft mud, and wet grasses, and my soul is in the sky.

FIFTEEN

Blooming

"I've spent hundreds of dollars on my garden," she said, rolling her eyes, "but the deer that lives under the deck keeps coming out and eating all the plants!"

Betsy lived several miles west of me and put an addition on her cabin the same summer I began mine, which I remember because we had to share builders. She worked in a school in Southern California and summered in Wyoming with her elderly father. She was a slim woman with slightly graying hair, a little older than I, with serious steel-blue eyes. At first I thought her "garden" was vegetables, but it was flowers.

"And if I do manage to plant something that she won't eat, it doesn't seem to survive more than a month. I don't know. Maybe it's the soil," she said. "I got so tired of nothing blooming around the front of the house that I stuck in some plastic flowers."

We were at a summer party held by mutual neighbors, the first time we'd met, though we'd heard about each other. We stood with glasses of wine on the expansive deck, light breezes coming up the broad hillside. We stood angled, side by side, so that the wind blew our hair back from our faces.

"Well what do *you* do—like about the deer, and gardening?" she asked.

Before I could reply, her father appeared and she introduced us.

But I kept thinking about her question. Up here in Wyoming, I would answer her as a naturalist: I don't really do anything about the deer, for they pass through and graze and that's just fine, for I don't have a yard but a wild place. If I were in Salt Lake, I might answer as the lifelong gardener that I am: plant deer-resistant plants. But in truth, my roles as naturalist and gardener are not that clear-cut, I realized, and are influenced by cultural norms and practices no matter where I am. Though I have approached the land around my cabin as a naturalist who wants to observe, identify, and understand, my impacts have also made me a gardener who tries to reseed and reclaim that which I have disturbed. And while wearing both these hats, over the summers I've learned a great deal about what it takes to bloom in the largest sense possible.

~~~~~~

When I was in junior high, I ordered from a catalog several small parchment hangings with wise sayings to decorate my room. The one that traveled with me to college and beyond said, "Bloom where you are planted." Even then, I knew that I was a nester, someone who liked to feather my dwelling inside and explore what lay outside. As a kid, my best friend Susie and I knew where Jack-in-the-pulpit grew in late spring in the gully near the train trestle. Near the fence lines we picked heads of milkweed blossoms and spent hours stringing the tiny blooms into delicate leis. From the creek, we brought home phlox bouquets for Mom. We learned, the hard way, what poison ivy looked like.

In my twenties and thirties I moved a lot, and the landlords of all those rentals were amazed at the effort I spent in the battered yards, planting gardens and bulbs, trimming, and tending. In all those domiciles, my blooming was as intertwined with the natural world as a sweet pea is to its fence. It was elemental and biological, not just a matter of preference; if you are in touch with your environment, there are simply some places where you grow and bloom best, and some where you are far less successful. I bloomed well in Port Angeles. In Moscow-Pullman, I liked the climate but never felt particularly connected to the land. I did not like the habitats of hot, dry cities like Boise and Salt Lake, nor hot and humid ones in the Midwest. And though there was much surrounding Idaho Falls that I enjoyed, the town was sprawling and unattractive. But in each place, I explored widely and sought to understand the natives that bloomed there.

The natural world has always figured large in my journey of becoming. I gained self-confidence, adaptability, and perseverance from backpacking in Washington and Idaho, especially in rain and snow. My healing after Nate left will forever be associated with the White Cloud Mountains and fishing on the St. Joe in Idaho. Acknowledgments for my academic success belong in no small part to the comfort and mind space I found on hiking trails in the Wasatch and beyond. Whereas some women call their mothers or best friends daily to talk things out, I call upon the woods.

~~~~~

Despite learning about native vegetation in each new region, I nevertheless treated each yard as interchangeable with any other. From the moment we are toddlers learning to walk on neatly shorn, lush green grass, we're inculcated as to the exact landscape that "belongs" around a house. So when I bought my very first house in Salt Lake after six years of grad school in Minneapolis, I trotted home from the garden center with my Minnesota favorites: hostas, forget-me-nots, and impatiens. My friend Camille gave me as a house-warming present one of her favorite mountain flowers, a lupine.

Snails devoured most of the hostas the first night, the culprit obvious from the slime trails the next morning. The lupine was entirely gone, with only the plastic stake to mark the spot. Despite watering, the forget-me-nots and impatiens died of thirst and intense dry heat. For several years, I was a slave of my hoses, watering something—grass, plants, flowers—every damn day. Minneapolis and Salt Lake—two cities that couldn't be more different in terms of humidity, precipitation, and temperature—yet I fell into the same trap of thinking I could make these habitats interchangeable with enough gardening.

That experience began a long, slow process of breaking down my notion of "yard" and the belief that yards consisted of the same general flora (geraniums to marigolds) regardless of highly specific habitats and climes. After learning my lesson with water-loving, high-maintenance foliage, I slowly transformed my Salt Lake yard to be "natural"—as much as was possible in a much-altered urbanscape. Over a few years, I dug up all the Kentucky bluegrass on my tenth acre and replaced it with buffalo grass, a drought-tolerant native that grew into a lush mat about four to six inches tall with tops bent over slightly; it required no mowing, what bliss. Gradually, I replaced the thirsty shrubs and flowers for natives that only sipped water.

When I bought the land in Wyoming and knew I would be summering there, I was already on the way to a Salt Lake yard that could survive its climate, though it still required watering. So I dug all the trenches for an automatic sprinkler and drip system ("How hard can it be?"). The timer was instructed to water the buffalo grass and all the perennials once a week and the parking strip of creeping thyme once every five days.

Nevertheless, the city yard required a fair amount of work in spring before I left for the cabin. Each May, I pulled weeds in the buffalo grass and tried to dig out stubborn invading patches of Kentucky blue-grass that traveled in on the wind from a neighbor's yard. I've tried to contain the nasty bindweed from spreading beyond the sidewalk, but I'm losing ground. It arrived from my neighbor's yard to the east, which is such a shambles that people walking by ask if the house is vacant. My yard may have been converted to "natives," but it is constantly invaded by outsiders.

At times, I felt engaged in the futile battle of Sisyphus, a king of Corinth in Greek mythology whose punishment in Hades was to push a large rock uphill, only to have it roll back down and be forced to begin again. Trying to make the yard "natural" when it was surrounded by exotics and invasives seemed hopeless, as if I needed to take part in this battle every dang year and every year hence.

To a casual observer, a city's yards look so lush and idyllic and belie the effort it takes to produce them. In reality, a city is one gigantic disturbance zone that would effortlessly revert to thistles, dandelions, and bindweed if each resident didn't engage in a ceaseless, continuous battle—native plants or not. As a landscape, a city has been too long altered and disturbed, and it's a crazy patchwork of flora from yard to yard, making it impossible to be a less vigilant gardener. The heavily watered yards have even altered the city's microclimate.

Much of my early-spring yard work in Salt Lake is deadheading last year's growth, which fills an entire green-waste bin with the dried growth of herbs and the spent heads of perennials. As I wheeled the heavy bin to the curb one spring, I thought that it would never occur to me to deadhead at the cabin! There when I arrive in late May, the fresh fuzzy shoots of balsamroot reach up through last year's leaves, which are splayed out in a perfect pressed and dried ring around the new. Grasses flattened and matted down by snows have new growth poking up just fine from underneath. Such old growth is nature's mulch and fertilizer. So why don't I leave it alone in the city? I asked myself. Why am I attached to the neat and manicured look in my city yard when it is unthinkable and out of place at the cabin? Yet year after year, I can't leave it alone. It would look too messy, too unkempt; no good city gardener could leave this be.

Nevertheless, in the summers I've lived at the cabin, I have more or less acquiesced maintenance of the Salt Lake yard to the plants themselves, save for a midsummer trip from cabin to city to run errands and to weed, deadhead, and spray the apple tree. Through the plants' survival—or not—and even their movement, they've educated me on what they want and need. The hummingbird vine is so happy it's attempting a takeover of the utility pole. The pari penstemon didn't really want to "bloom where it was planted"—I'm not sure why, too much water perhaps—and has moved itself to other locations. It seemed to like companions and took root under the rabbitbrush, next to the Indian rice grass, even tucked under the rim of the bench. All these places are near the sand path, so perhaps it's a drainage or soil issue. The Utah chokecherry tree wants to start an entire colony, sending up shoots for new trees up to ten feet away. The main tree has done remarkably well and in the process has increased the shade to an intolerable level for the once-sizable purple coneflower beneath it. Another coneflower in the front yard was both too shaded and too wet, thanks to the other neighbor's ultramoist yard. Once I became less attached and more absent from this city yard, it was a relief to become more an observer and less an active participant in their little plant lives.

Years ago, my mom gave me a sweatshirt with the words "Plant Manager" emblazoned across a landscape of bright, lush flowers. It's a great shirt that I still wear, but I have renounced the title. Thinking

I can (or should even try to) manage their lives is like thinking I can manage the rain. How liberating that is for us all.

~~~~~

Each year I ask students in my environmental studies class to name any of the first native wildflowers that bloom in spring. "Tulips? Daffodils?" they venture. "No, *native* flowers, ones that grow without us planting them." They are stumped, though many of them grew up in the valley and hike or mountain bike past these flowers routinely. When I offered an extra credit point for the answer, a couple of students Googled it but came up with a flower that grew elsewhere.

This saddens me greatly. The desert foothills around Salt Lake in springtime are, for a brief and shining month, riotous with the blooms of balsamroot, lomatium, and vetch. If we are ignorant of what grows without our meddling, "natural" habitats seem interchangeable, infinitely malleable, and unimportant. Tulips, wildflowers, plastic flowers—what's the difference? Perhaps the frenetic mobility of many Americans means we don't stay put long enough to put down our own roots and learn what native flora roots next to us. Or perhaps the cultural comfort we find in the neat green grass and pots of geraniums is extremely powerful, as much a symbol of "home" as the structure in the middle of the yard.

Once I was driving on the long, dusty road of the remote Upper Green River in Wyoming before a Fourth of July weekend, when I saw a midsize motor home parked near the river. A pot of plastic flowers sat on a table under the fold-out awning, and a satellite dish on a pole was stuck in the ground, searching for signals from home.

~~~~~

When my cabin shell was finished, the dirt envelope surrounding it was packed like cement and devoid of topsoil. Then Fred spread the topsoil he saved when he dug the foundation all around the cabin.

Some neighbors after cabin construction had seeded lawns, which they mowed and even watered, but I knew I didn't want a "yard" to tend. I also didn't want flower boxes or baskets of annuals. I wanted a seamless line from meadow and woods to cabin, a place that "fit in" to the greatest extent possible with its surroundings. I wanted to step to the background and pay attention to what bloomed where and then mimic that.

For the first three Octobers after cabin "dry-in" I seeded, beginning with the steepest pitches south of the cabin. I identified the grasses and flowers growing nearby and ordered a mixture of these seeds from a place in Colorado that specialized in Rocky Mountain habitats. After raking, sowing, raking, and compressing the soil with hundreds of my baby steps, I covered it with rolls of excelsior shavings pressed between photo-degradable green plastic mesh. It worked for the most part. Occasionally, a dog paw or deer hoof would pull up a corner, despite my anchors of rocks. But the cover held the seed in place and preserved moisture when the heat of summer came.

By the third autumn, there was new bare ground around the new septic tank and the line running down to the meadow bottom and spreading into three drainage seeps. I cut back on the yarrow in the seed mix (too prolific) and increased fireweed and grasses that I hoped would take root on the steep, dry slope. But the mesh cover was no longer manufactured for retail sale (though highway departments still manage to purchase it). The straw I used for mulch wasn't successful; what didn't blow away was consumed by deer and rodents. I hoped for a riotous bloom over the drain field, but despite what Erma Bombeck said, the grass and flowers didn't grow greener there, perhaps because of the sandy loam soils. Two consecutive summers of drought didn't help. Still, each year more grasses, flax, and yarrow spread, less ground was visible, and less soil was washing downhill.

One day I gleefully showed my neighbor Anne a seeded area with little bunchgrass shoots just poking up. She looked at me, smiled, and said, "You're just like a pig in mud up here, aren't you?" I grinned as widely as was possible for someone who is not a Cheshire cat.

~~~~~

One summer Tobie and I were following a deer trail well below the meadow's bottom edge when I noticed just below the trail hundreds of gray, twisted limbs of sagebrush, crisscrossed and jumbled, and tossed down the hill. The dead sage had sunk into a dense pile, compressed by snow and each other, their leaves fallen away like dry raindrops, leaving only the stiff trunks and bony twigs of hundreds of uprooted sagebrush. At least part of the mystery was solved as to why the meadow was strangely devoid of sagebrush in a state where 60 percent of the land grows some.

I'm betting that the sagebrush graveyard had something to do with William. William was the previous owner of my land, a professor of something from Arizona who summered in a tent and cut and cleared, and raked and hauled for several summers. William also left partway up the driveway an immense pile of long logs—probably eight feet high, forty feet long, and fifteen feet tall—which I christened the mother-of-all-woodpiles. Folks say he hauled away more than ten times that much. According to Bob and Betty, Willy worked on the place with a girlfriend, which was a factor in his eventual divorce. I imagined them making love in his tent as light left the meadow, warming the earth beneath them, their bodies tired and pliable after a day of hauling dense and fragrant fuel.

William's daytime labor mimicked what a fire would do, thinning the trees, clearing the understory and opening it to light. Thus, much of my land is an idyllic mountain meadow, thick with grasses and flowers. I can walk through the center four acres without climbing over a single piece of deadfall. It's easy to identify my south property line: on my side, arnica, asters, and lupine grow between scattered trees, and abruptly beyond, a flowerless jumble of logs and branches, tight trees, and a deep duff layer of needles and cones.

But his eradicating the sagebrush went beyond clearing deadfall and wasn't necessary for a clear view of the mountains. Maybe he thought sage was taking over the meadow; sagebrush does produce a chemical that keeps some plants at a distance. Perhaps he was allergic to it or simply didn't like it. Regardless of his reasons, removing the sage may have made the steep, sloping meadow drier and more barren. It receives the full glare of the south and west sun, and the steepest parts fight to hold moisture. Aspen have struggled to take their place in the succession; as the last piece of tender forage to be covered by snow and the first to be revealed, small aspens are repeatedly clipped and pruned by hungry ungulates. In summer, animals avoid the meadow's empty expanse, preferring to hug the sheltered edges. Thistles and dandelions have sought to fill the void in bare patches.

William also planted the knoll with what some call pasture grass, a chest-high, thick-stemmed grass that the horses of the horse logger I hired did indeed relish. It dwarfs the bunchgrasses and other natives, but would likely be impossible to eradicate.

~~~~~~

A constant challenge for both the naturalist and the gardener in my stewardship of this land is discerning where or how the natives like to bloom. I had no idea why the yarrow was so thick in one area and why the flax took hold in another. Or why the ground remained bare in several spots after several years, while the grasses went wild in what I considered unlikely places. Paintbrush seed never germinated, nor fireweed nor penstemon. They all grew elsewhere on my land but wouldn't deign to sprout where I planted them. It took three summers before I spied a tall variety of evening primrose that was in my seed mix. I discovered that the deer cropped its tops shortly after it bloomed and was using the grass for camouflage. The lessons made me feel like a hapless gardener and caretaker, as well I should.

When the potentilla were just starting to bloom along the little creek and pond, with their deep-yellow flowers and frilly green foliage, I thought about buying a couple of these shrubs to plant around the cabin. But walking home, I realized I'd never seen any growing anywhere near the cabin. Duh—they were growing near the pond because they liked to keep their feet wet! I laughed at myself. They, like every other shrub, tree, grass, and flower, knew best where to plant themselves and grow. Of course, I am free to try and rearrange that to suit my desires, and I may get lucky. But in all likelihood, it will take more effort, more water, and more tending by the gardener.

Each summer sego lilies bloom in the heat of July, right in the driest and barest and most sun-exposed part of meadow. In the morning, the three snow-white petals are closed, but the sun coaxes the petals to relax into a delicate bowl, revealing a pattern of deep maroon edging a bright-yellow center. There they are, surrounded by parched earth, not an ounce of shade, this flower on a wisp of a stalk—why this slight, genteel bloom, here? Their parched surroundings make me want to water them, to transplant them to what I perceive as a more hospitable location. But no, this is where they bloom.

Shortly after I arrived one year, I spied a fairy slipper orchid near the mother-of-all-woodpiles...and then another and another. For some reason unbeknownst to me, this was a good year for these rare woodland orchids. Was it the less frequent rainfall? The early warm spell in May? The precious pink things pushed up through the forest duff and thick needles, had little green competition, and needed little light. The flower guide noted that people have tried to dig them up and transplant them, which was a death sentence.

It's curious that homesteaders were required to "improve" their 'steads, defined as erecting a dwelling and planting acres of crops or ranging livestock. I don't consider the bit of planting I've done to be an improvement at all; I disturbed this patch of woods and meadow and am now clumsily trying to return it to some version of "natural." Thank goodness that whether I'm here or not, the grass will grow, the flowers will bloom, and the trees will sprout, grow, and die. After all, these plants took centuries to get it right, to find just the right magical combination of conditions—soil, sun, slope, moisture, temperature, wind, and neighbors—to root and bloom.

One of the most important reasons to reseed and play the active gardener instead of the hands-off naturalist has been to forestall weeds after the soil was left bare. Nevertheless, what grew best (and first) in my reseeded areas were these uninvited guests, the opportunists that were phenomenal at taking advantage of such a situation. Thistles, roadside clover, dandelions, and cheatgrass. I suppose I should admire the tenacity of these colonizers; this is cowboy country, after all. Some have ingenious designs for dispersal and reproduction. Deception was the ploy of tiny light-blue flowers splayed into several stems that I found around the cabin. How nice, they look like forget-me-nots, I thought, and I left them alone. Only when each tiny flower dried into a stick-tight seed that my socks and Tobie's fur carried everywhere did I realize I'd been duped. I now see them regularly along roadside cuts.

Salsify is also talented at dispersal. Although it's listed in a few wildflower books, it grows in dry, disturbed areas such as ditches and roadways. I know that "weed" is a cultural label, not a biological one, but I nevertheless want to even the odds for the natives over the invaders. Salsify is a single yellow flower on a stocky stem, which dries to a giant, golden, wispy ball of seed umbrellas. One summer, I pulled dozens of salsify up by their thick taproots and piled them in the meadow to die. A couple of days later, the wind sent hundreds of their umbrellas skyward. How clever: both the yellow flowers and the still-closed buds went straight to seed, using the last bit of moisture to burst and fly. Now, I pull up the stalk and pop off the tops, stuffing them in my shorts pockets until they bulge like chipmunk cheeks.

~~~~~

Then there is the rodent factor. I can only imagine how many of the thousands of the seeds I've scattered have been eaten, or stuffed into cheeks, carried down holes, and buried. I named this hillside Mouse Meadow for good reason. Every summer day, there are new mounds of fresh dirt between clumps of flowers, though tunnel openings are rarely visible in the undergrowth. I never see most of these soil engineers, an assortment of ground squirrels, moles, and voles. Tobie has uncovered pieces of tunnels (in her never-successful quest to dig a rodent out) that curve and snake great distances. In spring, extensive tunnels among the matted grasses are revealed by the melting snow. Rodent rooting no doubt provides excellent soil aeration—like teams of tiny rototillers—and the flowers and grasses don't seem to suffer. If I were watering and mowing a lawn here, their lumpy activities would probably drive me crazy. Also abundant are chipmunks and mice, which are far more efficient at seed collecting than excavating.

Thinking that the rodents were well occupied with the meadow, one summer I planted a few herbs outside the basement door; the gardener and the cook were yearning for some fresh additions to summer dishes. The next morning, the savory had disappeared without a trace; I guess it was. The following morning, a tunnel uprooted the chives. A few days later, the rosemary, mint, and tarragon were chewed to the ground and never recovered. The following summer, I put a few herbs in pots on the porch steps, where they grew untouched but did not thrive in the drying Wyoming wind.

Another aspect of yard control is the ability to make a yard look the same each and every summer, regardless of what the weather and season deliver. I didn't realize this until summers five and six at the cabin, when I watched but didn't intervene in two very different seasons.

By late June in the fifth summer, forest fires were burning and meadow grasses had gone to seed. Some early bloomers made an appearance; many others parched on the vine. I mourned the desiccated meadow as flower tops faded and stems lost their green, drooped, and turned crisp. I missed the blooms, and it seemed to signal a quicker passing of summer. Its length was unchanged, of course, but I felt pangs of sadness, remnants of my city life that say all growing things should be green, and if they're not, you should water them.

But ah, in summer number six an excellent snowpack and a month of rain and snow that pushed into mid-June produced a riotous progression of blooms. It looked like bloody Switzerland, with mounds of early mountain bluebells, then carpets of yellow—first balsamroot, then arnica, hawksbeard, buckwheat, and sunflowers. The dry slope that held at best a dozen sego lilies erupted with them. Lavender harebells propagated happily. For the first time, red was more than a wee accent when scarlet gilia produced an amazing display. By August, despite six rainless weeks, the flowers continued to hang on; only the seeded portion on the south side had faded for the year.

In retrospect, my distress with that dry summer was very curious (and highly cultural). Underneath the parched surface, down with the moles and salamanders, mixed with the scat of hoofed visitors, lay the dormant seeds, the roots, the stems, all waiting. For them, it's not a matter of patience or relinquishing control—just a simple accommodation of cycles, of taking the soft path of seasons, of living with what is.

It's a lesson to heed in my own life. When I work to take charge and direct my life course, it can feel like a hard path—hands on the wheel, steering over bumps and ruts toward distant destinations I deem important. But when I let go long enough, when I let my gaze broaden, there are all manner of bright bits of luck and happenstance on the path in front of me. Pausing to see them sparkle, to turn them in my hand, provides more guidance than any map I might have drawn. Rooting my life on Mouse Meadow was no doubt a soft path, surrendering to a strong but unshapen dream of how life could unfold and bloom at the pace of a season.

~~~~~~~

There was one more lesson of blooming in these woods and meadow that I needed to learn: to love dandelions. During my summers of reseeding, I spent considerable time digging and spot spraying dandelions. They will outcompete what I'm trying to reestablish, I reasoned, and they need to go. What was driving my reasoning, really, was the century-old cultural symbolism that having a "yard" full of dandelions meant you were a lax and delinquent gardener. Ha, a contradiction laid bare in my attempt to be "natural." So one summer, I ignored their blooms in the meadow but still felt compelled to spray some in the long driveway. Then finally, I ignored them entirely and was surprised how very hard that was. Next summer, as part of my dandelion rehabilitation program, I plan to pick and cook up some dandelion greens.

For the most part, the therapy I once got from growing a garden morphed into watching a wild garden do what it knows best. Nearly every day, I stroll through it to see who's blooming (ah, the first phacelia), who's seeding (look, the heartleaf arnica blooms have turned to white puffballs), and who's being invaded by pushy neighbors (the short-lived colomia have taken over the septic field). I wander and watch—that's my only tending, save for weeding the invaders from the seeded patches. No deadheading blooms, no mowing, no watering. I am marvelously unneeded.

Yet one summer I found myself yearning to dig in the dirt. Perhaps such a hankering is what drove Betsy's frustrating gardening experience. Perhaps it's larger than that. No matter the habitat or culture, humans like to grow things; tending and nurturing living plants is satisfying, and dirt under the fingernails is good therapy. But my foiled attempt to grow herbs made me hesitant.

I found a solution in a catalog: a self-watering planter on casters that I could wheel from deck to cabin at night to protect from frosts (the frost-free season here is only a month) and from rodents (and even deer if they became bold enough to walk up the three steps to the deck). The herbs and greens didn't really thrive until late June when the temperatures rose and the rainy skies cleared. The arugula and spinach were divine, the mint delicious. But by late July after several little harvests, the planter was invaded by small green caterpillars that annihilated all the greens in about twenty-four hours. But that could happen to a gardener—or a naturalist—anywhere.

SIXTEEN

Home Is Where Your Dead Are Buried

On a September afternoon on the sun-filtered deck, I was reading the last chapter of the novel *Sight Hound* and began to weep. As with the dog in the book, Tobie had been slowing down and I was loath to admit it. She was ten then (our fifth summer at the cabin) and started limping after shorter and shorter hikes; occasionally, a back leg would start shaking, presumably from muscle fatigue. It didn't matter that I was the general contractor, made the decisions, and paid the bills on this cabin; she and I felt like equal partners in the dream. She was a constant and steady presence and companion in our cabin life and our city life, indoors and out, winter spring summer and fall.

A friend (who sent me the book) asked me why I thought Tobie came into my life; the author's premise was that a particular dog comes into your life for a particular reason. Well, I said, she was an adoring and uncomplicated loving soul on the heels of my mother's death, my cat Cosmo's disappearance, and my uncle Don's death, boom boom boom, all within a month.

And, I told him, Tobie was good—unrelenting—in getting me to lighten up. I told him about her willful sabotage of the "exam" for intermediate dog obedience training; we had practiced religiously and Tobie had mastered every task. On the long recall when the examiner told me to call my dog, I called "Tobie, come!" but she didn't cross the long hall to sit obediently at my feet as she had a hundred times. Instead, she trotted over to the sidelines to visit her buddy Bodin, the rottweiler. At the hurdle, instead of jumping—like she did every blessed day into the truck—she walked around it, and set out once again for Bodin. I was beside myself—how could she! My face sank when the examiner handed me the evaluation—five points below the minimum passing score. She gently reminded me, "Stress travels down the leash." Only months later could I admit that I was far too concerned with performing and passing that test, and Tobie must have sensed it. Tobie continued to remind me not to sweat the small stuff, to stop and smell the flowers (and also the poop), to chill about hair and dirt in the house, and occasionally to abandon decorum and fart in public.

I set the book on the porch deck and called for Tobie, wanting to hug her and press my tear-stained face in her fur and tell her not to get old and die. And around the corner she came, with a dead rodent swinging from her jowls.

~~~~~~

But it was Kaya who left us the following spring, spry, in her prime, only twelve. When Tobie was a puppy, I brought the nine-month-old cat home from the shelter, hoping that they would grow together and be friends. They were; Tobie stood still to let Kaya sniff her after a hike, and they slept next to each other on the futon in my office.

It was a spindle cell sarcoma in Kaya's hind leg, difficult to remove or treat. I grieved intensely and immensely and knew I'd never have another cat like the sweet little ambassador who cordially greeted every guest at my parties, who growled at moose. After she died, I made a collage of Kaya photos, many of them from the cabin: Kaya on top of my book manuscript "helping" me write inside Dory, Kaya riding shotgun on top of the backseat to Wyoming, Kaya lying in the meadow with her belly to the sun. She adapted so easily to life in Dory and even seemed to enjoy cabin construction. The trucks, the noise, and the cast of workers didn't seem to faze her. One of my favorite pictures was Kaya sitting on top of the basement stem walls, eight feet off the ground, gazing at the sun sinking over the mountains.

Not having a kitty in my life was agony, and I kept seeing phantom cat shadows out of the corner of my eye. I have had cats in my life even more continuously than dogs; I needed one. Wise, sweet feline spirits, independent yet warm companions, seeking scratches and laps. When I returned from teaching for a month in Costa Rica—where I approached every cat who would have me—I went to the animal shelter.

Chica was a cute gray tabby with a white belly and white mittens on front paws and white boots on back paws, an attentive and affectionate kitty. But unlike her wild-savvy and friendly predecessor, during her first summer at the cabin (my sixth) she watched moose out the window with an indifferent ho-hum, yet burrowed under the bedspread whenever humans arrived. She seemed to believe that the woods held no danger and gave me no indication that she knew anything about life outdoors. She'll be an indoor kitty, I decided.

One morning at the cabin I found Chica crouched on the living room rug, eyes wide and wild, a shell-shocked little cat. Her fur was full of sap. Hmm. I partially reconstructed what must have been a night of terror for her: an open living-room window whose screen had fallen onto the porch. I surmised she was excited by mice cruising for crumbs on the porch (where I spied mouse turds) and had leaped at the screen, which gave way and delivered her into the dark night. Perhaps her adventure was, at first, exhilarating, and she ventured off the porch into the meadow and woods, rolling in pine duff. But something changed all that, something very frightening. An owl? A fox? I was glad she remembered how to get back inside. For the remainder of the day, she startled and jumped at the slightest sound, like a veteran with a bad case of PTSD.

The light on the answering machine blinked rapidly in the dark, hot house in Salt Lake. It was two in the morning, and my plane was four hours late touching down from Chicago, where I'd been at my annual academic August conference. In the first message, I heard the anxiety in Tasha's voice, calling from my cabin where she and her husband were vacationing and pet-sitting in my absence. "Tobie collapsed this morning. We called around and found a vet who could see her right away." With each beep and another message, the anguish in her voice crescendoed. "It's Tasha again. The vet just called, and she said it's cancer and it doesn't look good. Please call us." I stared at the phone; my heart raced. Message three. "Hi again. Call us as soon as you can." Message four. "Haven't heard from you yet…Maybe your plane was delayed. Call us just as soon as you get this. It doesn't matter what time it is, just call."

Tasha was the assistant director of the environmental studies program and a graduate student in my department, so our paths overlapped often. She was a warm and generous young woman, who knitted Kaya a little pouch for catnip and volunteered in schools teaching children to knit. Both she and her husband, Alf, a slight man with carrot-red hair finishing his doctorate in English, adored animals, and they jumped at the chance to spend a week in the woods with my pets.

I knew before Tasha answered the phone that Tobie was dead. But knowing it and spilling over the edge into feeling it were worlds apart. As she replayed the day's scenes, her words oozed in, deeper, into every fissure.

"Tobie didn't want to go for a walk in the morning, and I knew something was wrong. Then when she tried to stand, she collapsed and couldn't get up. We could tell she was in pain and that something was very wrong. There was only one vet—a woman in Boulder—who would see her right away…"

I sat on the edge of the couch. My mind traveled there, and I could see the road to Boulder east of Pinedale, undulating sagebrush plains, the crags of the Winds rising behind.

"The vet drew some blood and it was very watery, and she knew what had happened. A large tumor on the spleen had burst. She said this kind of cancer is very hard to detect, and a lot of the time you don't have any indication, no sign that anything is wrong. You couldn't have known…"

For much of the rest of that sultry August night, I wandered my house, sobbing. I wasn't there for her; I didn't get to say good-bye. My precious Tobie girl. I should have known—why didn't I feel something that big in her belly? I should have been there. She died alone, without me. We fit together like bread and jam; we knew each other's hearts and minds without speaking. I didn't get to say good-bye.

The next morning, the horizon blurred on the drive north. I was exhausted, spent, and raw, but the tears still came. I clutched the wheel with both hands and drove much of it from memory. At the junction, I turned toward Boulder. The women at the vet office showed such compassion, kindness, and empathy toward this stranger and her dog. The vet tech told me she was with Tobie when she died, that she was on morphine and not in pain. While I paid the bill, they loaded into my car a large black plastic bag with her body, heavy, cold, and stiff.

At the cabin, Tasha and Alf greeted me sweetly and hugged me. I called my neighbor Steve to dig a grave at the top of Mouse Meadow with his backhoe, eight feet down where no wild animal would unearth her. He came right over. "So sorry, Julia," he said. "It's tough to lose one, I know…" The yellow backhoe dug and dug, piling earth to one side. Tasha and Alf fed me, and told me the story again.

We carried the bag to the edge of the freshly mounded dirt. My friends walked back to the cabin and I opened the bag, pulling it gently away from her body. There was my girl, peaceful and still and cold. I pulled her head onto my lap, stroked her fur, smoothed her ears, smelled her feet. At first, I wasn't sure I wanted a reunion with her stiff, dead body, but with each run of my hand from head to tail, I found solace, her corporeal presence like a tonic, a chance for adieu. I was glad she would be buried here, her forest home and mine, but I couldn't fathom my faithful partner and sidekick not walking the woods with me, not greeting visitors, not racing around the meadow.

Tasha and Alf walked up the meadow to sit with me. The sky grew pink and ash blue and two does came to watch, their heads peering over the rise just ten feet away. I sprinkled Kaya's ashes at the bottom of the grave; I had retrieved them during my night of grief in Salt Lake, finally sure of their resting place, with her Tobie in that meadow full of mice. The three of us eased Tobie's body down, holding paws and head, but the hole was deep, and we reached the point when we needed to let go. Thud. The sound split me open. With each shovelful, as her body disappeared from view, from touch, from air, the heartache blossomed and I sobbed.

As August plodded along, I rarely ventured to the meadow top. I felt no comfort standing above the mounded earth, envisioning my dead dog down deep and the worms moving in. It was Tobie who was with me when we celebrated the purchase of this land with champagne and strawberries, who endured with me the drip, drip, drip of leaky Dory, who greeted every workman and every neighbor, who stayed close when I sanded and stained and sweated over this place. And it was Tobie who wasn't here now.

I tried my best to conjure up good memories, like Tobie at the Salt Lake City Library with all the children, where we volunteered as a certified animal-assisted therapy team. The kids would read to Tobie, who listened patiently and without correction, sometimes licking the reader or barking her encouragement. Or there was Tobie looking hilariously pitiful wearing the dreaded plastic collar, the cone of shame, our second summer in Dory. She had gotten a severe case of mosquito bites on her belly that became inflamed from her licking. The contraption was so wide she couldn't turn around in the motor home, so we tried various combination of T-shirts through legs and neck, pinned at the middle. But each memory was as brief as a 45 vinyl on the turntable, and when the needle reached the end, it sounded the scratchy refrain: she is dead, she is dead, she is dead.

When I took my first hike without her—a hike that felt wrong and empty but something to endure and get beyond—I brought back a rock and placed it at the top of her grave. I also deposited there her half-eaten rawhide bone. A couple of days later, the rawhide was gone, and in its place was a mound of scat. Probably one of the foxes that had been around here all summer. That felt better.

Although it took me years after my first dog's death to feel ready for Tobie, this time I couldn't stand the absence more than a month. It was worse than phantom kitty shadows—there was no greeting when I opened the door, no click of nails on the floor, no hiking companion, no companion on the office futon when I worked. And as a person living alone, there was no one to direct my comments to, to feel like I was talking to an actual being and wasn't just crazy.

I "went to look" at some puppies an hour south of Salt Lake and came home with Maddie, a fuzzy, fresh spirit—another golden retriever—who climbed into the front seat and onto my lap, where she slept for the long ride home, exhausted but seemingly not yearning for her siblings and mother. When I stopped the car in front of my house, she promptly threw up in my lap. In the mornings when I let her out of her kennel pen at the foot of my bed, she always trotted over to cuddle with me, rather than springing into the instant frenetic motion one expects of puppies. And bless her, she didn't bark like Tobie.

But the transition from old and easy dog to infant-toddler pup caught me by surprise. With needle-sharp teeth she nipped at my clothes and hands and chewed on everything from drawer handles to window blinds. She chased Chica and tried to elicit play but received only hisses and swats. I began to wonder if shaken-puppy syndrome existed, for at times I was ready to heave her across the kitchen. Despite long walks twice a day, it seemed impossible to tire her out, to get a moment of peace after dinner when I needed it.

One evening, after an entire day of puppy exasperation, bloody scratches on my arms and legs, and newly ripped jean shorts, I walked to Donna's house for dinner and sobbed, "What have I done?" I missed Tobie and her old, gentle ways, and this puppy was just too much. "I can't take it!" I cried. Was it this hard with Tobie? I think it was (I think it was actually far worse), but it was so very long ago. The list of forbidden items Tobie chewed was probably just as long, and the amount of time and energy spent on training that independent creature was extensive.

When I first took Maddie to the cabin in September, I walked with her across the meadow and found myself at Tobie's grave, bawling, longing for her, aching horribly. The second cabin visit with the puppy in late September was better. I took Maddie on the woods walk from the meadow south toward the peak—a favorite of Tobie's. I lifted her over logs too tall for her short fuzzy legs, clapping my hands on my thighs to get her to follow. That evening, she wiggled up to me and leaned into my body, sitting quietly and contentedly, her puppy breath warm and sweet.

The next day, she discovered grasshoppers, cautiously nosing them until they flew, then bounding after their flight. The day after that, she discovered she could jump; she flew over logs with an exaggerated spring that launched the front legs but often left the back legs a little short, and she slid off the log nose first into the dirt. I laughed, what a little clown, and it felt so good. She trotted over, wiggling, wagging, licking. In the cabin, she discovered that flies are good to eat, and if you visit the low west windows in late afternoon, you can have quite a good snack of them. She also discovered that the doorstop, those boingy things on the wall that keep the door from hitting the wall, are great toys that make delightful noises when you hit them with your paw—again, and again, and again. Everything was new and fun and exciting for her, and I needed a bit of that.

With the car loaded to return to Salt Lake, Maddie and I walked the meadow one last time. I wondered whether next summer she'd remember all this, and how soon she'd understand our seasonal migration and whether, like Tobie, she'd give a happy bark as soon as we turned onto the last four miles of gravel, followed by joyous little zooming circles through the meadow upon our arrival. Maddie left the ground squirrel hole she had been pawing and trotted over to Tobie's grave. She sniffed the fox scat, walked around it, and sniffed it again from the opposite side. She looked at me. Then she squatted right next to the scat, and added a fresh pile of poop.

SEVENTEEN

Going with the Grain

"Whup!" shouted Abe, and the massive horses strained into their harnesses, hooves raised then planted, metal clinking. The slack chains popped tight, and three thick, long logs began to move, sliding up the hillside, bumping over roots and rocks. Abe stood atop the two-wheeled chariot behind the horses, reins in hand, glancing forward past the horses for his route, then back at the tree trunks bouncing along behind. The horses snorted and panted, their chest muscles rippling as they ascended the meadow with their weighty load.

It was the second day of a week of horse logging on my land, and each time I heard the command hollered to haul another load, Whup!, I leaned toward the window from my work, mesmerized by the sleek and steady horsepower dragging giant dead pines out of the woods. Now in my seventh summer on the land, pine beetles had flown and infested in every direction, leaving dense pockets of dead lodgepole pines.

Abe was felling trees southwest of the cabin, trees that I had marked with neon pink flagging. One by one, I located a lodgepole pine with the telltale light-yellow tubes of sap protruding like bits of popcorn from the lower trunk. I wrapped my arms around each trunk and gently tied the pink flagging. When the trunk was broad, I leaned my chest against its scaly bark and stretched my arms around to pass the ribbon from hand to hand. Some infested trees sported deceivingly healthy-looking yellow-green growth, while some held evidence of what would come: a crown of red needles and finally a red carpet of needles beneath a bare tree. In a small area just south of the cabin, I moved from trunk to trunk and soon held two cardboard rolls empty of their flagging amidst a cemetery of pink-striped trunks.

The yellow sap tubes represented a valiant attempt of the lodgepole pines to push out mountain pine beetles, *Dendroctonus ponderosae,* that burrowed through their bark. When beetle numbers are low and trees are healthy, sap can pitch a beetle out. But when a few beetles becomes an infestation, and when trees are stressed by drought, disease, or competition in dense stands, this defense is futile. A couple of summers ago, we felled a dozen immense Douglas fir that lined my gravel drive, victims of a similar fate by another species of bark beetle, *Dendroctonus pseudotsugae.*

Entomologists remind us that bark beetles are a normal part of forest ecosystems, and studies of lake-sediment cores in the West show that periodic outbreaks are historic. It's true, but not comforting. When I look west across my meadow toward Forest Service land on a distant slope, I see a dense mosaic of green dotted with deep rust-red, like a book of green matches with built-in torches.

~~~~~~

The evening I finished flagging the dead trees before the loggers arrived, I walked back up to the cabin and opened the basement door. The smell was intoxicating—the bright, fresh smell of newly sawn pine. I'd spent the past several weeks nailing up tongue-and-groove pine paneling to cover the cement walls and provide added insulation. Last summer, I finished the ceilings downstairs (the main room with drywall and the bedroom and bathroom with antique-looking tin) and had finished the cement floor with an adobe-colored soy-based etch. The walls were one of the last steps for a finished basement.

Woodworkers call it blue pine. Patterns of blue-gray streaks and stripes swirl against the light yellow-tan background, flowing around knots and invisible channels. An artist could have done no better. Some boards are stained with solid patterns, some are clear, but most carry wisps, like syrup slightly stirred into maple ice cream. All of this beauty was created by saliva—the fungus-carrying saliva of bark beetles that flowed through the veins of sap in the trunk. The lumberyard sells blue pine for a bit less than regular knotty pine, but that's not the reason I prefer it. This gorgeous work of destruction deserves an honored and functional reuse.

The sweet piney scent is also the first one that greets me when I open the door upstairs, especially if the cabin has been closed for a day, a week, a winter. When I trudge from the car, heavy with bags and larder, and push open the door, ahh, there it is, the smell of fresh wood. The smell is fainter now, not raw and new, but still reminiscent of recently milled wood. It's softened and mingled, gotten comfortable. Smells of cabin life—garlic and onions sautéing, dog and cat dander, mud and needles tracked in—have been absorbed into the log walls, dampening their edges and giving the wood age and experience. Wood smoke adds another scent as it escapes the wood-stove door when I add a log or turn a smoldering one. The cabin's woody scent—one of the most welcoming and soothing smells I've ever known—means that I never forget I live in a log cabin, indeed, a structure of wood.

Yet the buzz of saws outside in the forest of red trees and me in this log cabin hold such circular irony: trees killed by beetles have made my cabin a thing of great beauty and joy. While the trees outside represent that which I most love about this land, they also are the surest threat to this dwelling and my life in it. I burn wood inside to stay warm; flames outside may extinguish it all. Horses haul out log after log from the forest, and I haul beetle-killed milled lumber into the cabin.

～～～～

The sound of heavy clatter on metal—the massive hooves of the Suffolks as they exited their horse trailer—announced the arrival of Abe and his two horses on the first day of logging. Trace was a young chestnut female, and Dewey an older and experienced chocolate-brown male. Their hooves were the size of small dinner plates, their chests like giant barrels.

Maddie, just shy of a year old, had never seen a horse, let alone one that weighed a ton. She thought them wild beasts and cautiously inched forward, uttering a soft woof-chuff at them and an occasional bark for good measure. Every time they moved or snorted, she jumped and spooked, racing back to me or the cabin. We watched Abe put the pair in their harnesses and traces and then watched them work.

Abe was a nice, good-looking young man (and patient with all my questions) who grew up on a farm in the hills of Virginia and answered an ad for a horse logger that Ted placed. Ted, who lived about thirty minutes away, had once logged with his own horses but now preferred to hire an extra hand who worked with his own team. Both Abe and Ted felled and limbed the trees, and both directed the trees' descents with impeccable accuracy. A half-circle wedge was cut from the base of large trees, then a cut made from the opposite side in just far enough to convince the tree to abandon its vertical life. If the tree needed additional encouragement, a plastic wedge was tapped into the second cut, and tapped and tapped until the tree began to lean.

When a tree first started to lean, it often did so silently in what seemed like a slow-motion sweep. A few trees protested loudly, the wood at the base groaning and creaking in tortured twists until the final bands of wood at the trunk's center snapped. As the treetop leaned ever closer to the earth, a rapid, syncopated series of crack-crack-cracks issued forth as limbs broke on neighboring trees during its journey to the ground. Finally, there was a magnificent and thunderous thud as the entire trunk struck and sunk into the duff, a sound that Ted said he loved and never tired of.

I was amazed that the birds seemed totally unfazed by the considerable cacophony of sawing and falling trees. There was an unabated stream of birds to and from the feeders each day. Perhaps they quickly discerned that the disturbance didn't chase them or that they could fly from it. Maybe their minds were stuck on food and their own little bird lives. I did wonder and worry whether birds had built nests in any dead trees, though lodgepoles had few branches on their tall trunks and probably weren't good choices.

As thrilling as it was to watch trees fall, I preferred to watch the horses haul. Trace and Dewey were attached to a chariot of sorts, a metal frame with a tractor-type seat mounted above what looked like two oversize mountain-bike tires. From the back of the frame hung chains and massive hooks to attach to the big end of the tree trunks. The chains were attached high on the chariot, which raised the front of each tree a foot or more off the ground when the trunk was dragged. Abe backed or turned the horses and chariot into position beside each felled tree, as much with verbal commands as with reins. Haw! Gee! Whoa! Foot! Back! While he attached the trunks, he kept admonishing them "whoa" because they were ready, anticipating their eruption up the hill, dragging the massive logs. To me anyway, they truly seemed eager and happy to work. Upon Abe's command, a quick and high-pitched "Whup!" they charged forward and the logs began to slide.

I told Abe he must have an incredible sense of geometry, for he was able to find a relatively straight path through the woods all the way back to the flatbed truck and maneuver horses and several forty- to eighty-foot trunks through all the other trees en route.

He just shrugged. "Lots of practice, I guess."

~~~~~~

When I was probably nine or ten, my friend Susie and I wrote away to get our very own Smokey Bear Junior Ranger badges, and we signed pledges to help prevent forest fires. We wore our badges proudly and took our mission seriously, combing our rural wooded and cornfield-encircled neighborhood for fires, warning neighbors to extinguish leaf fires and slash burns. I imagine they found us earnest but annoying. Many decades later, my neighbors and I know that Smokey's de rigueur policy of fast, complete fire suppression has not served us well, and its consequences are not simply or casually righted in our little corner of the West. We are "overdue" for a big fire, they say.

In the early 1980s when I worked for the Bureau of Land Management in eastern Idaho, each summer I traded my normal media and information duties for that of fire information officer. I'd set up shop near the fire dispatch with maps and push pins, telephones and blackboards, and wait for the phone to ring. I fed the news media steady updates of acres burned, number of structures threatened or destroyed, and expected containment times. There was admittedly a thrill to it, an adrenaline rush from the massing of equipment and firefighters and danger—but all of it was far away and mostly burning flat sagebrush plains. I learned about up- and downslope winds, about setting backfires and using a silver emergency shelter. But I didn't learn anything, really, about living on the other end of fire danger.

These days, my neighbors and I are fluent in the language of "defensible space." Many of us have done what we can: gotten fire assessments, run the chain saws, and had friends snowmobile in to burn slash piles in winter. William, who owned this land before me—though he never built a cabin—gave me a good head start by clearing massive amounts of deadfall. The remaining vulnerable side was south of my cabin, where the pink cemetery of trees was now falling one by one. Last summer, Dad and I thinned dozens of the scraggly crowded pines south of the cabin and limbed all trees around the cabin about ten feet up. Each summer, I trim down to nubs the grass and flowers right around the cabin. And I've pondered buying fire-resistant gel to spray on the cabin if I'm called to evacuate.

Several weeks ago, the ruddy-faced UPS man delivered the box of scent packets. Some neighbors and I pooled our resources for a large order of pheromone patches from a company in Canada, one kind of patch to protect lodgepoles, another kind to protect Douglas firs.

The idea of fighting scent with scent appeals to me. When bark beetles find a good tree and start boring through the bark, they release pheromones that attract more beetles to that tree, like flashing a neon sign that says "Eats!" When enough beetles have massed, they release a repellent scent to deter any more beetles—in essence, turning the "Eats!" sign off—an effective dual strategy for fully utilizing a tree for egg laying, but not killing the host tree and its food supply before new beetles can emerge. Researchers have copied the repellent scent in the pheromone patches, telling beetles from the outset that "this tree is not available."

I donned latex gloves and leaned a short ladder against a large Doug fir north of the cabin, the tree with the nest box that hosts mountain chickadees each year. About eight feet up the trunk, I tapped a small nail through the colored strip at the top of the packet. One by one, I climbed and tacked packets on my chosen few—sixty trees among thousands.

As any species will do, bark beetles are simply optimizing a favorable set of circumstances. It is the human species that has made the forests thick and dense with even-aged stands of fuel. My species has also warmed the climate and sped up the life cycle of the mountain pine beetle. A life cycle that used to take two summers to complete—from adults laying eggs to larvae, pupae, brood adults, and back to egg-laying adults—can now finish in just one summer, doubling the population and the damage. And warmer winters don't kill larvae like they used to. Forests need to burn—as terrifying as that is to me—and they will burn. If not this summer, then the next or the one after. In summer when thunderclouds form and the air begins to conduct electricity and excess electrons seek a discharge, one by one, they will find targets to strike. It's physics, not politics or desire or fear. And physics doesn't recognize the brass monuments that mark the corners of my property.

<hr />

While Abe skidded logs from the woods to the staging area, Ted cut logs to lengths that would fit on his flatbed truck and trailer. He used a little Bobcat tractor to hoist each log onto the truck bed, which they drove away fully loaded each evening. Each time the little Bobcat turned and pivoted, it gouged the soil, turning the staging area into a powdery black pit. The drag trails through the woods were similarly scarred, though I knew by next summer new growth would begin.

I walked down to the staging area and found Ted putting the chain back on his saw. He was easy to talk to; I asked him about regrowth on the disturbed areas, and he asked how my tongue-and-groove work in the basement was progressing. Abe wouldn't be returning next summer, and I asked Ted if he was worried about finding a replacement. He smiled and shook his head.

"When I first started logging, I tried to plan everything out, to figure out exactly how to approach a job or a season. I tried to think how I'd juggle jobs—I just thought and thought and thought about everything. And ya know, it wasn't working. My mom suggested I file for bankruptcy—that's how bad it was going. But I really didn't want to do that."

"What did you do?"

He chuckled, "I decided I needed to quit worrying about everything. It wasn't working and it was making me nuts. And I did."

"You quit worrying about *everything*?" I found that hard to believe.

"Pretty much. I just decided, whatever happens, happens. And sure enough, things just kinda fell into place; things just worked out. I always had enough work, and not too much."

"You must have great karma or something," I said.

"I don't know 'bout that, but everything does seem to come out just right. Even the last few years, when I hired a third man with horses, we had lots of work. One spring I hired one but he backed out—some medical thing with his neighbor—and ya know, that was good too because we ended up having just the right amount of work that summer for two, but not for three."

"Wow, that's amazing," I said. I paused. "I worry too much, I know I do. But I figure a little bit of worry can motivate somebody—like me worrying about forest fires prompted me to hire you. But not worry at all—about anything? I wish I could do that."

"Well," he said, stroking his long, wavy beard, "you can," and he carried his saw back to the truck.

～～～～

On the way back from the lumberyard last week with paneling for the basement, I was grinning like a cheeky schoolgirl. The smell of all that fresh wood stacked inside the SUV from the front dashboard across the folded-back seats to the rear window was intoxicating and ambrosial. I wondered if the average person would have the same reaction, or if it was just me who had such wood lust. And the more I worked with wood, the more I desired it, was drawn to its smell, its feel, its responsiveness.

Later that day, I was cutting a pine board with the jigsaw to make an opening for a light-switch plate, sawdust flying in every direction, when the blade hit a big knot. Wow! The intense sappy smell rose up, and it felt like I had opened a magical box that connected wood to tree, dead to living, an instant sensory reminder that this knot once held a tree branch and sap flowed from trunk to branch like blood through veins. I don't know why they call a dead tree "wood" and not just "tree." Perhaps similarly we call dead pig "pork" because we desire a distance, a disconnection between living and dead. But when I work with wood, "tree" is very much in the room, creating a seamless connection between naturalist and woodworker.

I asked Ted whether he ever worked with the wood he felled and hauled away.

"Like building stuff?" he asked. "Some, not so much now. But this weekend I'm finally making a railing for our loft. For years, we've had dressers and stuff blocking the edge. Figured it was time."

When cabin building commenced six summers ago, I yearned to participate in woody creations. So I signed up for community education wood-shop class (several times) to get more comfortable working with wood and the tools that shaped it. And practically, I needed some furniture for the cabin.

When I went to MacBeath's lumberyard in Salt Lake for material for my first project, I fairly danced through it like a kid in a candy store—smelling, touching, and holding all these delicious pieces. Exotic dark and rusty mahogany, light and airy cedar, dense and brilliant hickory. Each board told a story, chronicled a history—its scars and injuries, where branches hung, where beetles chewed—in a way like our skin carried our histories.

For the coffee table I chose wormy maple, a wood that was not too soft like pine, not too hard like hickory or oak, and it had such stories in it. In a nod to the beetles staining my pine walls, the worms stained the warm, golden maple with small stripes of dark gray and brown, complete with tiny holes where the worms ate their way in and then back out. I later made matching end tables and a small bookcase. Then I made a bathroom wall cabinet out of yellow-green poplar with cherry dowels and a matching mirror frame and towel bars. Finally, I made picture frames: a beech frame for a poster print of Picasso's *Girl and Flower,* hickory for a print of O'Keefe's iris, and reclaimed tropical woods that smelled like black pepper under the saw for batiks of African women dancing.

In wood shop, we learned about the qualities of wood and how those translated into what wood "liked" and didn't. The miter or chop-saw cut wood across the grain, but most machines in the shop were meant to work with the grain, not against it: planer, joiner, sander. A few machines—like the lathe, router, and jigsaw—did a bit of both. But every piece that was created, from cabinet door to table leg, was the result of learning to respect and work with the grain—grain that was once a tree trunk that inched and stretched its way to the sky.

It was amazing how worked wood possessed such great and enduring strength at the same time that it was malleable and delicate. A massive beam of glued strips of wood held up the very cabin, after all, and wood walls held up the roof. Even logs that supported the deck and porch, though they developed splits as they dried, did not lose their strength. Depending on the type of wood, its thickness, and shape, wood could be remarkably flexible, able to bend and be worked and shaped. A long but slightly warped board of tongue-and-groove pine could, with a few well-placed taps from a rubber mallet, suddenly ease and bend to fit its neighbor's path. How many substances can build both houses and ships, oboes and cellos, and be pressed into wafer-thin delicacies like typing paper and coffee filters?

As wood ages, dries, and settles into a life of little moisture running through its capillaries, its underlying characteristics may come to life, including a knot or a grain that was crooked becoming more so. A couple of years after it was placed, one corner of a fir board on the deck twisted up like a sneer, pulling out long screws and rising above its neighboring boards. To prevent such a twist in the cabin walls as they were laid, in addition to a fitted notch smeared with glue that held the logs firmly together, wooden dowels were driven down between two log ends so one wouldn't dry, settle, and twist differently than its neighbor. The utility of being able to bend and adjust yet lie comfortably side by side for the sake of a union has lessons for relationships of all kinds.

~~~~~~

By the end of the second day of horse logging, Maddie was captivated with Trace and Dewey and thought them fantastical creatures. She crept closer and closer, nose working the air, and sat and watched them. With a sudden hoof stamp or snort, Maddie would still spook and race backward, but that could have just been respect at their size. At night, Abe selected a portion of my meadow to pasture them, rigging up a thin wire connected to ground stakes—a solar-powered electric fence. They could have easily outwitted or outmuscled it but didn't. While washing dishes, I'd look up and see the pair cropping the tall pasture grass with pleasurable mouthfuls. After dishes, Maddie and I walked out to visit them and feed them carrots. Maddie learned that she could duck under the hot wire and cautiously weave around the pair, while sneaking mouthfuls of fresh manure. If one of them suddenly turned a giant head in her direction and took quick steps toward her, Maddie zoomed under the wire with haste. To this day, Maddie likes horses.

The next afternoon, distracted from my desk work by the saws and tromping of horses and drawn by the bright, warm sun, I went outside to gather the remaining scattered limbs from two dead aspen and a lodgepole that Abe had felled and removed right outside the cabin. The aspen limbs were bumpy, jointed like knuckles. The lodgepole boughs were heavy with yellowing needles and wafted resin and sap, belying the tree's imminent death. The more limbs I gathered, the more tiny aspens I saw sprouting up through the undergrowth. Closer to the woods' edge were several saplings already several feet tall. Their delicate yellow-green new leaves glowed as they fluttered gently on their stems. My thinning and limbing and the dying lodgepoles had allowed more sunlight to reach the forest floor, though aspens are a fairly short-lived species and are continually resprouting and replacing. Even if I hadn't been here, hadn't lifted a finger, hadn't thinned or logged, something would have cleared and made way for aspens—eventually.

I tacked on the fridge a news story that fascinated me: forest officials estimated that each day, one hundred thousand trees fell down in this region, trees killed in the past few years by bark beetles. One hundred thousand trees, crashing down each and every day, simply astounding. The article was meant to warn people who camped, hiked, and were near all these dead trees, but all I could think about was the sound of tree after tree after tree smashing down. In just Colorado and parts of Wyoming, pine beetles have killed 3.6 million acres of trees, enough to cover the state of Connecticut. I got out my calculator: more than four thousand trees an hour—about seventy trees a minute—were falling, crack, crack, thud. When winds picked up, trees fell in rapid bursts, the officials said. Bam, bang, boom! they went in the howling wind. I kept imagining this boisterous symphony. Boom, boom-boom like timpani, crack-tatta-tat like snare drums, groans like bassoons, whines like clarinets. Dead trees, rotting roots, wet spring soils, and wind—biology and physics set to music. Trees root, grow, die, and fall down.

Nothing you could do except stand clear, watch, listen, and not worry about it. And wait for their replacements to sprout.

EIGHTEEN

All Is Forgiven at the Ceiling

Thhh-chhung! The nail gun delivered its spike through the top tongue of the pine panel into the stud behind it. I stepped down the ladder and lay the gun on the floor. Only one more board to go to reach the ceiling.

Last summer and this summer, my seventh at the cabin, I'd been finishing the cement walk-out basement. I hired some workmen to frame out the walls—two-by-fours from ceiling to floor spaced vertically—onto which I nailed tongue-and-groove planks of pine. The nail gun was thrilling and amazing, and I still sucked in my breath slightly each time I squeezed the trigger. But I no longer jumped each time the small red compressor kicked on with a thunderous eruption.

I cut the plank to length—6'8" and 5/16ths—on the chop saw and climbed the ladder with it. The top board was the hardest to set onto the tongue below because it lacked much clearance on top to tap it down and seat the bottom groove of the new board firmly onto the tongue of its neighbor below. There wasn't enough space to use the rubber mallet, so I used a screwdriver to lever and wedge the pieces together.

Before I retrieved the nail gun, I stepped back to look at this, my final wall in the basement. The left end of the top board was just an inch below the ceiling, but at the opposite end, the gap between board and ceiling was a good three inches.

"Well, shit," I said. I sat down on the basement steps, rubbed my face with my hands, and thought about my brother Scott.

This wasn't the first time this had happened. On my first basement walls the previous summer—in what is now a guest room—I had uneven gaps at the ceiling, and the ends of the boards on two adjacent walls didn't match at the corner. A workman (there to install some drywall on the ceiling of the utility area) pointed this out and said, "I woulda tore that out." I called Scott to ask what to do about the gap at the ceiling.

"Aah, don't worry about it," he said. "Once you get the ceiling tin nailed up in that room, your trim piece—a one-by-four—will cover the gap and you'll never know the difference. And when you put a trim piece in the corner, the mismatch won't be noticeable either."

Well, here I was at the last wall in the basement, my twelfth wall, with much-honed skills, and there was still a gap.

"Yep Scott," I said softly, "all is forgiven at the ceiling."

~~~~~

Five summers ago, Scott nailed the very first tongue and groove in this cabin—in the high ceilings in the main room upstairs, standing upon some borrowed scaffolding. He and my younger brother, Jim, had gifted me with a week of work that second summer on the land.

Scott showed me how to sight down a long board—hold it out flat away from you, rest the opposite end on the ground, look for a sway from end to end, then turn it on its end, and check for a bend to the left or right. Both brothers were skilled woodworkers, and they took delight in pitching the rejected warped boards off the porch into the meadow below where they'd land with a twang and a thud. "Boys," I'd thought.

Scott also taught me how to use his nail gun. He was a good teacher, patient but exacting, big on safety. He sunk nails in rapid succession—bap, bap, thh-chung—but I cautiously positioned the gun, sucked in my breath, and squeezed the trigger. The ceiling was a difficult training ground, working with arms and gun raised high, creating aching work.

I bought my own nail gun and little air compressor when I began to finish the basement. First, I stapled in tall batts of insulation into the spaces between the studs. I debated buying another tool for this chore—a little staple gun that you hit like a hammer to sink a staple. I had used Scott's at his wedding reception when his new wife, Brenda, and I stapled plastic table covers over the picnic tables—whack, whack, whack, very satisfying.

"Wow, this is a great little tool," I said to him.

He smiled, "You might need to get yourself one, huh."

~~~~~

The summer after he got sick, Scott and Brenda considered a trip to my cabin but opted for a salmon fishing trip to Alaska, a lifelong wish of his. "Maybe next summer," he said.

That fall back in Salt Lake, I was on my way out the door to campus, briefcase and lunch in hand, when the phone rang. Puzzled who would be calling at this early hour, I answered.

"Hey Sis," Scott said. "Got a moment?"

The chemotherapy was not working, and the specialists in Iowa City said surgery for his rare cancer was really the only remaining option, and even then, the odds were long. Scott sounded uncharacteristically pessimistic. He asked me if I were religious, whether I believed in an afterlife.

I sat down on the kitchen tile, my back against the cupboard doors, my satchels puddling around me. Though Mom and Dad had taken all three of us to church for years, none of us became churchgoers. Scott and I talked and talked, punctuated by long, silent pauses. I bit my lip and blinked hard and fast, but the tears welled up, my voice cracked; he sounded stoic. I told him about my carbon theory, how I believed that our basic elements were returned to the earth, but that the energy, the spirit that was who we are, like energy, lived on and couldn't be destroyed.

After a moment of silence, the phone line humming, I said, "That's the biggest revelation I got out of an entire semester of physics—energy can't be created or destroyed."

He chuckled, then grew silent. "Sounds a bit like some of the Buddhism stuff I've been reading."

We talked about Buddhism, two kids who grew up in an Episcopal church full of community, yes, but also pomp and circumstance and odd-sounding English. In my sixth grade confirmation class, the priest asked me to rewrite my assigned essay on Death, that's how poorly I'd understood it (at least according to church doctrine), despite a year's worth of religious study. Scott and I agreed that Buddhism to us novices made more sense: no creation story, no beginning, and no end. Just one continual, continuous unfolding and coming into being. When you're living it, it's about life and all its interdependencies.

~~~~~

The following spring, Dad called as I was making coffee. "You'd better come," he said. "Now."

Scott waited until February for the surgery (a delay none of us fully understood), and he never bounced back from it. Each phone call with him was shorter, more fogged and pain-filled, more centered on the day's energy level and what food, if any, tasted good. The doctors were baffled at the edema, the extreme fatigue, his struggling heart.

Jim and I were on the same flight that night into Des Moines; we shared a drink, memories of Scott, and disbelief at our journey. Dad drove us directly to the hospital, but we arrived three minutes too late.

~~~~~

If you began with a poor foundation—that is, a board that didn't sit level against the basement floor—it affected every other board on that wall even though it wasn't touching it. It was almost impossible to make level that which started out so flawed. If the first board had the slightest bend or warp in it, it rippled up and exacerbated in each successive board (even if it was straight) all the way to the ceiling.

That's something I learned during wall number four. Although Scott taught me to sight a board, I didn't notice the slight upward bow right in the center of the first one. For every board on top of it, I'd tap on one end to seat its groove, and the opposite end would pop out of joint. Wall number four had no windows or door to cut around, which I thought would make it a fast and easy wall, but it actually made it far harder to get some wiggle room in the long boards. Finally, I cut several boards into shorter lengths, for each cut added some play. It was an amateurish solution, but I was an amateur. There was no easy solution, amateurish or otherwise, for the foundation underlying the relationship with my brother.

~~~~~

The day after the memorial gathering at Dad's house, we drove to Scott's house thirty minutes away, where Brenda was sorting through papers with her son. It was an old farmhouse Scott had been renovating, slowly. The entry had bare drywall, and above the stairwell, new furnace pipes emerged from a large hole. Off the long porch-turned-sunroom with its large red tiles lay the rented hospital bed.

The first time I met Brenda was at the wedding; the second time I met her was the night Scott died. I really liked this sister-in-law and didn't know how subsequent meetings would take place, but I hoped they would. Like Scott, Brenda was an obstetrics nurse, which was where they met many years ago. Brenda had long, poofy blonde-gray hair that she often wore twisted back in a way that was highly functional and a bit hippie-throwback. I liked that she looked at you intently when you talked, with nods and smiles and heart, all good nurse qualities. From the first time I met her, there was something in the way she said Scott's name—time spent on each letter, rounded and full, soft and sure—that was astonishingly full of love, acceptance, and gratitude. Scott was so lucky to have found that, and her.

Brenda had a house in town with her two teenagers. When she and Scott married, she didn't want to move so far from town and into a two-bedroom house under significant remodeling construction, and Scott couldn't part with the little farmhouse in the country, surrounded by fields and horizon, with his chickens and his tractor. Scott told me he thought he got this marriage right, in part because of the separate domiciles. "Hey, I'm hard to live with," he acknowledged. They had "date nights" every weekend. I had accompanied Brenda to the funeral home, which prepared and transported Scott's body to the medical school to which he donated it; their two separate addresses took a bit of explaining to the funeral director.

Scott's usual clutter had deepened in his illness. Brenda and Dad sat down with a drawer of papers, looking for PINs, accounts to be closed. Brenda urged me and Jim to take whatever we wanted, whatever reminded us of him. I walked room to room, touching coats in his closet, petting his cat, looking out the windows to the chicken coops where his "girls" had clucked and scratched and followed Scott like schoolgirls.

It was an uncomfortable experience walking through someone's house—even your own brother's—when all of the possessions had suddenly become stuff for others to sort, disperse, and dispose. The stuff of one's life, the final accounting, the remainders, the leavings. Now just stuff. The wooden tray where he kept his loose change. A case of canned tomatoes. The antique hall tree with boot bench. The glass-topped end table, a castoff from Mom and Dad. Most of it was not that valuable, save the extensive collection of tools. Jim volunteered to inventory the tools and attach some prices, though he said it didn't feel right to take one; they were Scott's. I took a sauté pan; we shared a love of food. To busy myself, I began to vacuum, first in the sunroom, then the main room, and all around the hospital bed. I stripped the sheets.

<hr />

It had been almost two months since Scott died, and I wanted to finish the basement before Jim came with his family, their first visit to the cabin. But when I started working with my power tools, I often thought of Scott and got weepy. Not a safe combination.

When Mom died seven years before I bought the land, the grief was different—expansive, raw, encompassing. We were so very close and I so lost without her. But this? There were long periods in our lives when Scott and I didn't really communicate. The foundational warp began in childhood with things he did that remained unvoiced, unnamed, things that once given voice in adulthood grew larger before they grew smaller. Even at their smallest, they were hard to lose in tall grass. By adulthood, I lived in the West. He'd had four wives and only two we liked. Until the past few decades or so, he drank, used drugs. Until the last decade or so, he never remembered my birthday.

But by the time the first piece of lumber arrived on my land, Scott had appeared in my life once again. He called sometimes. He sent me chunks of cedar from his land to burn in my woodstove because it smelled so good. He nailed tongue and groove on the cabin ceiling. He felt like a brother again.

Now, there was this hole where my brother had been. I couldn't pick up the phone and ask cabin-construction questions. He wouldn't be there at Christmas, coming through the door with a happy ho-ho-ho. There were things I should have asked him, things we should have talked about, things I didn't know about him. I wished we were closer, like he and Jim became as adults, talking on the phone for hours. I wished I'd meant more to him. I wished that we had been able to move more fully and cleanly out of the past. Now it was all "the past."

For the last decade or so when I'd ask Scott what he wanted for Christmas, he'd say, "Nothing. I've got everything I need, and then some." When pressed, he'd say, "Make me something—I love the stuff you make me. Do you still make that salsa? Or that jalapeño jelly?" Last Christmas when he was sick, I sent applesauce and jam that I had canned and in his name bought ten baby chicks for a poor family in a developing country. I also sent the chapter "If You Want to Make God Laugh," which Brenda said filled his eyes with tears.

Scott had gotten beyond stuff. Even before he got sick, possessions and material things mattered less and less. He loved Brenda, he loved his land, he loved his sons (whom wife-number-three had taken to Florida and then Michigan), he loved his job as a neonatal nurse (a "baby catcher"). And over the years, he did a better and better job of loving himself.

~~~~~~

I wiped my eyes and went upstairs to make a sandwich. I took it outside onto the deck where I ate every meal, weather permitting. The heavy blanket of morning fog in the valley below had evaporated into the day and revealed once again the angles and inclines in the distant forest before the mountains. Tree swallows dipped and rose above the meadow, sometimes darting under the roof above the deck, catching insects that had warmed enough to fly. I wondered how swallows could eat while zipping around like that—must be like eating on a roller coaster. Maddie bounded onto the deck, dirt on her snout from rooting around in the meadow, happy that I had left the basement and joined her outside. She leaned into my leg, panting, and watched the swallows with me.

〰〰〰

For the memorial gathering at Dad's house, Brenda wanted to have a display of photos of Scott that spanned his life. From the hall closet, I retrieved photo albums and two boxes of photos that hadn't found their way into albums. The prints spanned half a century and told the transformation of Scott. Scott on his trike with his little sister standing on the back, arms around his waist, her cheek resting on his back. Scott with a bulldog puppy, his seventh-birthday present. Long-haired high school Scott raking leaves with Mom, followed by the crewcut, uniformed Scott fresh from army boot camp (a transformation that surprised all of us). Dressy pictures from three weddings.

Just as striking as the photos of his journey were the photos of the pretty brunette sister. From square black-and-white prints with wavy white edges to gaudy Polaroids and poorly preserved color prints, this young woman with shimmering hair and bright smile amid soft features kept staring back. I had some of these pictures and was familiar with them, but the face looking out at me looked so surprisingly foreign that day. Death gives us fresh eyes, a perspective rewound after standing so close to the edge of a life.

There was one photo of me and my brothers in front of the fireplace one Christmas that I held for a long time. I was wearing a plaid shirt, long hair falling from my shoulders, and flashing a big, endearing smile. I was indeed pretty, wasn't I—especially after I shed the cat-eye glasses and braces. But the strangest thing was that I never thought I was pretty; I don't remember a time when I looked in the mirror and thought, "Yes, I'm pretty." Was it just adolescent anxiety masking this innocent truth? A feeling of inadequacy based on constant criticism from my father?

I remember looking in the mirror this past winter and scowling at the sag in my chin line, with a sense of regret that these muscles had been stretched by time and gravity. So this is why women have facelifts, I thought. Yet I wondered if perhaps twenty or thirty years hence, I'd look at pictures of this face now, at fifty-three still relatively wrinkle free, and think, "I was still pretty then, wasn't I?"

How stupefying that in my half-century journey, this unreconciled piece remained. With all I had done, experienced, gained, and lost, with all the wisdom that was mine, such a simple, skin-deep hang-up remained. Of course, virtually all Western women are taught by our cultures to hate our bodies, despise our wrinkles, and defy each and every way that lessons and laughter and days reveling in sun and wind are carried forth in our bodies. That fresh, young face in the Christmas photo is still learning after all these years that there are manifestations that matter far, far more than the history written on her body.

My favorite photo of women homesteaders is a pair of young women linked elbow to elbow in front of a distant shack. The woman on the right has her hands on her hips, her eyes and nose scrunched up in the sunlight, a broad, toothy smile across her face, and her long, dark skirt brushing the tall grass. Her wide straw hat is bent up in front and hair billows forth; a kerchief is knotted around her neck. She looks so happy, so content and at home. She was raised in a culture with a Victorian sense of the chaste and a cloaked female form with a diminutive, corseted waist. On that wide-open grassy plain, she looked like she left so much of that behind, but it's not that simple, is it, leaving one's culture and its pronouncements of what's proper and ideal and valued. I envied that she lived before the fashion world chose one Barbie body type above all others. Before plastic surgery, before Lycra, before high heels. But she would have envied my shorts, my jeans, my cowboy boots.

～～～

I stood from my deck chair and said, "Come on Maddie, let's drive into town and the lumberyard. I need some more trim pieces."

She cocked her head, unable to piece the words into an action.

"Let's go for a ride in the car!"

Maddie zoomed off the deck and stood by the truck.

At the lumberyard, I picked out the straightest one-by-twos and one-by-fours I could find. The woman at the desk remembered my name; I'd made numerous trips that summer because I could fit only a limited amount of lumber inside my SUV.

I walked the long pieces of pine down around the cabin and in through the basement door. Maddie returned to the meadow. I turned on the compressor and it roared, dancing a little across the floor on its red feet. While it filled with air, I went upstairs to get a soda. As I leaned against the counter, tipping my head back to drink, I saw the white patch near the ceiling.

"You're still there," I laughed.

At the apex of my high ceiling, a crack developed in the drywall after the second winter from the settling of logs and roof beams. Not desiring to add drywall work to my repertoire, I hired Daisy to fill the crack with plaster, but an even bigger crack appeared the next winter. Daisy came back, dug it out, put in more mud, and smoothed it. I laughed. Here it was, now, what, three or four summers later, and I hadn't repainted it. Maybe I'll wait until someone looks way up there and notices it, whatever.

When I began finishing the inside of the cabin—sanding, sealing, varnishing, painting, and tiling—I decided it was time to replace my old catchphrase "How hard can it be?" It was funny, and perhaps necessary to help me naively dive into tasks far above my skill level, but now it sounded cocky, a bit arrogant, like charging in with guns blazing. That saying got me into trouble, thinking that I could whip out some brand-new project in a jiffy, master a new skill in a minute, all just a proverbial piece of cake. Even my first room upstairs, the bathroom, took me five solid days to sand and varnish—not a quick weekend as I originally planned. But it's true what people say about sweat equity and the sense of ownership and pride it engenders. I have touched virtually every square inch of this cabin, except the roof. I've either sanded it, stained it, covered it, painted it, caulked it, etched it, or insulated it—and oftentimes several of each.

"It takes as long as it takes" was my new phrase. Without grand expectations, I felt freer to work a little bit, then stop and do something else. It was easier on my body and more enjoyable, easier to accept things that cropped up along the way. I enjoyed watching the tone of the wood change from one wall to the next after sanding, then again after one coat of sealer, then a second. I perfected using the little tank sprayer to apply sealer to the ceilings. I enjoyed thinking about where furniture might go. It all took as long as it took, no less, no more.

My neighbor and hiking friend Janet gave me another phrase: "It's just a cabin." When my dream of a cabin started to materialize, it was The Cabin. It all felt really serious and weighty—if not a matter of life and death, at least money and stress and possible bodily injury. When the sprayer couldn't reach the tip-top of the underside of the vaulted roof over the outside deck—even standing on the tip-top of my extension ladder—she looked at the odd pattern of dark drops and said, "It's just a cabin." When I bemoaned the uneven gap at the ceiling from the first wall of tongue-and-groove pine, I said to her, "I know, I know, it's just a cabin."

～～～～

Later this summer, Dad would visit for a week. In a sense, my relationship with him began after Mom died almost fourteen years ago, for she'd always played mediator between us. He was the taskmaster, the critic, and I struggled to be seen, to be heard, and like Mom to please. Sometimes after he visited, I felt emotionally beat up.

You don't change a man like that, but you can learn not to let things stick, and to stick up for yourself. On the phone, after he monopolized the conversation and said, "I've got to get back to work," I would say, "Wait a minute, Dad—at least ask me how I am first." When I called to tell him of a sad experience and he started criticizing or telling me how to fix it, I said, "Dad, please just say 'poor baby,'" and he would. I once asked him to write down some nice things about me and send them to me, and the next week I got a card with a painting of a heart on the front and sweet little awkward compliments inside. Some of his visits to the cabin were pretty good, others very trying. It also got harder to separate symptoms of his aging from normal exasperation; was it his hearing aids, or was he simply not paying attention to me? Jim and I worried that what Dad called his "fierce and sometimes foolish independence" would get him into trouble—like walking on his roof to clean out the gutters, and chainsawing alone. Scott had always been nearby to monitor such things.

When he turned eighty, I asked Dad if there were any things he hadn't done or seen in his life that he still wanted to; he said a cruise of the Inside Passage in Alaska with some fishing thrown in. "Your mom always wanted to do that," he said softly. I am taking him on that cruise next summer.

Despite the occasional rockiness in our relationship, he is my most faithful ally, the solid guy in my corner. He's the only person who visited each of my seven summers, and we always chainsawed some and did some fishing. No one has pitched in and worked up here like he has, from perc tests to concrete work. Besides me, he is the person most invested in this place, psychically and through some generous gifts.

His singular focus on work has also forced me to examine my own ideas of work and worth, the value of play, and the importance of friends and relationships. The cabin has helped me do that. However, I know that the cabin can seem like an automatic escape from city and job, and I can just as easily transport my stressors up there as I can a sack of potatoes. But if I let it, this captivating place tempts me to sit in the deck chairs and watch the sky go by, to walk through the woods daily, to linger over sunsets and good wine. I work hard—mentally and physically—but I also play and hike every single day and feel not a whit of guilt about it. My internal accounting scheme—what matters and what doesn't, what fills me and gives me joy, what needs to be washed away in the morning dew—is tallied in a way quite different than it was seven summers ago.

<hr />

When I began my posttenure sabbatical—the year I bought the land after spending a few weeks in Dennis's cabin—my department chair, Ann, urged me to go look up the word *sabbatical.* We were standing in the hallway, and I had been racing through my writing plans for my first academic book.

"Why do I need to look it up?" I asked. "It means you won a semester of leave to go work on a new research project."

"Just go look it up," she repeated.

Sabbatical is from the Latin *sabbaticus* or Hebrew *shabbat,* and is literally a "ceasing," a rest from work, a hiatus. It's described several

places in the Bible, such as a commandment to desist from working the fields in the seventh year, or when God rested after seven
days spent creating the universe. Biblical Sabbath is the origin of the
present-day practice of "the weekend" to give the faithful time to prepare for a proper observance. An academic sabbatical is not an automatic break every seventh year; it's a competitive process awarded to
the most promising research proposals that requires sustained effort.
But it is a break, a hiatus nonetheless.

Only at the end of that sabbatical did I truly understand the definition. Yes, it was about embarking on an exciting research project and
having the luxury of solid, undistracted time to work on it, but the
very act of so doing was indeed restful and rejuvenating. My batteries
were fully recharged. During that sabbatical I bought the land, and
then I spent seven summers following a dream of woods and cabin;
now it was time once again to rest and take stock.

For so many years I thought my life would follow a familiar story
line: get married, have a few kids. No doubt, mine has been the path
less traveled for a woman. But the rest of the story line that was always
in the back of my mind—and rarely said out loud—was to write in a
cabin in the woods. How curious, and how right, that the unvoiced
dream was the one that was born. It makes me wonder if it was always
the stronger dream—or just the dream that met fewer sharp stones,
that distilled and fermented in dark corners for many years before it
faced the light of day.

~~~~~~

I headed back downstairs with my soda and sat on the bottom step,
the compressor now charged and waiting. Outside the basement windows, dozens of electric-blue dragonflies caught the afternoon sun as
they coursed by. Snow was melting from the peaks in the Wyoming
Range, their newly bare flanks maroon in the angled light.

This was my seventh summer on this magnificent land. People still asked me if my cabin was done. I always replied, "It'll never be done." Literally, there are dozens of little (and medium) tasks awaiting me. Figuratively, this cabin and its naturalist-homesteader have a lot more unfolding and becoming ahead, as the Buddha would say. A lot more carbon will be recycled—from mouse and moose, flower and pine, brother and pets. More migrations from city to cabin, more summers of snow and fire. More loving and losing, more loving and gaining.

I measured the length of the wall (twice) and then put the measuring tape on the one-by-four trim piece. I added one-eighth of an inch for the saw cut, then penciled a line along the T-square. I pushed the board level against the back of the chop saw, and pulled the blade down twice to check the alignment with my mark. Then I squeezed the handle and drew the spinning blade quickly down and back up. I stood, long board in one hand and nail gun in the other, and looked at the wall. It was a beautiful wall, the stain of beetle fungus swirling in circles and streams of wispy gray against the creamy background. Better than a museum painting. I climbed the ladder and pushed the trim piece firmly against the ceiling, completely covering and forgiving the gap between board and ceiling. I hoisted the nail gun over my head, sucked in my breath, and squeezed the trigger.